A CENTURY

of

AMERICAN ALPINISM

2002

by

FAY

BENT

PALMER

THORINGTON

KAUFFMAN

PUTNAM

A Centennial Publication of
THE AMERICAN ALPINE CLUB–2002
710 10th St. • Boulder, CO 80401
(303) 384-0110

Front cover: Angelo Heilprin (1853-1907)
Founder of the American Alpine Club
Back cover: Charles Ernest Fay (1846-1931)
1st, 2nd and 5th President of the American Alpine Club

Printed by
SEDONA COLOR GRAPHICS
Sedona, Arizona 86339
(800) 450-0985

A CENTURY

of

AMERICAN ALPINISM

CONTENTS

FOREWORD
C. James Frush, President
The American Alpine Club

Our club is now beginning its second century. We want to remember the past for numerous reasons. We wish to honor those who have gone before and blazed our trail. We wish to learn from what has occurred. We wish to avoid repeating our mistakes or reinventing the wheel. And we wish to celebrate the past as we appreciate our successes and our failures.

Hardly a Board meeting of The American Alpine Club occurs but there is some question about the Club's history. Whatever the reason, our usual source remains the same: Past President William L. Putnam. For many years, he has been our "unofficial" Club historian. The fact that he was alive and present at a majority of our meetings over our entire history gives his recollections added credibility. Listening to him, who had the pleasure of knowing many of our founders and early members, gives an added dimension to our life as a club.

Bill has been one of the moving forces behind the celebration of our club's centennial. He originated the idea of the Centennial Dinner to be held in September of 2002 in Denver, and has helped us plan and implement many of the celebrations and functions commemorating our first 100 years.

An avid writer and editor, Bill has contributed to our Centennial in other ways as well. He was instrumental in creating and publishing the *Year of the Mountains, 2002, Commemorative Calendar*. Now, he has completed and helped us publish a chronicle of our first 100 years: *A Century of American Alpinism*. The list of authors given attribution for our Centennial history includes three others of our Past Presidents, but he remains the sole living Past President listed as an author, and there is no question that his hand is behind all portions of the manuscript.

As with so many of his labors for our Club, the compilation of our centennial history has been a labor of love for Bill. Those of us who know him appreciate that he has his own perspective and viewpoint, not only on events but on issues and personalities.

We take this gift of our history from Bill's hands with a keen appreciation not only for his writing it, but for helping to fund its publication. As with the Commemorative Calendar, it is certainly "Putnam-esque" in character. That its emphasis might be more on the first 50 years of our Club history than its last is both understandable and appreciated. Rather than some dry textbook chronicling in dreary recitation an exhaustive history of our Club, with no stone unturned, we are instead treated to a conversation with our predecessors, all channeled through the delightful and illuminating intelligence of Mr. Putnam.

I wish to thank him on behalf of the Board of Directors, our membership, and the climbing community, for all of his efforts over the years, and most recently for the Centennial history which, through his efforts, we now give to our membership and our posterity.

PREFACE
About the Authors

Charles Ernest Fay (1846–1931), the "Mr. American Mountaineering" of his day, was chairman of the meeting that led to the foundation of the Appalachian Mountain Club in 1876. Thereafter he served several terms as that club's president and was the editor of its Journal, APPALACHIA, for 40 years. In 1902 he was elected as the first president of The American Alpine Club, and reelected for a second three-year term. In 1917, he was elected president once more, thus becoming not only the Club's first president but also its longest serving. During all this period he was Professor of Modern Languages at Tufts College in Medford, Massachusetts, where he shared offices with the junior editor – albeit with a hiatus of 18 years between their respective occupancies.

Allen Herbert Bent (1867–1926), a native of Boston, Massachusetts, started his life of scholarly research into alpinism by dropping our of college – anything but a promising beginning. Soon, however, he began the serious study of the history of mountaineering, ultimately writing extensively on this topic. He became the first person elected to The American Alpine Club, during its days of "exclusivity," under the *"or the equivalent"* clause of membership prerequisites, for he was never a serious alpinist – always contenting himself with the study of its literature.

Howard Palmer (1883–1944), a lawyer by training, inherited the management of his family's mattress manufacturing business in New London, Connecticut. Starting in 1907, he compiled an enviable record of first ascents in the mountains of western Canada and in 1914 published the North American classic, MOUNTAINEERING AND EXPLORATION IN THE SELKIRKS. He served as editor of the Club's first guidebook and several editions of its JOURNAL. He also furthered the organization as its secretary, a director and as its president.

James Monroe Thorington (1894–1989), of Philadelphia, was an ophthalmologist by profession, following in the footsteps of his father. After the end of World War I, Roy, as he was known to his intimates, spent most of his vacation time in the mountains of western Canada and served as editor of the Club's guidebooks to that region for several editions. A diligent student of alpine literature, he compiled a number of scholarly researches into the history of American alpinism, served many years as a director of the Club, one term as its president, then for 10 years as editor of the AMERICAN ALPINE JOURNAL, and gave the Club some of the most valuable items in its museum. In 2000, the UIAA gave its first award for research into the history of alpinism under the name of James Monroe Thorington.

After graduating from Harvard in 1942, Andrew John Kauffman (b. 1921) the son of two distinguished American literary figures, spent his entire working career in various diplomatic capacities. Between State Department assignments in Washington, Paris, Managua and Calcutta, he spent weekends and holidays in the Alps and the mountains of Peru, Colombia, Alaska, Canada, and finally in the Karakoram, where he demonstrated a high level of acromania by becoming one of the only two Americans to make the first ascent of an 8000 meter peak. He also served the Club as a counselor and as vice-president and was elected to Honorary Membership.

William Lowell Putnam (b. 1924) has been an official of the Harvard Mountaineering Club, the Appalachian Mountain Club, then The American Alpine Club and finally the International Association of Alpine Societies (UIAA), and has been honored by several other mountaineering societies. His major employment was in television broadcasting, but his heart remains in the mountains of western Canada. At this writing he is the sole trustee of Lowell Observatory in Flagstaff, Arizona. While many have wished for the opportunity, people have not yet read his obituary.

*   *   *

At the outset, the junior compiler wishes to exercise his rights of survivorship by acknowledging an enormous debt to the above-named distinguished co-authors, whose labors for American alpinism and its national organization continue to bear fruit long after their lives have ended. Their original works form the basis of several chapters of this volume and are appropriately cited at the start of each; they have, however, been slightly amended and supplemented in order to form a coherent and updated, yet major part of this chronicle. For further biographical data on these authors, consult – inter alia – the following mountaineering journals: *Appalachia* XX-499 – Bent; *AAJ* I-373 – Fay; *AAJ* V-406 – Palmer; *AAJ* XXXII-337 – Thorington.

On. Page 62; Merriam/Webster's Third International Dictionary - one can read "`Alpine:' *resembling or relating to the Alps or any lofty mountain or mountain system...*"*often cap: devoted to mountaineering activities.*" "American" on page 68 as: *"belonging to, inhabiting, coming from, or forming a part of America..."* And on page 430, under `club' one reads; *"an association of persons for social and recreational purposes or for the promotion of some common object..."* The common object of The American Alpine Club is clearly stated in its 1915 Charter and By-Laws, both of which derive in great part from the language used in the founding documents of the original Alpine society, which was formed in London in 1857: *"The cultivation of mountain craft; the encouragement of mountain climbing and exploration; the promotion of good fellowship among climbers; the dissemination of knowledge concerning mountains and mountaineering through its meetings, publications and library."*

* * *

T here was an interesting episode at the close of the 51st Annual Meeting of the American Alpine Club, held in New York, on 6 December, 1952 – definitely not on the agenda.

Henry Snow Hall, Jr. – in his final appearance as president – had called the meeting to order in the clubhouse at 2 p.m. and then asked for the reports of the officers and committee chairmen. Between 55 and 80 members were present, more coming in during the course of the meeting. There was little of controversy in the offing – all that was two years behind us, the insurgents having been roundly trounced – and the meeting was proceeding peacefully. The committees were called upon in alphabetical order, and all the officers' reports accepted without significant discussion.

At the close of the business meeting – there was a general mingling of people while chairs were rearranged for the afternoon's program. During this break, the Club's Honorary Member and resident scholar, James Monroe Thorington, approached one of the younger alpinists scheduled for the final talk of the evening's program. Roy Thorington, a prolific writer on mountaineering topics, was notoriously crusty, a condition that Hall generously blamed on shyness. A year earlier, W. V. Graham Matthews, in company with Club members Dr. George Bell, Judge David Michael and others, had made several interesting ascents in the vicinity of Fortress Lake in the Canadian Rockies. For the past 30 years Thorington had been editor of the Club's Canadian guidebooks and was widely regarded as "the authority" on that region. This year, however, Matthews and Bell were to speak on their ascent of Salcantay in the Andes of Peru.

"How long were you in at Fortress Lake last summer?" asked the aging but still spry alpinist.

"About two weeks, Doctor," replied Matthews.

"I was in there twice, close to 20 years ago, but could stay only a few days each time."

"It's great country, Doctor; you should have stayed longer."

"I'd have liked to, but it took our pack train almost 10 days to get there from Lake Louise."

"Well!" Matthews rejoined, *"we used a float plane and landed right on the lake."*

"Damned tourists!" huffed Thorington, turning on his heel.

Mountaineering had changed in the 35 years that Roy had been a member of the AAC, and it was to change a lot more in the next half century.

*   *   *

The 56th Annual Meeting of The American Alpine Club was called to order on 7 December 1957, also on the main floor of the old private fire company building that past president Dr. William Sargent Ladd had given to the Club a dozen years earlier. Looking up, one could still make out the patch in the corner of the metal ceiling masking the hole where the traditional brass pole had once stood. New York City bureaucrats had insisted it be removed, alleging that it constituted a hazard for persons unfamiliar with making quick descents – at the time thought to be a laughable condition to impose on members of this organization.

The officers made their reports and President John Oberlin then called on the various committee representatives, in alphabetical order. While Christine Orcutt, the Chairman of Research, was making her report, it was noticed that Dr. Benjamin Ferris, the Chairman of Safety, was absent – possibly still upstairs in the office getting his statistics in order. A friend stepped out of the door at the rear of the hall and called up the stairwell,   *"Ben! You're on next."*

Ben's voice came from up around the corner; *"Tell John to go ahead with the first program and put me on later; I just got a whole bunch of new material from the West Coast handed to me."*

The messenger moved back into the meeting room and passed a note forward to the president that Dr. Ferris would not be available until later. Oberlin announced a slight change of program and introduced the first speaker of the afternoon program, Jack Graham, who had made an interesting traverse of the Matterhorn the previous season. Part way through his lecture, as a view across the fearsome east face of the Matterhorn was on the screen, an equally fearsome rumbling crash reverberated through the wall separating the meeting room from the adjacent stairway – something seemed to have fallen down the steep passage from the offices on the second floor.

Several members near the back door rushed to open it and see what had happened. There – on the floor, trying to rehabilitate his composure – was the chairman of the Safety Committee who had just completed the most serious accident of his long, and still unfinished, climbing career. Maybe the New York City bureaucrats had been right after all.

ACKNOWLEDGMENTS

While much of this volume owes its genesis to its distinguished co-authors and to the archives and library of The American Alpine Club, many others have helped to flesh it out with details and bring the narrative up to date. These include several other past-presidents of The American Alpine Club, in particular, Nicholas Bayard Clinch, James Peter McCarthy, and Thomas Callendar Price Zimmermann. We were also aided by an old pen pal, A. J. Francis of the Royal Naval Historical Branch in London, and some good friends at the Western History section of the Denver Public Library. Many other research libraries have been especially gracious, in Boston both at the Atheneum and the Public Library; in the Public Library of Springfield, MA. where I was born; in Flagstaff, that of Lowell Observatory and Northern Arizona University; as well as the University of Calgary. Suzanne Brown helped us with a scholarly insight into the life of William Osgood Field. At the end of the editorial process, Lloyd Athearn, of the Club's staff, gave a number of very helpful suggestions.

The pictures used herewith are all taken [with one exception] from the files of The American Alpine Club and have been carefully scanned and enhanced through the painstaking work of Club member Peter Rosenthal and his talented wife, Darlene. My own long-suffering and beloved wife, Kitty, helped diligently with the Index.

...Of all the activities in which men seek wholesome enjoyment, none may be said to be healthier, for the strength of body and soul alike, than the ascent of mountains, provided all recklessness be avoided. For while one's strength is renewed and increased through hard labor and the struggle to reach the purer and more rarified regions of the air, it also happens that the soul, by wrestling with every type of difficulty, becomes more persistent in its handling of the burdens and duties of life, and the mind, through the contemplation of the immense and beautiful view that presents itself to those who look around from the summits of the Alps, easily rises toward God, the Author and Lord of nature.

From the apostolic letter of Damiano Ambrogio Achille Ratti (1857-1939) [Pope Pius XI] to the Bishop of Annecy, France – 20 August, 1923

++

Pure on the frozen snows, the glacier-steep
Slept moonlight with the tense unearthly charm
Of spells that have no power to bless or harm;
But when we touched the ridge which tempests sweep,
Death o'er the murky vale, yawning wide and deep,
Clung to frost-slippery shelves, and sharp alarm,
Shuddering in eager air drove life's blood warm
Back to stout hearts and staunch wills fortress-keep,
Upward we clomb."

John Addington Symonds

From the program of the 11th Annual Meeting of The American Alpine Club 27 December, 1912. Symonds (1840–1893), an expatriate English essayist generally resident in Davos, also wrote the first serious works on homosexuality.

I – PRE-HISTORY
EARLIEST AMERICAN MOUNTAINEERING
Bent & Fay

The original of this chapter was published by request of The American Alpine Club in accordance with its publishing agreement with the Appalachian Mountain Club and can be found in APPALACHIA XIII, pp 45 - 67.

For further toponymic information, the interested student is referred to the scholarly work by Francis Peloubert Farquhar, NAMING AMERICA'S MOUNTAINS - THE COLORADO ROCKIES that appeared in the AMERICAN ALPINE JOURNAL X-319.

Along the western parts of North and South America, sweeping from Alaska to Patagonia, runs the longest mountain system in the world. From Mount McKinley (6187m) to Aconcagua (7035m), the culminating points in the north and south, is over 13,685 Km, and the mountains still extend 2500 km. farther to the south. In eastern North America, stretching from the Gaspé Peninsula to Georgia, is another long range, containing some of the oldest mountain uplifts in the world but, because of their orogenic age, relatively low. Both of these systems contain many interesting high points.

While only in the last 200 years have the full beauty and majesty of mountains been widely appreciated, mountain climbing in the Western Hemisphere began early. For untold centuries prior to 1519, the year that conquering Spaniards climbed 5340m Popocatepetl, even after 1818, when the young Scot, Captain Alexander Gerard, reached 19,411 feet (5916m)[1] on Mount Tahigung in the Himalaya, the global supremacy, as far as recorded attainment of altitude is concerned, remained in South America. Prior to 1818, the Himalayan chain was practically unknown to the modern western world, though Marco Polo had made numerous references to high points in the Karakoram. Sir George Everest did not start doing his thing until 1830 and nomenclature remained uncertain for another century.

Recent archeological finds indicate that Inca religious

---

1. See ACCOUNT OF KOONAWUR IN THE HIMALAYA, ETC, ETC, ETC by the late Capt. Alexander Gerard, edited by George Lloyd; London, 1841; pp 160-2.

ceremonies – banned once the Spanish conquest was virtually complete by 1535 – were held on the crest of Llullaillaco, some 6,700 meters above sea level. There has been similar and specific evidence for many years; much of it was acquired on 28 March, 1677, when the 5852m Peruvian volcano, El Misti (3566m above the city of Arequipa), was ascended by a group under the leadership of Fr. Alvaro Melendez. This expedition had been

". . .sent by ecclesiastic and royal authority to investigate the cause of a dense column of smoke seen rising from its summit... They exorcised the crater, cast in holy relics, celebrated mass and set up a great cross on the highest place."[2]

More relevant to our point, they also found vestiges of a small stone structure on the crater's edge, indicating that others had made the ascent prior to their arrival.

The story of the earliest ascent of Popocatepetl is told in a long official letter written by Hernando Cortes (1485-1547) from Mexico City on 30 October, 1520, to Holy Roman Emperor Charles V,[3] and printed in Seville in 1522. The conquistador, who at this time was barely able to hang on to his position in Mexico, stated:

"Eight leagues from the city of Cholula are two very lofty and remarkable mountains; in the latter part of August their summits are covered with snow; and from the highest, by night as well as by day, a volume of smoke arises, equal in bulk to a spacious house; it ascends above the mountain to the clouds as straight as an arrow, and with such force, that although a very strong wind is always blowing on the mountain, it does not turn the smoke from its course. As I have desired to render your Highness a very minute account of everything in this part of the world, I wished to ascertain the cause of this phenomenon, and I despatched ten of my companions... with several natives of the country for guides, charging them to use every endeavor to ascend the mountain and find out the cause of that smoke, whence and how it was produced. They went, and struggled with all their might to reach the summit, but were unable on account of the

---

2. In 1893, the Harvard University Astronomical Observatory, whose director, Edward Charles Pickering, was the first president of the Appalachian Mountain Club, built a meteorological station on this point as a function of its original "Boyden Station." This quotation comes from the annals of that observatory.

3. An avowed and forceful enemy of Protestantism, his Most Catholic Majesty, Charles (1500-1558), finally abdicated his reign over half of Europe and the New World in 1557.

great quantity of snow that lay on the mountain, and the whirlwinds of ashes that swept over it, and also because they found the cold above insupportable; but they reached very near the summit, and while they were there, the smoke began to issue forth with such force and noise that it seemed as if the whole Sierra was crumbling to the ground; so they descended and brought with them a considerable quantity of snow and icicles, that we might see them, as it was something quite new in this region on account of its being so warm a latitude."

In a later letter, written on 15 May, 1522, and printed in 1523, Cortes gives further particulars:

"In my former relation I informed your Majesty of a conical mountain of great height, from which smoke issues almost continually. As the Indians told us it was... fatal to those who made the attempt, I caused several Spaniards to... examine the character of the summit. At the time they went up, so much smoke proceeded from it, accompanied by loud noises, that they were either unable or afraid to reach the mouth. Afterwards I sent up some other Spaniards, who made two attempts, and finally reached the aperture of the mountain, whence the smoke issued, which was two bow-shots wide, and about three-fourths of a league in circumference; and they discovered some sulfur around it, which the smoke deposited. During one of their visits they heard a tremendous noise, followed by smoke, when they made haste to descend; but before they reached the middle of the mountain there fell around them a heavy shower of stones, from which they were in no little danger..."

The leader of this party, Francisco de Montano, a native of Cuidad Real, had volunteered to have himself lowered down inside the crater in a basket in order to fill a number of containers with sulfur to help alleviate the gunpowder shortage that was beginning to slow down the Spanish conquest.[4] These climbers deserve more recognition from subsequent alpinists than they have received, for the 3548m Roche Melon, on the French-Italian border, some 1800 meters less in altitude, was the highest point previously recorded as having been ascended. In this regard, however, one should note the late Mr. Palmer's advice on page 73 of this narrative.

The natives of the high plateaux of Mexico and the Andes

---

4. The original account (written in 1913) contains the line: *"Thus, the time-honored story that Cortes sent men up Popocatepetl to get sulfur for gunpowder was not the cause of this first, well-recorded, high mountain ascent."* Subsequent research indicates more conclusively that there was indeed much truth to the *"time-honored story."*

obviously had done considerable adapting to their environment. Physiological studies of them conducted in more recent times have shown several accommodations to the thinner air, of which an expanded chest cavity is the most pronounced. Modern archaeological studies have also shown that they had no fear of visiting the heights, particularly in the Andes.

Thirty-four year-old Diego de Ordaz, who led the first party of 10 scouts to Popocatepetl in 1519, was born at Castro Verde, Portugal, and died 14 years later in Venezuela. He went to South America while still a youth, served under Governor Diego Velasquez in Cuba, and in 1518 joined Cortes, under whose command he remained for a dozen years. After 1531 he was in South America, where he explored the Orinoco River for some 300 kilometers. Little else is known of Francisco Montano, leader of the expedition that finally reached the crater, except that he remained in Mexico after the Spanish conquest and his daughter received a royal pension.

Three centuries and more later, during the American occupation of Mexico in 1848, a party of Yanqui officers made the same ascent. A number of other officers, including Ulysses Grant (who became snowblind during the ascent) went part way to the summit but turned back after a bad and stormy night in a half-roofed hut. Three of those who made the top wrote accounts of their climb, Richard Heron Anderson, Samuel Bolivar Buckner,[5] and Charles Pomeroy Stone.

A native of Greenfield, Massachusetts, Stone graduated from West Point in 1845 at age 21. He resigned his commission in 1856 but came back to duty as a major general of volunteers early in the Civil War. Accused of improper actions during the Battle of Ball's Bluff (that resulted in the death of a fellow commander, 50-year-old Senator Edward Baker, of Oregon, who had also been an officer during the Mexican War), Stone was imprisoned late in 1861, but released a few months later. He returned to active duty, but resigned again in 1864. Appointed Lt. General in the Egyptian Army, he

---

5. Fourteen years later Anderson (1821-1879) became the hero of the Battle of Spotsylvania.

Buckner (1821-1914) became governor of Kentucky in 1887. His son of the same name played a secondary but important role in the development of American Mountain Troops in World War II, but was killed in the capture of Okinawa.

served as Chief of the Khedive's staff from 1870 to 1883, then returned home to become chief engineer of the Florida Ship Canal. At the time of his death in 1887 he was in charge of building the foundation structures for the Statue of Liberty on Bedloe's Island.

In June, 1802, Alexander von Humboldt, the widely traveled German naturalist, accompanied by his frequent companion, the eminent French botanist Aimé Jacques Alexander Bonpland,[6] accompanied by the Ecuadorian grandee, Carlos Montufar, claimed to have reached an altitude of 5878m on Chimborazo in Ecuador, and certainly wrote accurately about the effects of thin air on the human physiology. But Edward Whymper, the British engraver and alpinist, who finally conquered it in 1880 at age 40, proved conclusively that the earlier climbers did not reach the altitude they had supposed. Whymper's book, TRAVELS AMONGST THE GREAT ANDES OF THE EQUATOR, published in London in 1892, also offers an excellent summary of the physiological problems associated with high altitude of which the following is from the opening paragraphs:

It will be within the knowledge of most ... that it has long been debated whether human life can be sustained at great altitudes above the level of the sea in such a manner as will permit of the accomplishment of useful work. . .

. . . the evidence is overwhelming that, from 14,000 feet above the level of the sea and upwards, serious inconveniences have occurred; that prostration (amounting in the more extreme cases to incapacitation) has been experienced; and that, in a few instances, perhaps, even death has resulted through some cause which operates at great elevations.

This evidence has come from all parts of the world, and has accumulated during several centuries. It has been afforded, independently, by multitudes of persons of diverse conditions – by the cultured men of science down to illiterate peasants, the latter of whom cannot have heard of experiences beyond their own; and, though the testimony often differs in detail, it agrees in the general, leading features. Nausea and vomiting; headaches of most severe character; feverishness; hemorrhages; lassitude, depression and weakness, and an indescribable feeling of illness, have been

---

6. Friedrich Wilhelm Heinrich Alexander, Freiherr von Humboldt (1769-1859), was the son of a Prussian Army officer and blew much of his inheritance during his five years in the Andes.

The family name of Bonpland (1773-1858) was Goujaud, but he adopted this more fulsome handle.

repeatedly mentioned at great elevations, and have only been cured by descending into lower zones. To these maladies the term Mountain-sickness is now commonly applied.

* * *

From the "Smoking Mountain" and the adjacent "Sleeping Lady" (Ixtaccihuatl - 5285m) of Mexico northeastward to the White Mountains of New Hampshire is some 4000 kilometers, as the smoke blows.   The highest peak of that area, Mount Washington – Agiocochook to the earlier residents – rises merely 1400m above its surrounding valleys and only 1917m above the sea. Yet it has been heavily glaciated and is the home of the worst weather recorded on Earth as well as being the first significant mountain to be climbed by the invading whites in what is now the United States. In 1642 the ascent was a significant undertaking, but the only documented account of it is in Governor John Winthrop's journal which was not published until 1790. A Puritan, Winthrop (1578-1649) was the first governor of the Company of Massachusetts Bay, elected in 1629 and for a number of further terms in the years that followed. His JOURNAL OF THE TRANSACTIONS AND OCCURRENCES IN THE SETTLEMENT OF MASSACHUSETTS – 1630 TO 1644 is a source book of great historic value.

Among the entries for June, 1640, is found:

One Darby Field, an Irishman living about Piscataquack, [near later day Portsmouth, NH] *being accompanied with two indians, went to the top of the white hill. He made his journey in eighteen days. His relation, at his return was, that it was about one hundred miles from Saco, that after forty miles travel, he did, for the most part, ascend, and within twelve miles of the top was neither tree nor grass, but low savins[7] which they went on the top of sometimes, but a continual ascent upon rocks, on a ridge between two vallie, filled with snow, out of which came two branches of Saco river which met at the foot of the hill where was an indian town of some 200 people* [Pigwakit]; *some of them accompanied him within eight miles of the top, but durst go no further, telling him that no indian dared to go higher, and that he would die if he went. So they staid there 'till his return, and his two indians took courage by his example and went with him. They went divers times thro' the thick clouds for a good space, and within four miles*

---

7. "*Any of several trees, shrubs, or shrubby herbs somewhat resembling plants of the genus Juniperus;*" Merriam/Webster's 3rd International Dictionary, p. 2020.

of the top they had no clouds, but very cold. By the way, among the rocks, there were two ponds, one a blackish water and the other reddish [Lakes of the Clouds]. *The top of all was a plain about sixty feet square. On the North side there was such a precipice as they could scarce discern to the bottom* [Great Gulf]... *About a month after he went again with five or six in his company."*

Later that year Winthrop noted that Field's report of seeing various shining stones and "muscovy glass" [mica] *"caused divers others to travel thither, but they found nothing worth their pains."* Little else is known about Field (1610-1649) or his party. He appears to have died near Portsmouth, NH, and an oblique biographical reference indicates only that he enjoyed a short life *"...its merriness marred by insanity,"* a statement that might apply equally well to any number of mountain climbers.

The other high alpine points of New Hampshire's Presidential Range may well have been reached earlier but were not accurately measured until 1820, when Major John Wingate Weeks (1781-1853) who subsequently became a member of Congress from the northern portion of New Hampshire, and his brother-in-law, Adino Nye Brackett (1777-1847), a professional surveyor as well as clerk of the Coos County court, spent four nights on the range, the last one, 31 August, being on top of Mount Washington. Week's grand-nephew and namesake was born 40 years later and became a representative in Congress from Massachusetts. In 1909, with the support of all mountaineering organizations of the nation, he was responsible for the passage of the most far-sighted conservation legislation in American, if not world, history – the Weeks Act. This law brought most of the White Mountains and many other cut-over and despoiled areas of eastern American forests and mountains under the regenerative custody of the newly formed United States Forest Service.

The first white men to see the slightly higher but less inhospitable summits of the Southern Appalachian mountains were probably those unfortunates led by Panfilo de Narvaes (1480-1528) who had spent several prior years imprisoned by Cortes. Released from custody, he was granted a royal permit to conquer Florida, then a poorly defined area that included most of the Gulf of Mexico coast of the United States, and marched northward from near modern Pensacola in 1528. Panfilo would have done a lot better to have gone south with his brother, Diego, who accompanied Pizarro to Peru and received 113 marcos of silver and 2,775 pesos of gold as his share of the enormous loot taken by the invaders for the non-ransom of the Inca king, Atahuallpa, in 1530. Before the summer was over several of Panfilo's party had been killed by hostile natives and most others drowned while attempting to escape by sea at Apalachee Bay. Four men, however, got away from the unreceptive natives and made their way west across the Mississippi River and through Texas and Mexico to the Gulf of California, thus likely becoming the first persons to cross the North American continent.

The leader of these survivors was Alvar Nuñez Cabeza de Vaca (1490-1557) a soldier of fortune born in Jerez, who had been the treasurer of the expedition. De Vaca's reports, upon his belated return to the safer environs of Mexico six years later, led directly to the more fruitful expeditions of Niza in 1539 and Coronado in 1540-42. The man never let up; he was subsequently involved in military adventures in Brazil and Paraguay, but ultimately was imprisoned after King Charles V received too many complaints about his governorship of the latter region.

While the eastern mountains of North America were indicated on maps as early as 1540 and Richard Hakluyt[8] first showed them with the name "Apalchen" in 1582, they did not receive much formal attention until André Michaux,[9] the French botanist, visited North Carolina in 1795 and climbed Roan and Grandfather Mountains. A generation later Elisha Mitchell[10] went to the University of North Carolina as professor of mathematics and determined that the mountain upon which he ultimately lost his life was the highest of the entire Appalachian system. Soon after moving to his adopted home,

---

8. The name of Hakluyt (1522-1616), a forerunner of modern geographical science, is commemorated in the Hakluyt Society, English publishers of original works of exploration.

9. Michaux (1746-1802) had been sent to North America in 1786 to collect plants for the depleted forests near Paris. Shipwrecked on his return, almost all of his collection was lost and his grandson, François (1770-1855) was sent on a follow-up visit in 1802 while the elder was in Madagascar, where he contracted a tropical fever and died.

10. Mitchell (1770-1855) was a native of Connecticut and graduate of Yale. He wrote in the AMERICAN JOURNAL OF SCIENCE AND ARTS, Vol 35, January 1839. This publication was commonly referred to as "Silliman's Journal," a tribute to its long-time editor, Yale professor Benjamin Silliman (1779-1864).

he began a series of botanical and geologic excursions and in July, 1835, stood atop 2046m Mount Mitchell with two local guides. He wrote:

. . . The Black Mountain is a long ridge... and has some peaks of greater elevation than any point that has hitherto been measured in North America east of the Rocky Mountains... The ascent... is very difficult on account of the thick laurels, which are so closely set and their strong branches so interwoven, that a path cannot be forced by pushing them aside... At the time of our visit, the mountain was enveloped in mist... and we were so uncomfortable from cold, that some of the company urged a return with the least possible delay, and this when it was clear weather at a small distance below the ridge, and the thermometer at 80 °.

Professor Mitchell visited the mountain on four subsequent occasions, in 1838, 1844, 1856 and 1857. During a storm on his last visit he was killed, evidently by a fall in the darkness, and was buried in Asheville. A year later his body was removed and carried to the top of his mountain, where a funeral address was made by the first Episcopal bishop of Tennessee, James Hervey Otey (1800-1863), an opponent of secession who had been one of Mitchell's first pupils. A stone monument 12 feet high was erected in 1888.

* * *

The Rocky Mountains or, as another of these authors put it in 1925, THE GLITTERING MOUNTAINS [OF CANADA], were first reported seen by white men on 1 January, 1743. On that date 58-eight-year-old Pierre Gaultier de Varennes, Sieur de la Vérendrye and two of his sons, who explored the plains country west of the Great Lakes, were visiting the Mandan settlements along the upper Missouri River. The mountains they saw were probably the Bighorn Range of north central Wyoming, but of course, many years earlier various Spanish travelers had seen the equally high, though less continuous and more barren, mountains of the American Southwest.

When much of the central Rocky Mountains became part of the United States, after the Louisiana Purchase of 1803, various official expeditions started moving into them. The first of them was that led by two Army captains famous in American history, Merriwether Lewis and William Clark which crossed Idaho's Bitterroot Mountains to reach the Pacific Ocean in 1805.

A year later, on 15 November, Captain Zebulon Montgomery Pike, followed the Arkansas River up towards what, at 4301m, he called *the Grand Peak in the Mexican Mountains*. Then 34, Pike bercame a brevet Brigadier General in the War of 1812, and was killed while leading an assault on York (now Toronto) in 1813. Major Stephen Harriman Long, whose own explorations were notable, called this "James Peak," at the time of its first ascent. By the time of his retirement in 1863, Long (1784-1864) had become chief of the Army Corps of Engineers and was the leading American authority on railroad layout. But John Charles Frémont, a slightly later explorer, soon renamed that prominent peak for Pike and, as such, a half-century afterwards it became one of the most celebrated place names and objective goals in North America. Frémont (1813-1890), obviously a free spirit, was later court martialed for mutiny and disobedience while military governor of California in 1848, but was then elected one of the first senators from that state. Edwin James (1797-1861) was a native of Vermont and graduate of Middlebury College where he studied botany and geology made the peak's first ascent on 30 July, 1820. He was only 23 years of age when he was sent west under Major Long's command, and, as he subsequently reported to Secretary of War John Caldwell Calhoun:

. . . On the morning of the 14th [of July] *as soon as daylight appeared... we continued the ascent... A little above the point where the timber disappears entirely, commences a region of astonishing beauty... It was about four o'clock P.M. when the party arrived on the summit... The party remained only about half an hour; in this time the mercury fell to 42 °.*

James spent most of his later life in the West, for some years as a military surgeon and later as a farmer in Iowa. The Army's records[11] show that his companions on this initial ascent of an American 14,000 foot peak, were Private Wilson and the civilian hunter, Verplank; the latter being described by Major Long as *faithful and indefatigable.*

A dozen years after that climb, Benjamin Louis Eulalie de Bonneville (1796-1878) came by. He was a native of France but an 1815 graduate of West Point. Though perhaps somewhat over-glorified by Washington Irving, he did explore a lot of the American West. In September, 1833, he climbed what he claimed to be the highest peak in the Wind River Mountains of Wyoming. In

---

11. Other authoritative sources indicate that James was accompanied by Lt. William Henry Swift and a Quebecoise trapper-guide named Bijeau.

fact, he stated it to be the highest point in North America, a form of self-induced hallucination that has possessed many other climbers, at many other times and places. Irving described his view from the summit:

> . . . *Here a scene burst upon the view of Captain Bonneville, that for a time astonished and overwhelmed him with its immensity... Beneath him the Rocky Mountains seemed to open all their secret recesses... The Indian fable seemed realized: he had attained that height from which the Blackfoot warrior, after death, first catches a view of the land of souls, and beholds the happy hunting grounds spread out below him, brightening with the abodes of the free and generous spirits.*[12]

In August 1843, Frémont, who became a major general and candidate for president but was then a humble lieutenant in the United States Army, appeared in the same region. He climbed and measured one of the summits that was for many years called "Frémont Peak" (4189m) and claimed that he too had climbed the loftiest peak of the Rocky Mountains.

Two dozen years later, Major John Wesley Powell (1834-1902) who had been through the Civil War and lost an arm at the Battle of Shiloh distinguished himself further by leading a party in boats down through the Grand Canyon of the Colorado River. In 1869 he conquered Major Long's 4345m Peak in northern Colorado. However, in later years more than a dozen peaks in this region were found to be higher than Pike's and Long's and many dozens turned out to be higher than Frémont's. As of 1913, 39 peaks over 14,000 feet (4267m) had been surveyed in Colorado, 12 in California and one in Washington, but none at all in Wyoming. There are 55 summits higher than Frémont's in the central Rockies alone.

For many years Blanca Peak (4370m) in the Sangre de Cristo Range was supposed to be the highest of the Rockies, but a redaction of arithmetic caused it to lose the title in 1911 to Mounts Massive and Elbert in the Sawatch Range, both at about 4399m. These latter peaks were easily attainable from Leadville and had been climbed by 1874; Massive by 28-year-old Henry Gannett, subsequently chief geographer of the Geological Survey and for whom the more prominent 4202m peak near Mount Frémont was later named, and

---

12. This is from Irving's ASTORIA, published in 1836; THE ADVENTURES OF CAPTAIN BONNEVILLE came out a year later.

Elbert by his assistant, Henry Stuckle. The latter peak was named for Samuel Hitt Elbert, the 40-year-old governor of the Colorado Territory in 1873. Gold having been discovered in this region in 1859 and prospecting actively prosecuted, these high but relatively easy peaks may well have been climbed even earlier.

Blanca Peak, which is more distinctively a climb, was first ascended in 1875 by topographers (and half-brothers) Franklin Rhoda and Allen David Wilson, members of the Hayden Survey [discussed further in Chapter IX]. This pair was not alone in their surveying years among the mountains, there were cooks and packers regularly in their party, frequently visiting Indians, and in 1878 the 40 year-old British gentleman alpinist, James J. Eccles, with guide Michel Payot and two packers, accompanied the surveyors for much of the summer.[13] The lives of Rhoda (1854-1929) and Wilson (1844-1920) took diverse turns when the two left off surveying and returned to California in 1880; Rhoda became a revivalist preacher and Wilson a prominent Oakland businessman.

13. See also the ALPINE JOURNAL IX-24.

II – PACIFIC CRESTS
Bent & Fay

The original of this article was published by request of The American Alpine Club in accordance with its agreement with the AMC and can be found in APPALACHIA XIII, pp 45 - 67.

The interested student of toponymy is referred to the authoritative article by Francis Peloubert Farquhar, NAMING AMERICA'S MOUNTAINS - THE CASCADES *that appeared in the* AMERICAN ALPINE JOURNAL, *XII-49.*

The high, glacier-clad volcanoes of the Cascade Range in Oregon and Washington were seen and named by Captain George Vancouver during his epic voyage of 1792. Vancouver (1757-1798) was a successor to Captain James Cook in surveying the coastlines of the Pacific Ocean. The quotations that follow are from his five-volume VOYAGE OF DISCOVERY TO THE NORTH PACIFIC OCEAN AND ROUND THE WORLD, London; 1798. From his report, published in the year of his death, besides various engravings of the notable summits in this region as seen from the ocean, one can read the log kept during his visit to the body of water he named after his subordinate, Lt. Peter Puget:

April 30, 1792. "The lofty mountain discovered in the afternoon by the third lieutenant,[14] and in compliment to him called by me Mount Baker, rose a very conspicuous object, bearing by compass N 43 ° E, apparently at a very remote distance...

May 8, 1792. "The round snowy mountain now forming the southern extremity [Tahoma to the natives] *and which, after my friend Rear Admiral Rainier,[15] I distinguished by the name of Mount Rainier, bore N 42 E...*

October 20, 1792. "The clearness of the atmosphere enabled us to see the high round snowy mountain, noticed when in the southern parts of Admiralty inlet, to the southward of Mount Rainier... This I have distinguished by the name of Mount St. Helens, in honor of his Britannic

---

14. Joseph Baker (d. 1817), navigator and one of Vancouver's ablest officers, later commanded HMS Castor and Tartar in action against the Danish Navy.

15. Peter Rainier (1741-1808) entered the Royal Navy in 1756, did quite well financially in prize capture, retired from active duty in 1805 and left 10 percent of his estate to help retire His Majesty's national debt.

Majesty's ambassador at the court of Madrid [Alleyne Fitzherbert, Baron St. Helens (1753-1839)]. *It is situated in Latitude 46 ° 9' and in Longitude 238 ° 4'* [E. of Greenwich] *according to our observations.*

October 29, 1792. "A very distant high snowy mountain now appeared rising beautifully conspicuous in the midst of an extensive tract of low, or moderately elevated, land, lying S 67 ° E...

October 30, 1792. "The same remarkable mountain that had been seen from Belle Vue point, again presented itself, and though the party were now nearer it by 7 leagues, yet its lofty summit was scarcely more distinct. Lieut. Broughton honored it with Lord Hood's[16] name; its appearance was magnificent; and it was clothed in snow from its summit, as low down as the high land, by which it was intercepted, rendered it visible."

The first of these mountains to be successfully climbed was the then more classically symmetrical cone of 2972m Mt. St. Helens. In the summer of 1850, Thomas Jefferson Dryer, founder and editor of the newly established Portland OREGONIAN, made the ascent with three companions, whose names he gratuitously omitted in his published account of the climb. Four years later, Dryer claimed to have reached the summit of 3421m Mount Hood, although he estimated its height at 5596m, *even more lofty than Mount Shasta and heretofore unexplored.* The journalist and his companions, William Barlow,[17] Wells Lake and an unnamed Amerind, went on horseback to the foot of the mountain and were gone from Portland just a week. There were three other persons in this Dryer party (Captain Otto Travaillot, Judge Cyrus Olney and Major Granville Owen Haller) but they turned back before reaching the top. Dryer's description of the summit area, as reported in the OREGONIAN of 19 August, 1854, was vague and at variance with the observations of later visitors by way of the subsequently named Wy'east Trail. Dryer had spurned the offer of

16. William Robert Broughton (1762-1821) surveyed the northeast coast of Asia in the years 1794-97 and retired in 1812.

This was intended to honor Samuel Hood (1724-1816), one of several British naval figures by this surname, who had commanded much of the British fleet on the North American station during the American Revolution.

17. Barlow (1822-1904) arrived from Indiana at Christmas, 1845, and established himself in various aspects of the transportation business. He has been among those given credit for the first ascent of Mount Hood, though recent research indicates that General Joel Palmer (1816-1881) may have been there earlier.

a barometer that was available from Peter Skene Ogden, the now elderly agent for the Hudsons Bay Company; instead he relied for his estimates of altitude on tables of latitude and snow depth compiled by Baron Humboldt to arrive at a height of 18,361 feet for the "north pinnacle" of Mount Hood.

A more creditable claim for the first ascent of this peak came in 1857 when the 23-year-old mathematician, L. J. Powell, organized an ascent that was recorded in considerable detail by the Reverend T. A. Wood. This party included Lyman Chittenden, Wilbur Cornell and Henry Lewis Pittock (1836-1919). The latter was to take over the OREGONIAN when Dryer encountered financial difficulties in 1860, and build it into a newspaper of national repute before retiring to the unofficial position of United States minister to the Sandwich (Hawaiian) Islands.

Worthy of more than passing note regarding this summit is the account given by the Rev. Harvey Hines (1828-1902), a widely traveled Methodist minister, educator, historian and politician in Oregon, of his fearsome ascent of Mount Hood on 25 July of the year before. Hines wrote, beginning on page 83 in the 11 February, 1867, PROCEEDINGS of the Royal Geographical Society, that the climb brought him to *17,640 feet* [220 meters less than Dryer had found it] *. . . the pinnacle of the highest mountain in North America.* Hines' highest mountain in North America was in fact some 2000 feet lower even than that of Fremont, nevertheless he felt safe in reporting:

. . . The summit was so sharp that it was impossible to stand erect upon it... Its northern face is an escarpment several thousand feet high. I could only lie down on the southern slope, and, holding firmly to its rocks, look down the awful depth.

Mount Rainier, 4392m, a continual source of artistic inspiration, is considered by many to be the grandest mountain in the "lower 48" In 1857, Lieutenant (later Brigadier General) August Valentine Kautz led a party to within 1000 feet of its top, but the actual summit was not reached until 17 August, 1870, when General Hazard Stevens[18] and sometime prospector Philemon Beecher van

---

18. Kautz (1828-1895) was a member of the staff of the then territorial governor, General Isaac Stevens, father of General Hazard Stevens (1842-1918). While the father was killed at Chantilly in the Civil War, the son received the Medal of Honor for his conspicuous bravery. Interestingly, though he died a prominent member of the Washington (state)

Trump, a 31-year-old erstwhile gold seeker who was then secretary to the territorial governor of Washington, accomplished the ascent. James Longmire (1820-1897), a farmer near the west base of the mountain who had merchandised the hot springs flowing onto his property, provided a guide. Sluiskin, a Yakima Indian, led the party through the bush to the foot of the mountain, and then they still had 11 hours of hard work before they reached the top, near which they spent a miserable night in an ice cavern *freezing on one side, and in a hot steam sulphur bath on the other.*

The party initially included the English-born artist, Edmund Thomas Coleman, then in his 48th year, who had to turn back after his heavy pack fell down a declivity some hundreds of feet. Coleman (1832-1892) had previously written and illustrated the classic volume, SCENES FROM THE SNOWFIELDS; BEING ILLUSTRATIONS OF THE UPPER ICE WORLD OF MONT BLANC, based on his experiences on that mountain in 1855 and 1856 and the Dome de Miage in 1858. An alpinist of distinction, he had been among the founders of The Alpine Club [London], but was more attuned to the gentlemanly aspects of climbing, as done in the Alps, not the bush-whacking, back-packing variety of necessity practiced in North America.

Mount Baker (3262m), the navigator's peak and a far less strenuous ascent than Mount Rainier, was climbed by Coleman on 8 August, 1868. It was his fourth attempt on the summit and the event was reported in considerable, if somewhat overblown, detail by the BRITISH COLUMBIA COLONIST five days later. However, the local competition, the BRITISH COLUMBIAN, never mentioned the climb.

* * *

The Sierra Nevada, where exploration and climbing began so late, was curiously enough the first mountain system in North America to appear by name on any of the early maps. It is shown on Sebastian Münster's map of 1540, but without a name. On 1556 map of

---

establishment, he had also served as a member of the Massachusetts General Court in 1885-6.

Stevens Pass, another landmark of the region, was named for the railroad location engineer, John Frank Stevens (1853-1943), who worked for "empire builder" James Jerome Hill in pushing the Great Northern through these mountains in the 1890's and then went on to even greater engineering fame in connection with the Panama Canal.

Giovanni Battista Ramusio,[19] a Venetian geographer and collector of travel accounts, it is given its present name – a transplant from the mountains of southern Spain, of which the highest point is 3461m Mulhacén.

General Frémont, returning from his first exploring tour to the Pacific Coast in the winter of 1844, was perhaps the first to climb any of the mountains of California. On 5 February, his party camped at an elevation of 7,400 feet (2255m), in latitude 38° 42' 26". The next day, as he reported to then Secretary of War William Wilkins, a former senator from Pennsylvania:

. . . we set out with a reconnoitring party on snow shoes... and in a march of about ten miles we reached the top of one of the peaks. Far below us, dimmed by the distance, was a large snowless valley, bounded on the western side, at a distance of about a hundred miles, by a low range of mountains, which Carson [Kit, his guide] *recognized with delight as the mountains bordering the coast.*

Mount Shasta (4317m), the only major peak of the region to retain its Indian name, was first reported seen by white men in the year 1826. Peter Ogden (1794-1854), born in Quebec, had been with the Northwest Company from 1811 until its amalgamation into the Hudsons Bay Company in 1821. This son of a United Empire Loyalist wandered by while searching for good beaver country accessible from the company's newly acquired post at Astoria. However, its true first ascent was unknown to Josiah Dwight Whitney, chief of the Geological Survey of California 1860-74, who climbed it with his two assistants, William Henry Brewer and Charles Averill in September, 1863.[20] Hoping to make a first ascent, Brewer was disgusted to find *a mixture of tin cans and broken bottles, a newspaper, a Methodist hymn-book, a pack of cards, an empty bottle, and various other evidences*

---

19. Ramusio (1495-1557) wrote DELLA NAVIGATIONE ET VIAGGI which appeared in three volumes between 1550 and 1559.

20. Whitney (1819-1896) had been born in Northampton, MA. He continued for another dozen years as head of the California Geological Survey, then returned east to become professor of geology at Harvard.

Brewer (1828-1910) was a graduate of the Sheffield Scientific School at Yale to which he returned as professor of agriculture after 1864. He subsequently became president of the Arctic Club of America. His book, UP AND DOWN CALIFORNIA IN 1860-1864 was edited by F. P. Farquhar and published by Yale University Press in 1930.

of a bygone civilization. These *other evidences* appear to have been left behind on 14 August, 1854, when a 15-person party led by Captain E. D. Pearce attained the summit. Their climb was noted in the San Francisco DAILY HERALD of two weeks later.[21]

In 1863, Clarence King (1842-1901), one of the most enthusiastic of 19th century American mountaineers, joined the California Survey as an assistant in geological field work. A native of Rhode Island, he had spent his summers among the Green Mountains of Vermont and became one of the organizers of the U. S. Geological Survey. He also exposed the notorious Arizona diamond hoax. After graduation from Yale he studied under the famous Swiss-born naturalist, Louis Agassiz, but in May, 1863, drawn by Whitney and Brewer's account of Mount Shasta, set out for California with his college friend James Terry Gardiner (1842-1912), a native of Troy, NY, and a civil engineering graduate of Rensselaer Polytechnic who had taken further courses at the Yale Sheffield School. In September, King and Brewer climbed 3187m Lassen's Peak,[22] for years stated to be the only active volcano in the United States. The following year they all went into the High Sierra.

In July, 1864, with Gardiner and Charles Frederick Hoffman, the German-born topographer of the Survey, they ascended 3543m Mount Silliman and named it after their professor who remains one of the greater names of American science. Brewer and Hoffman went up 4232m Mount Brewer and King went up a still higher summit with Richard Cotter. This was Mount Tyndall, at 4273m, the highest peak that had up to that time been ascended in the United States, and which they named after John Tyndall (1820-1893), an accomplished alpinist, noted natural philosopher and physicist of Irish ancestry who authored a total of 145 scientific papers. From its top they could see two even higher points one of which they named Mount Whitney, after their distinguished chief, and the other Mount Williamson (4384m), after

---

21. The interested student of these placenames is referred to the article by Francis Farquhar, NAMING AMERICA'S MOUNTAINS - THE SIERRA NEVADA OF CALIFORNIA in the AMERICAN ALPINE JOURNAL XIV-131. For more on the Pearce ascent, see MAZAMA VI-54.

22. Named for Peter Lassen (1793-1859), a Danish-born blacksmith and trapper occasionally in the employ of John Sutter, but better known for his colonizing efforts in Northern California.

Major Robert Williamson (1824-1882) who later became most notable for his mapping of the harbors of the Pacific Coast. While with the U.S. Army Engineers.

Mount Whitney (4418m), proved to really be the highest summit in what was then the United States. King, only 22 years of age at the time, though destined to become the first chief of the U S Geological Survey at age 39, was ambitious to climb it and started for it in the summer of 1864, but had to turn back in storm when only about 400 feet below the crest. It was seven years before he had a chance to try again. His time was short and the weather was bad. In the mist and rain, he arrived at what two years later was proven by W. A. Goodyear[23] to be the wrong peak, with an altitude several hundred feet less than seemed correct. Furthermore the summit was adorned with a cairn, embedded in which was an Indian arrow shaft pointing due west. Hastening westward again in 1873, he climbed the real Mount Whitney on 19 September, via the north only to find that it, too, had been visited – twice before, both times within the prior month.

It is interesting that none of these early explorers and alpinists managed to share (or perhaps even find) the awe that others later found in the magnificent, glacially scoured terrain of the Yosemite and Hetch-Hetchy valleys.

---

23. See the PROCEEDINGS of the California Academy of Sciences; 4 August, 1873.

III – LATER AND FARTHER NORTH
Putnam

This chapter was adapted from portions of several passages that appeared in the Club's earlier guidebooks and the Club's 1982 volume, THE GREAT GLACIER AND ITS HOUSE.

The interested student of toponymy is referred to the 1990 work, PLACE NAMES OF THE CANADIAN ALPS, by Boles, Laurilla and Putnam; Revelstoke, BC.

D avid Douglas (1798-1834), the Scots botanist for whom the most famous of North American lumber trees is named, was the first to leave a record of alpine climbing in Canada before which he served as the official collector in the United States for the Royal Horticultural Society. After a long journey up the Columbia from Astoria and thence up the Wood River with a Hudsons Bay Company fur brigade, he reached Athabasca Pass at the end of April, 1827, and on May 1 climbed the peak to its north. He wrote (though published posthumously in the_COMPANION TO THE BOTANICAL MAGAZINE, Vol II, London, 1836):

Its height does not appear to be less than 16,000 or 17,000 feet above the level of the sea. After passing over the lower ridge I came to about 1200 feet of by far the most difficult and fatiguing walking I have ever experienced and the utmost care was required... The view from the summit is of too awful a cast to afford pleasure. Nothing can be seen in every direction except mountains towering above each other, rugged beyond description. The peak, the highest yet known in the northern continent of America, I feel sincere pleasure in naming Mount Brown in honour of R. Brown, Esq., the illustrious botanist... A little to the southward is one of nearly the same height, rising into a sharper point; this I named Mount Hooker, in honour of my early patron, the Professor of Botany in the University of Glasgow. This mountain, however, I was not able to climb.

Robert Brown (1773-1858), the Scots-born curator of the Botanical Department of the British Museum, had been botanist of Matthew Flinders' Australian expedition of 1801 to 1805. Sir William Jackson Hooker (1785-1865), the 1821 author of FLORA SCOTIA and subsequently of FLORA BOREALI AMERICANA, was the first director of Kew Gardens. Both of these gentlemen were, more than coincidentally, supporters of Charles Darwin in the great controversy over evolution in which he soon became embroiled. For over half a century after Douglas's visit Mts. Brown and Hooker were shown on maps as the culminating points of the Rocky Mountains. But in 1892, Professor Arthur Philemon Coleman, the first Canadian to become president of the Geological Society of America,[24] made several visits to the area with his brother Lucius, who owned a ranch in southern Alberta near Cochrane. In the course of these months-long journeys (on which Lucius's wife, Frances, did the cooking) they conclusively proved these peaks to be only about 9,000 feet high – and another false icon of alpinism was shattered. More recent surveys have lowered Brown to 2799m and Hooker to 3286m, some 2000m less than Douglas had generously given his patrons. Worth of note is the fact that the Stoney Indians felt that Mount Murchison (3311m and named by John Palliser for the distinguished geologist, Sir Roderick Impey Murchison), in the drier, frontal ranges of the Canadian Rockies, was the highest peak of the world. As with most North American aboriginals, they made no attempt to scale it, being content to wander respectfully around its peripheral valleys.

The crowning peak of the "Canadian Alps," long a favorite playground of American climbers, is indisputably 3954m Mount Robson, which was described in the 1899 Report of the Geological Survey of Canada by James McEvoy:

. . . *Looking* [north] *up Grand Fork is the most imposing view met with on the whole route. Great mountains are on every hand, but over all stands Robson Peak, 'a giant among giants and immeasurably supreme.*[25]

The mountain survived numerous attempts by the Coleman brothers, the Reverend George Brown Kinney (1872-1961) and Arnold Mumm (1859-1927) although the great Swiss-Canadian guide, Edward Feuz, Jr,[26] and others contended it really had been conquered

---

24. Coleman (1852-1939) was one of Canada's most outstanding scientists as well as alpinists. President and subsequently honourary president of the Alpine Club of Canada, he fully deserved the six-page obituary in CAJ XXVI-127.

25. McEvoy quoted this last phrase from Milton & Cheadle's THE NORTHWEST PASSAGE BY LAND, London, 1865; page 252.

26. Kinney, a Presbyterian missionary, wrote a thrilling account of the climb in CAJ II #1, p 1.
   Arnold Louis Mumm was an English lawyer and publisher (though descended from the champagne family) and a frequent climbing companion of John Norman Collie.
   Edward Feuz, Jr (1884-1981), the dean of North American alpine guides, became the

by Kinney in 1909 with his guide/packer Curly Phillips (1884-1936) a native of Lake of the Bays, Ontario. Nevertheless, their claim did not stick for they took no photo and building a cairn on the rime-coated crest was clearly impossible [See again, Howard Palmer's dictum on page 73], but they did describe the summit area quite accurately. When faced with disbelief regarding his ascent, Kinney, though a leading member of the Alpine Club of Canada, retired from alpinism and spent the rest of his life attending to his church's missions on Kootenay Lake. Phillips, unfortunately, died in an avalanche on Mt. Elysium, a lesser peak only a short distance from the great mountain.

However, no one expressed doubt about the 1913 ascent by William Wasborough Foster and Albert Henry MacCarthy, then of Summit, New Jersey, led by the noted Austrian-born guide, Conrad Kain.[27] Only four years from his native land, Kain chopped hundreds of steps up the steep snow/ice of what is now called the "Kain Face,"(which has since been descended on skis) whence the party continued along the east ridge to where, . . . *a little cap of cloud covered the exact summit, and when after a short, steep piece of work Conrad turned and said, "I will take you no further;" it was difficult for a moment to realize that Robson was won . . .*[28]

Instead of descending by their already established route, Kain led his party down the drier ledges on the southern aspect of the great mountain, thereby achieving not only a first ascent, but also the first traverse of the mountain.

*   *   *

The "Mystery Mountain" of British Columbia's Coast Range had been rumored to exist for more than a century before it was

---

topic of a 1986 biography, by A. J. Kauffman and W. L. Putnam entitled THE GUIDING SPIRIT.

27. A military officer, Foster (1875-1954) served with distinction in both World Wars. See AAJ IX-220.

   For more on MacCarthy (1876-1956) see AAJ X(2)-137.

   Conrad Kain (1883-1934) is lovingly described in a semi-autobiographical work (edited by J. M. Thorington) WHERE THE CLOUDS CAN GO, first published by the AAC in 1935 and since reprinted twice. See also CAJ XXI-217.

28. From Foster's account in the CANADIAN ALPINE JOURNAL, XIV-15.

definitely sighted in 1925 from Mount Arrowsmith on Vancouver Island by the indomitable mountaineering and exploratory team of Don and Phyllis Munday. Its altitude, at 4059m, was considerably higher than Mount Robson and its unique original name had been suggested by Canada's great geographer, George Mercer Dawson. However, in 1927, a generation after Dawson's death, the peak was officially named Mount Waddington, after Alfred Penderil Waddington, an early white exploiter of British Columbian real estate who was also an alpinist of some competence, having made the 20th recorded ascent of Mont Blanc on 10 July, 1836.[29]

The observer from a later generation cannot help being struck by the vastly different cultural approach towards the land that others already lived on which was taken by the whites invading North America. The prior inhabitants subscribed to a tradition holding there to be no private ownership of land. People, as well as other animals, were merely "tenants at will" under the benign overlordship of variously named Great Spirits who dwelt among the high places. Land could only be lived on – never owned. The basic conflict between these two cultures was further exacerbated by the invaders' insistence on written treaties which the natives never comprehended and had no use for, even if they could have read them, due to their age-old, aboriginal reliance on oral tradition. In any case, Waddington was neither the first nor the last to speculate handsomely in aboriginal (in this case Salish) real estate.

Phyllis Beatrice Munday became one of the greater figures of North American alpinism. Born in Ceylon [modern Sri Lanka], she was the first woman to ascend Mount Robson and participated in dozens of first ascents in the Coast Range. Editor of the CANADIAN ALPINE JOURNAL from 1953 to 1969, she outlived her husband, Don, by over 30 years and received the Order of Canada as well as Honorary Membership in The American Alpine Club, the Ladies Alpine Club and the honourary presidency of the Alpine Club of

---

29. Dawson (1849-1901) has a 3386m high point of the Selkirk Range as well as the city in the Yukon named in his honor.

Waddington (1801-1872) was among the early members of The Alpine Club and became a great promoter of British Columbian union with Canada. His cousin, William Henry Waddington (1826-1894) was briefly the president of France and then French ambassador to England for 10 years after 1883.

Canada. After several exploratory trips, in 1927 the Mundays managed to attain the heavily glaciated region surrounding the peak by taking a boat up Knight Inlet, a stretch of water that had been named in 1792 by Lt. Broughton for Admiral Sir John Knight. It was a laborious venture, enlivened by the malfunction of their boat's motor, after which they made it . . . *about eight miles more to Grouse Point where we spent the night in an old Indian smoke house. In the morning we rowed the remaining twenty miles against the tide and the current produced by the two big glacial rivers . . .*[30]

Soon this mountain came to be widely regarded as one of the great unclimbed – if not unclimbable – challenges left in North America, and the Mundays attempted it several times, often with other friends. The most notable and persistent of these was Henry Snow Hall, Jr. (1897-1989) the great American patron of alpinism who, in appreciation for his unfailing support, was created the first Honorary President of The American Alpine Club.[31] The ascent of this dramatic peak was finally accomplished in 1936 by Fritz Hermann Ernst Wiessner and William Pendleton House, two Americans that were soon to leave divergent marks on K2, the world's second highest peak [See Chapter X]. Giving first crack at the ascent to a ski-equipped team from the Sierra Club that was also on the scene, the Wiessner party moved their camp somewhat closer to the base of the peak. When Bestor Robinson's group failed in its attempt, the easterners took over before dawn the next day. Arriving on Waddington's crest on 21 July, 13 hours after leaving their camp at 2:45A.M. . . . *We were rewarded with a grand view of the beautiful Coast mountains which extended around us. Large smoke clouds covered raging forest fires in the interior of British Columbia. In the southeast and south parts of the Inland [sic] Passage and Pacific Ocean were visible . . .*[32]

---

30. From their account in the CANADIAN ALPINE JOURNAL XVI-4. For more on Mrs. Munday (1894-1990) see AAJ XXXIII-341.

31. See AAJ XXIX-341 and AANews 181.

32. From Wiessner and House's account in the CANADIAN ALPINE JOURNAL; XXIV-15. It is fitting that, some 50 years later, a film was made of ascending K2, on which both Wiessner and House later climbed separately, major portions of which were filmed in the vicinity of the Waddington massif.

Wiessner (1900-1988), a native of Dresden and chemist, became an American citizen

*   *   *

     The first ascent of the dominant peak of the Interior Ranges of British Columbia (since formally renamed as the "Columbia Mountains") was an epic of exploration that predated the Waddington climb by two dozen years. Mount Sir Sandford (3529m) had been seen and thought about from the earliest days of exploration for the Canadian Pacific Railway and had been given its name to honor the railway's original chief engineer, Sandford Fleming.[33] The mountain had been seen from several high points by many travelers, but until 1908 no serious attempt had been made to climb it. That year two American patrons of the CPR's Glacier House, Howard Palmer, one of these authors, and New York businessman Benjamin Sayre Comstock,[34] went down the Columbia by canoe from Beavermouth to the Gold River. Paddling a short distance westward up the tributary, they ascended a nearby lesser summit to the north, which they named Mount Stockmer in honor of themselves, from which they could pick out a means of access towards their goal.

     In the succeeding three years, Palmer kept at it, generally in company with two vigorous companions, Edward Willett Dorland Holway, a retired banker from the Norwegian settlement of Decorah, Iowa, who was a professor of botany at the University of Minnesota, and Frederick King Butters, a younger associate in filicology at the same school. On these trips the trio was aided by several local woodsmen and packers -- one of them being the redoubtable Annie Bergenham[35] -- in following this route to the base of their peak.

---

in 1935 and brought a new and much higher standard to North American rock climbing. See AAJ XXXI-321.

    Robinson (1898-1987), an engineer, was primarily a skier in his mountaineering activities.

33. Fleming (1827-1915), Scots-born, became the first honourary president of the Alpine Club of Canada. He had earlier distinguished himself as chief engineer of the InterColonial Railway, prior to his work with the CPR. In 1884, Fleming was the prime mover behind the establishment of Standard Time zones.

34. For more on Comstock (1859-1941) see AAJ IV-481.

35. For more on Holway (1853-1923), see the monograph, EDWARD WILLET DORLAND HOLWAY, published by Palmer after his friend's death.

    Though not the senior in age, Butters (1878-1945) had the greatest tenure in alpinism

Nevertheless, despite Holway's considerable climbing skill and their collective ability to make strenuous marches and good maps, Palmer's team felt unable to scale Mount Sir Sandford's glacier-hung north face which was, in their minds, the only possible route.

After their 1911 visit, a party organized by George Culver an amateur alpinist of Winnipeg and including Edward Feuz, Jr. and Rudolph Aemmer, two of the Canadian Pacific Railway's Swiss guides,[36] made a tedious overland approach from Beavermouth and Palmer's elusive goal was saved only by their shortage of supplies. Palmer, however, got the message; he and Holway were waiting on the station platform of Golden the following June when the guides returned to Canada, this time to take up permanent residence. After time out for a wedding, all but the guides climbed into Palmer's waiting canoes for the trip down the Columbia and into the bush. Feuz had almost drowned a few years earlier in an attempted crossing of the Columbia below Revelstoke – he and Aemmer bushwhacked along the riverbank.

Twenty miles downstream from Beavermouth the climbers turned up the Gold River tributary along the route Palmer and his colleagues had already pioneered to their established campsite at the north base of the peak. The guides then spent a day out on the glacier (an area from which over 600m of ice has since melted, leaving a barren rocky expanse) studying the snow-clad face and determining their route. It would zig-zag across the steep snow-ice of the north face and then go through a tenuous area known as "the hourglass."

The preceding winter had been light, so a great deal of step cutting was in order after the party left camp at 2 A.M. on 24 June, 1912. Eight hours later and high on the west ridge, Aemmer reached a position to which his less experienced clients felt they could not safely follow. He and Feuz conspired briefly in SchweizerDeutsch and then, with Aemmer pulling sharply from above and Feuz giving Palmer

---

of the three. For more on him see CAJ XXIX-283.

Annie was the wife of Peter Bergenham (1886-1971), one of the area's most notorious poachers and woodsmen, whose name was subsequently given to a conservation area along the Columbia River.

36. Aemmer (1883-1973) and Feuz were childhood friends from the Interlaken area of the Oberland.

an unexpected push, the problem was solved. Holway – a more confident climber – followed easily enough. Aemmer soon attained a point in the snow which was exceeded in altitude only by a massive cornice jutting out over the cliffs to the northeast, a line of attack on this summit that had turned back one attempt by Palmer's team and several subsequent attacks.

"Here is the top," he said.[37]

---

37. Palmer's report of this ascent can be found in his classic opus, MOUNTAINEERING AND EXPLORATION IN THE SELKIRKS, New York, 1914. Feuz's slightly less respectful version can be found in THE GUIDING SPIRIT, op cit, pp 172-176.

IV – TIDEWATER ALASKA
Putnam

The text of this chapter first appeared in several sources, many of them published in various alpine journals, and earlier accounts by some of these authors in the publications of the Royal Geographical Society.

The scholar interested in some of this nomenclature is referred to the work of Francis Farquhar in the AMERICAN ALPINE JOURNAL, XI-211; NAMING ALASKA'S MOUNTAINS.

The first mountain ascent recorded in Alaska seems to have been that organized by George Davidson, who became the first vice-president of The American Alpine Club 35 years later. Davidson (1825-1911), a British-born geodesist and astronomer associated with the U. S. Coast & Geodetic Survey, was engaged for 50 years in primary triangulation and had established the location of Sir Francis Drake's 1579 landing on the California coast. On 9 September, 1867, very shortly after Alaska was formally transferred from Russia to the United States, he led a 10-man party to the crest of the 6,680 foot (2033m) volcano, Makushin, on Unalaska Island.

Davidson noted in his diary that his party consisted of Theodore Blake, geologist; Dr. Albert Kellogg, botanist; Lieutenant Hodgson; Engineer Ball, and two seamen, Walsh and Penny Two of these men had further distinguished careers; Kellogg, a native of Hartford, Connecticut, became a founder of the California Academy of Sciences and authored FOREST TREES OF CALIFORNIA, while Hodgson rose to the rank of Captain and was on the bridge with Admiral Dewey at the battle of Manilla Bay.[38] Picking up a guide and three packers at the village of Illiouliouk, they marched inland for two days to attain a campsite at an altitude of 3,287 feet. In his account, Davidson stated that their . . . *course lay along the sides of steep mountains and steeper ravines . . . After a most uncomfortable night's rest, made somewhat solemn by the subterranean rumblings . . . while the smell of sulphurous vapors was very strong . . . At seven o'clock the*

---

38. Kellogg (1813-1887) was both a trained botanist and a medical doctor.

Hodgson (1836-1916), a native of New York, stayed with the Treasury's Revenue Service and retired in 1906.

Davidson's original account can be found in APPALACHIA IV-8.

elevation attained was 4,379 feet, and one barometer had reached its limit of action . . . At nine o'clock the crater was discovered, shaped like an immense bowl, and about three hundred yards in diameter, with inner sloping sides composed of snow . . . This was the summit of the mountain, and it is 5,691 feet above the ocean. For a few minutes the clouds broke away, and almost beneath the feet of the party lay the crater, rolling out volumes of smoke and yellow sulphurous vapors . . .

They were all safely back on board the U. S. Revenue steamer *Lincoln* by the afternoon of 10 September, having made a decidedly unique contribution to alpinism by not overstating the altitude or the difficulty of their ascent.

Mount Saint Elias, at 5489m the giant of the Alaskan coast, was named in 1740 by Vitus Jonassen Bering (a Danish navigator who had been in the employ of Peter the Great and the Russian-American Fur Company since 1724) for the Biblical prophet on whose feast day [Old Style] he sighted land off the long cape lying west of the mountain.[39] This highly visible summit was imperfectly measured in 1786, 45 years after Bering's visit, by the expedition commanded by Jean François de Galaup Comte de LaPerouse during his visit to this coast in 1786. The ongoing navigational imperfections of LaPerouse led to his shipwreck and death among the Santa Cruz Islands two years later.[40] Members of Admiral Vancouver's party sketched the impressive summit in 1794, but did not venture a definitive estimate of its altitude.

At over 18,000 feet, this peak so dominates the view from the Gulf of Alaska that its nearby companions, Mounts Augusta, Cook and Vancouver, have tended to be overlooked. Close to a century after Vancouver's visit, the latter two summits were formally named by Smithsonian biologist William Healey Dall (1845-1927), honoring the British navigators who had mapped this coastline so effectively. The first of these neighboring peaks, however, was named by geologist/explorer Israel Cook Russell (1852-1906) whose own name

---

39. Bering (1681-1741) never made it home to report. He was shipwrecked en route and died on the bleak shores of Komandorski Island, which was named for him by his crew. His journals were saved by his men a few of whom constructed an open boat from the timbers of the wreck and returned to their base at Petropavlovsk.

40. LaPerouse (1741-1788) had earlier distinguished himself by capturing the Hudsons Bay Company trading posts during the last of the French and Indian Wars.

is on the fiord at the head of Disenchantment Bay, for his wife, née Julia Augusta Olmstead. This line of peaks manages to block the view from the ocean of North America's second highest summit, Mount Logan, about which much more below and which was named for Sir William Edmond Logan (1798-1875), "the father of Canadian science," an authority on stratigraphy who headed the Geological Survey of Canada for 28 years after 1842.

The ascent of Mount Saint Elias was not attempted until 1886, when the NEW YORK TIMES bankrolled a trip by explorer Frederick Schwatka, geologist William Libbey, of Princeton, and the British explorer/artist Heywood Walter Seton-Karr. Several other attempts, including one in 1888, led by the noted British climbers Harold and Edwin Topham, and containing the then 24-year-old William Williams of New York, were equally unsuccessful. Finally, in 1897 and simultaneously in the field with another American attempt led by Henry Grier Bryant, the celebrated Duke of the Abruzzi laid a well planned and equipped assault on the peak, including among the porters' loads, folding iron bedframes for use by the seven-man climbing team.[41]

True to now well-established American custom, the Duke hired four local Indians to help carry his supplies through several miles of bush to the westerly edge of the Malaspina Glacier. In so doing, he was using their muscle-power and expertise in the same manner as had almost every other exploratory alpinist for the preceding 400 years. The aboriginals had a non-exploitive, hand off, reverence for mountain heights that bordered on religion – and certainly was religion among

---

41. Schwatka (1849-1892) was a man of many parts. A 1871 graduate of West Point, he acquired a medical degree in 1876 and was admitted to the Nebraska bar in 1875. He had resigned his military commission in 1885.

Libbey (1855-1927), a professor of geology most of his life, was also the chief of rifle instruction for the U. S. Army during World War I.

Seton-Karr (1859-1938), was also a big game hunter, making 19 such trips to Africa, 20 to India and 20 to the Arctic.

Bryant (1859-1932) was to become the fourth person elected president of the AAC.

Luigi Amadeo di Savoia/Aosta (1873-1933) was born as the son of the (briefly) King of Spain. His accomplishments as an alpinist and explorer remain the stuff of legend: after Saint Elias he went on to establish a "farthest North" (at 86° 34") in 1899, climb Ruwenzori in 1906 and leave his place names all over the Karakoram landscape in 1909. He died in Mogodishu, a place name that became unhappily familiar to members of the American 10th Mountain Division 60 years later.

the Incas – as palefaces of a later generation have found out to their dismay on summits like Wyoming's Devils Tower and New Mexico's Shiprock. One of us [Bent] noted in APPALACHIA XIII-265 an example of that attitudinal difference:

. . . A wise old man, who killed many elk, made a sort of pick of their horns and went to the top of a high mountain to look for shell money, which Tamanous gave him to understand was there. He arrived at the top and found a great lake with much otter, but giving no thought to those, he set himself to digging this wampum, or hioqua. He dug twenty strings of it and started down the mountain, a rich man. On his way down, he was overtaken by a violent snow storm, and was in danger of death. To propitiate the tamanous' anger, he threw away one string after another, but the storm did not abate until he had cast away the very last. He then returned sadder and wiser, sure that the tamanous of the mountain did not wish his hoards to be taken . . .

The Duke also hired a 10-man team of whites (One of whom, Sidney Lawrence, reminisced with members of the 1946 American team that made the second ascent of Mount Saint Elias) to assist in moving his impedimenta across the wide expanse of glacier to the base of the peak. In this, as in everything else, he was a class operator and some of his porters, such as 37-year-old Clarence Andrews, a native of Astabula, Ohio, eventually made it into WHO'S WHO. There was plenty of man power at large in coastal Alaska in those days, frustrated in their attempts to get inland so as to strike it rich in the Klondike and too broke to purchase passage home. The Duke's porters dragged their laden sleds across the ice from near the Osar River to where the guides could work a way up the southeast side of the peak. There were no technical difficulties, though the guides set the pace throughout and led the party to within a few feet of the crest. Upon reaching that spot the Duke's Fortin barometer gave an altitude of 18,090 feet, agreeing closely with Russell's triangulation of 1891 at 18,100 feet.

However, Filippo di Filippi, Abruzzi's amanuensis, noted that *. . . All preceding calculations had proved discordant and untrustworthy. Only one gave an approximately correct result; namely that made by the Italian navigator, Malaspina, in 1792, fixing the altitude of Mount Saint*

Elias at 17,847 feet . . .[42]

Despite the mountain's sharp appearance, Abruzzi's party observed that:

. . . the summit of Mount Saint Elias consists of a spacious plateau stretching with slight inclination from southeast to northwest. The highest point stands north and forms a raised platform about forty square yards in extent.

Di Filippi's comment on the accuracy of previous surveys is hardly to be taken as a sign of Italian chauvinism; Malaspina had done pretty well -- far better than his successors over the next century. Mark Brickell Kerr, naturalist and topographer of the 1890 National Geographic Society/U. S. Geological Survey party, which went part way up the mountain, stated that:

. . . a mean of all the observations taken on Saint Elias gives a result of 16,693 feet and the writer is inclined to the belief that its true elevation, when determined, will not vary much from this mean.[43]

That Kerr's naviguessing was considerably off the mark may do much to account for the lack of esteem in which he was held by some of his more notable contemporaries. Israel Russell, for example, in a letter of 8 July, 1897 to Professor Davidson, states:

. . . What you say about Kerr does not surprise me. If all the lies he told about our expedition could be collected they would make a large volume. He was a total failure . . .

The Bryant expedition, to which reference was made above, had an ambitious plan for their season after climbing Mount Saint Elias. In a letter to Davidson, Bryant gave his itinerary:

. . . We shall land at Point Manby, and, sledging our supplies over the Malaspina Glacier, shall establish a base camp probably on the Southern edge of the Hitchcock Range. Our further advance will be regulated by the conditions which prevail at the time. My present intention is, however, to advance up the Agassiz Glacier and make my highest camp on the ridge connecting Mount Newton with Mount St. Elias . . . We shall first attack

---

42. Alessandro Malaspina (1750-1810), a scion of the great feudal lords of the Apennines and another Italian navigator in Spanish employ, had explored this coast in 1791 leaving his name on the largest non-polar glacier in the world.

This, and the immediately following quotation are from THE ASCENT OF MOUNT SAINT ELIAS, by Filippo de Filippi, London, 1900; p 156.

43. TRANSACTIONS of the Technical Society of the Pacific Coast, San Francisco; IX-8

Their initial objective, in fact, at 5489m, is the fourth highest summit of North America, exceeded only by Denali, Mount Logan and Citlaltepetl. But after the Duke's well-earned triumph, this spectacular Alaskan peak remained untouched for another 49 years and for the next century was visited by only another dozen parties, less than half of which were successful, though the last of them managed to make a winter ascent. Meanwhile the main focus of North American, high-altitude alpinism shifted inland to Denali and Mount Logan, as recounted in Chapter X, below. Worthy of more than a note, however, is the fact that, one year before his death, 84-year-old William Williams attended the 1946 Annual Meeting of the AAC. As an honored guest, he heard the account of the second ascent of Mount Saint Elias, by a wholly American party on a wholly American route -- the same line up the Tyndall Glacier which he, Bryant and others had tried and which, at this writing, is accessible by boat up the Taan Fiord, but over what had then been a dozen miles of heavily crevassed glacier. Soon after their visit to the crest in 1946, the Molenaar brothers,[44] visited with Andrews at his home in Eugene, Oregon, and found his recollections of that spectacular mountain to be as sharp as their own.

*   *   *

Mount Fairweather, at 4663m the crowning peak of the Alaska panhandle, owes its name to Captain James Cook, who, on 28 April, 1778, enjoyed a brief respite from the weather traditionally associated with the Gulf of Alaska and its shores. The clearing was so unusual that the great navigator promptly and appropriately named the cape off which his vessels were standing – and the spectacular peak behind it. LaPerouse, coming along a few years later, noted the same features under the name "Beautemps."

Many generations later, in the years after the first World War, a number of alpinists began to turn their eyes toward this and the other untrodden summits of Alaska. Of these persons, one of the most vigorous was 37-year-old Allen Carpé, a telephone engineer by profession but an alpinist by preference. In 1931 he gathered an

---

44. Both Dee (b. 1918) and Cornelius (K) Molenaar (1922-1994) became long-time employees of the U. S. Geological Survey.

impressive company – Andrew Morrison Taylor, Dr. William Sargent Ladd and Terris Moore. Carpé met his death the following year by falling into a crevasse on his way up Mount McKinley; Taylor had already left his mark on that summit as well as Mount Logan; Moore was to become president of the University of Alaska and Dr. Ladd was soon to become AAC president.[45]

Opting for an early season attempt, they left Juneau by boat on 4 April. After 10 days at sea, and following several failed attempts at finding a decent landing spot, the party disembarked on the shore of Lituya Bay, where LaPerouse had beached and careened his vessels almost a century and a half earlier. Several days were spent in preparing a route through the considerable growth of alder (alnus rhombifolia) and finally, on 19 April, the four-man team started packing their supplies through the bush from tidewater and up the glaciers towards their mountain.

The preceding winter had been light, but now snow commenced to fall in earnest and the party was further delayed by having to return to the bay for the skis that were in their initial plan but had – on second thought – been left behind on the beach. Anyone who has ever tried to carry skis through a growth of slide alder will fully comprehend the party's problems, decisions and revisions. Seven weeks later, recurring snow storms having hampered their upward progress and with supplies depleted almost to exhaustion, Ladd and Taylor opted to go down so that the younger members of the party could stay for one final attempt.

Blessed at last by clearing skies, the early morning of 8 June saw Moore and Carpé high on the rime and snow-covered southeast ridge. After climbing to the summit through what passed for the night at this exalted latitude Carpé noted:

. . . *The going was pretty steep. We crawled, Indian fashion on all fours, distributing our weight on knees and forearms. It was very cold, certainly well below zero. As we approached the arête we measured the*

---

45. For more on Taylor (1875-1945), a sometime riverboat captain on the upper Columbia, see AAJ VI-411.

Ladd (1887-1947) was one of the AAC's greater benefactors. The building he gave the Club was sold 40 years later for well into seven figures. For more on him see AAJ VII-476.

Elected an Honorary Member of the AAC in 1976, more on Moore (1908-1994) can be found in AAJ XXXVI-317.

grade with a clinometer. 55 ° was maintained over a long slope and the steepest touched 60 °.[46]

Many Alaskan climbers, including two of these authors, have found that better progress is made on the high snowfields in the summer by turning the clock around and starting one's climbing "day" in the early evening. Moore, then an amateur geologist, always carried his Brunton compass and could thus measure the slope with considerable accuracy.

---

46. From Carpe's account in the ALPINE JOURNAL, XL; III-229

V – PRE-HISTORY
EARLY AMERICAN ASCENTS in the ALPS
Thorington

The interested scholar is referred to the AAC's 1943 publication bearing the same title as this chapter, also authored by Dr. Thorington. Copies of this small volume can be found in most good mountaineering libraries but are unfortunately no longer available for sale by the Club.

In 1943, one of these authors, after completing his three-year term as president of The American Alpine Club, updated his notes on early American mountaineering in the Alps, which had previously appeared piecemeal in the AMERICAN ALPINE JOURNAL.[47] In their earlier form they had contained some errors that were corrected in this revision. Dr. Thorington's survey, which had occupied moments of his spare time during the preceding 15 years, was intended as a reference for those interested in the mountaineering activities of their forerunners who crossed the Atlantic to climb mountains.

The original AAC publications on this topic contained a recitation of the essential facts pertinent to each ascent. In some cases these accounts extended to many paragraphs compiled from study of FÜHRERBÜCHER and other factual repositories, all of which this author had personally verified, but in the unearthing of which he was greatly aided by others.

The above statements notwithstanding, any attempt to present the development of American mountaineering in the Alps must be fragmentary, as most records were inadequately kept and much material is buried in crumbling press reports, forgotten diaries and incomprehensible entries in many FÜHRERBÜCHER. It is obvious, though, that American travel in and around the Alps began at an early date.

The first such visit of which we have credible record is that of Dr. John Morgan[48] who had served as a lieutenant in the expedition of

---

47. The pertinent AAJ references are : II-353; II-360; II-508; IV-97; IV 248; IV-460.

48. In 1775, Morgan (1735-1789) succeeded America's first traitor, the Bostonian Dr. Benjamin Church, as Director of Hospitals for the United States.

General John Forbes that captured Fort Duquesne in 1758. He resigned from the British army in 1760 and went abroad for medical study. Receiving his doctorate in medicine from the University of Edinburgh in 1763, he followed this up with the soon-to-be traditional grand tour of "the continent" in the company of his fellow Philadelphian, Samuel Powel (whose son and namesake was elected to the 14th Congress from Tennessee). Morgan later founded the Medical School of the University of Pennsylvania. His diary is preserved in the library of that school and an excerpt was printed on page 460 of the first volume of the AMERICAN ALPINE JOURNAL. It describes his trip from Rome to London across the Mont Cenis Pass, the earliest description of the crossing of an alpine pass by a native of the New World:

Saturday, Sep'r ye 8th, – We proceeded ab't 2 leagues[49] forward to a little town called Novalese at the foot of Mont Cenis, the highest passable Mountain of the Alps. Here we dined. After dinner mounted ourselves and baggage on Mules. We climbed this arduous steep & in the space of five or six hours – thro' a rugged uneven, steep & often dangerous Road, we at last reached the summit. A rude but sublime Picture presented itself all around – Hills highing their Heads in Clouds – Some seeming to pierce, & seem above the Clouds in the upper regions of Air covered with Snow – Water precipitating itself down the sides of the Hills forming innumerable Cascades & running with impetuous force to the foot of the Hill. They join as they proceed & at length form a River w'ch takes the Name of the Po & washes the Walls of Turin.

This was the most traveled pass of the western Alps and the primitive road referred to by Morgan was improved 40 years later by order of the Emperor Napoleon in order to expedite military access to northern Italy. In the year 1871, 108 years after Morgan's trip, the Mont Cenis bore, first of the great railway tunnels of the Alps, was holed through 13 kilometers of rock, concluding 14 years of work. The historically inclined reader is referred to a diminutive volume entitled THE MONT CENIS TUNNEL – ITS CONSTRUCTION AND PROBABLE CONSEQUENCES, published in London in 1873.

Peter Irving, older brother of Washington Irving, graduated

---

49. Merriam/Webster offers the following (page 1285) relative to a league: *1: any of various units of distance from about 2.4 to 4.6 statute miles; esp: an English unit of about three miles..."*

in medicine at Columbia in 1794, but, like his brother, soon became more interested in literature. He made a tour of Europe in 1807, also crossed the Mont Cenis from Milan to Geneva (more precisely, from Turin to Grenoble), and then visited Chamonix to see the glaciers. He *... rambled thro' the valley along the Arve. A considerable stream rushing to that river from the mountains over rocky channels. Rude & variegated scenery – green mountains cultivated to the summit – others with summits of naked rock – dome of Mont Blanc covered with snow.*[50]

Friday morning [26 July] *at 4 set out on Mules to Montanvert – a distance of two or three miles to the foot – ascend the mountain Montanvert on mules by winding path for considerable distance – then proceed by a zigzag path to master the ascent. The steepness made the marquis's* [the marquis Decius Arrigoni of Milan had joined them two days earlier] *head turn – he & his companion had to rely on the assistance of the guide to help them – The rest of us found no difficulty, each being furnished by the Guide with a stout staff armed with a point of iron.*

"On the top of the ascent a herdsman's cottage [This hut had been built in 1779 by Charles Blair, an Englishman resident in Geneva and was referred to by Fanny Hall as "l'Hopital de Blair."] *a little stone octagon building of one room, built for the accommodation of travelers. Over the door of this little temple were the words "a la nature." Here we were furnished with cream, strawberries, bread, & excellent butter. We had brought some cold roast meat from the hotel...*

"The view of the glacier from Montanvert very interesting – like a rough sea in huge waves & ridges, the ice in some parts transparent & blue – in others covered with snow – large rocks lying on it which have fallen from the mountains. Environed by mountains terminating in very elevated spires of granite called "aiguilles" – some of these shaped like sugar loaves but with sharper apex – other pointed like needles – some grouped together like the steeples & turrets of Gothic churches.

"Descend into the Chamouny valley to view the source of the Aveyron, a river that rises here & joins the Arve at some distance. It comes out from under the Glacier – a cavern of Ice from whence it issues – is at particular seasons particularly beautiful – being large – transparent – with huge blocks of ice fallen or pendant from the roof. It has been called the

---

50. This appears to be the first mention of Mont Blanc by an American. Heretofore, the massif had commonly been referred to in European circles as *Mont Maudit* (Accursed Mountain).

temple of the Genius of ice."[51]

The above passage makes it understandable that this Irving, having flopped in the hardware business, did little better as a writer. At the time of his visit, the climate of western Europe in particular, was still strongly affected by what historians have since come to call "The Little Ice Age," a period of sunspot quietude when mountain glaciers were reaching post-Pleistocene maxima and extending well down into areas not covered by ice during the 10th through 14th centuries but which are again bare of ice due to the climatic warming that became apparent in the later half of the 20th century.

When Irving was at Geneva, he saw Léonard Gaudin's models of the glaciers near Mont Blanc and also ascended the Salève. A week later, when at Lucerne, he examined the late General Pfyffer's 12 by 22 foot relief map of Switzerland.[52] Chamounix had been "discovered" as a tourist locale in 1741 by a group of eight Englishmen (led by Rev. Richard Pococke (1704-1765) and William Windham, the father of Dr. Johnson's frequent companion) who climbed up the glacier leading over towards Aosta and drank to the health of Admiral Edward Vernon (1684-1757). One year earlier Vernon had introduced watered rum as a standard beverage for seamen under his command and was henceforth known as "Old Grog." However, he was cashiered in 1746 for his part in publishing pamphlets critical of the conduct of the Admiralty.

James Fennimore Cooper toured Switzerland in 1828 and, while staying at Lauterbrunnen, saw the flag on the summit of the Jungfrau, which had been planted by several colleagues in honor of Caspar Rohrdorf of Bern, a 55-year-old zoologist who had recently led an extensive exploratory party across the glaciers of the Oberland. Cooper (1789-1851) served in the U. S. Navy for three years after 1808, but only became a writer after being challenged by his wife. Rohrdorf (1773-1843) spent most of his life in association with the

---

51. These excerpts are from page 81 of Irving's diary (p. 30 of MS #7) now in the Yale University Library – much of which was published in the BULLETIN of the New York Public Library for August-November, 1941.

52. Franz Ludwig Pfyffer (1716-1802), a native of Luzern, was a Lt. General in the French army and in the forefront of modern cartography. His wax and stone relief model of the Swiss Confederation, completed in 1785, remains a leading attraction of his home town's Gletscher Garten.

University of Bern and its predecessor School of Theology.

Cooper was followed three years later by his friend Samuel Finley Breese Morse Though the latter is best remembered for his invention of the telegraph he was equally notable as an artist and many of his murals still adorn the United States Capitol Building in Washington. While returning from Rome to Paris by way of Lago Maggiore, Morse ascended the Rigi and witnessed the sunrise on 28 August, 1831. He wrote:

"I am alone on the mountain, . . . with such a scene spread before me that I might adore, and weak, indeed, must be that faith which, on this day, in such a scene, does not lift the heart from nature up to Nature's God."

Morse had graduated from Yale in 1810, where he, like so many other distinguished American scientists and early mountaineers, had been a pupil of the illustrious Benjamin Silliman but had then gone to England to study art. Morse also introduced Louis Daguerre's method of photography to America.[53]

In his IMPRESSIONS DE VOYAGE SUISSE, [Paris, 1841; page 146] Alexander Dumas, père,(1803-1870) mentions a party of 10 Americans wandering through the night in the summer of 1832, on the Faulhorn above Grindelwald, complete with women, children, horses, mules and dogs. This volume also contains the account of Jacques Balmat's first ascent of Mont Blanc, taken down by Dumas 46 years after the event, in which Balmat denigrates the part played by Dr. Paccard in that epic of alpinism. Dumas was a dramatist and historical novelist who enjoyed the patronage of Louis-Philippe. 1832 was also the year that the Faulhorn summit hotel was first opened after two seasons of construction.

But, in a preview of many things to come, James David Forbes (1809-1868) the Scots physicist whose studies of glacial banding were to place his name firmly in scientific literature, mentions that on 17 September, 1842, he and his regular guide, the celebrated Auguste Balmat, having been alerted by two local lads, rescued an American

---

53. Morse (1791-1872), born in Charleston, SC, was also the founder of the National Academy of Design. This excerpt is from his LETTERS AND JOURNALS, I; p 402. A half century later, Morse could have ridden the cog railway to this summit – the second such aid to tourism in the world – the first being that of Sylvester Marsh up the west side of New Hampshire's Mount Washington, from which many of the patents were adapted to subsequent mountain railways.

traveller on the Trélaporte precipice above the Mer de Glace. In a telling footnote to this account, Forbes *"regretted to learn afterwards that he* [the American] *had not shown himself generously sensible of the great effort used in his preservation."[54]*

Among the first American women to visit Chamonix was 40-year-old Fanny W. Hall, a school teacher of Grafton, Vermont, whose book, RAMBLES IN EUROPE, contains the account of her excursion to the Mer de Glace:

. . . Having been reared in the cold climate of New England I had, at an early age, acquired the somewhat unfeminine accomplishment of sliding on ice, and though out of practice for many years, I found on this occasion the benefit of my early discipline... The guide paid me the compliment to say, 'Vous etes une chamoise...' When I told her [a peasant at l'Hopital de Blair] *I had come all the way from America to see her wild mountains her astonishment was unbounded.[55]*

In 1842, Rev. John Price Durbin, then president of Dickinson College, paid a visit to "the Jardin," an area of vegetation at some 3000m on the edge of the Tallefre Glacier, probably the first by an American, where he recorded his emotions.

. . . Never had I such a conception of the wonderful power of God, as when standing in the midst of the Alpine world... It thoroughly cured me of my earnest desire to ascend to the summit of Mont Blanc.

Durbin (1800-1876) had been an itinerant Methodist preacher in the Midwest but managed to get off the ground by selection as chaplain of the U. S. Senate in 1831. This passage is from his OBSERVATIONS IN EUROPE [2 vols, New York, 1844, p. 79].

* * *

Everyone who was anyone – or about to become so – got into the act. The future historian of Canada, Samuel Parkman (1823-1893) who was to follow the Oregon Trail in 1846, crossed the Splügen Pass from Como to Chur in the spring of 1844, but noted that

54. Forbes (1809-1858) was also the discoverer in 1834 of the polarization of radiant heat.

The grandnephew of Jacques, Auguste Balmat (1806-1862) also became the chief of the restrictive trade union, Le Compagnie des Guides de Chamounix and traveled much with John Tyndall.

This excerpt is from Forbes' TRAVELS THROUGH THE ALPS OF SAVOY; Edinburgh, 1843; page 82.

55. Two volumes; New York, 1836. The preceding quotation is from Vol II, p. 81.

the scenery was *"inferior to that of Crawford Notch"* in the White Mountains of New Hampshire. In making this observation, Parkman was reflecting a certain amount of Yankee provincialism for, other than in the final pitch of its southerly approach, Crawford Notch is definitely less fearsome in appearance than any aspect of either approach to the Splügen, then or now.

The militant Presbyterian clergyman, George Barrell Cheever (1807-1890) thought the distant peaks were the only thing to take a *"powerful hold on the soul"* after he had ascended the Salève and made the Tour of Mont Blanc. Benjamin Silliman, Jr., son, collaborator with, and successor to, his father at Yale's Sheffield Scientific School, turned up and made a crossing of the Simplon Pass but, in keeping with his heritage, was mostly interested in further study of the local geology. Crystals found near the crest of this pass had been the subject of considerable dissertation by Johann Jacob Scherzer of Zurich on his 1705 journey. The younger Silliman (1816-1885) is best known for his 1855 report on uses of crude oil which furnished the scientific basis for establishment of the modern petroleum industry.

Harriet Elizabeth (Beecher) Stowe, already the mother of six children, wrote of her 1853 visit to Chamonix and the Oberland. Mrs. Stowe (1811-1896) was sister to Rev. Henry Ward Beecher and had completed her most famous work, UNCLE TOM'S CABIN, the year before this trip. The following passage is from her SUNNY MEMORIES OF FOREIGN LANDS; [2 vols, Boston, 1854, letter 32, p 203]: *"We had entered Sardinia,* [recently united politically with the mainland under the rule of Emmanuel II, of the House of Savoy]:

. . . and the [customs] *officers, being duly satisfied that we were not going to Chamonix to levy an army among the glaciers, or raise a sedition among the avalanches, let us pass free. The discretion and wisdom of the passport system can never be sufficiently admired. It must be entirely owing to this, that the Alps do not break out on Europe generally, and tear it in pieces..*

I look at the strange old cloudy mountains, the Eiger, the Wetterhorn, the Schreckhorn. A kind of hazy ether floats around them – an indescribable aerial halo – which no painter ever represents. Who can paint the air – that vivid blue in which these strange peaks cut their glittering images? Of all peaks, the Eiger is the most impressive to me.

In researching this topic, we found records of over one hundred ascents of Mont Blanc by Americans prior to the founding of The American Alpine Club, beginning with the 10th recorded ascent of the mountain, that of William Howard (1793-1834) of Baltimore, professor of anatomy at the University of Maryland. Howard was also a mathematician and in 1829 laid out part of the route for America's original railroad, the Baltimore & Ohio. He made his ascent on 12 July, 1819, after having made suitable "warmup" climbs on Mounts Etna and Vesuvius in company with Jeremiah Van Rensselaer, II, physician grandson of General John Van Rensselaer and scion of the last patroon of upstate New York. They hired a total of eight guides for the Mont Blanc climb – including Jacques Balmat, who had been party to the first ascent of the mountain and was now 57 years old. Howard's party passed each night at the Grands Mulets, thereby cutting the time for the ascent from four to three days. Nevertheless they suffered from altitude and ultimately snowblindness, the latter problem not at all uncommon among early alpinists: *". . . If we attempted to go more than twelve or fifteen steps without halting, a horrible oppression as of approaching death seized on us, our limbs became excessively painful and threatened to sink under us. . ."*[56]

Other notable Americans who scaled Mont Blanc over the next two generations included Henry Fairbanks (1830-1918), on 5 August, 1856. This was the son of Thaddeus, who, with his brother Erastus, had patented their platform scale in 1831. [See Chapter VIII for Henry's grandson's distinguished place in service to American mountaineering.] His sister, Charlotte, frail and younger by seven years, went only as far as the Grands Mulets. They were both members of a St. Johnsbury, Vermont, family that became famous and wealthy for success in a different sort of scaling. Charlotte (Catty, who died at age 32) reported to her mother that, upon her brother's return:

". . . the rarity of the atmosphere and the summit did not affect him unfavorably but the wind and the hail blistered his face and eyes so that he is suffering a good deal. . . On the descent, however, the lady committed the unforgivable and dropped her alpenstock into a crevice [sic] *for several hundred feet. . ."*

Almost a year later, on 20 July, 1857, the mountain was climbed by James Kent Stone of Boston, who later became a Catholic

---

56. Van Rensselaer (1793-1871) published a series of lectures on geology in 1825. Howard's account was published in the AMERICAN JOURNAL OF SCIENCE AND ART for November, 1820; Vol 1, p 375. For a fuller discussion, see AAJ I-329.

priest under the name of Father Fidelis and spent much of his subsequent life as a missionary among the mountain peoples of South America. Stone (1840-1921) made the first ascent of the Blümlisalphorn with Leslie Stephen in 1860 and was also the first American to become a member of London's prestigious Alpine Club.[57]

On 2 October, 1865, Margaret Claudia (Meta) Brevoort (1825-1876), aunt and surrogate mother to W. A. B. Coolidge and one of the most accomplished women alpinists of the 19th Century, was the first American woman to make the ascent of Mont Blanc. Her famous nephew was only 14 years of age at the time and did not accompany her, but certainly made up for this dereliction in later years. Coolidge was to make his initial ascent of this peak in 1869.

On 4 July, 1872, Richard Morse Colgate, who later became president of the pharmaceutical company bearing his name, climbed the mountain with his uncle Richard Cary Morse. Morse was a nephew of the inventor of the telegraph and became the first General Secretary of the Y M C A in America, an office he held for almost half a century. They held a typically American celebration on the summit, complete with fireworks, 41 years after their more famous relative had visited the area.[58]

Analysis of the early American Mont Blanc ascents brings out some interesting, if mildly irrelevant, facts. The accounts written by Howard and Van Rennselaer were the first printed descriptions in America of an ascent of an Alpine snow mountain. No American ascent was made in 1858, perhaps because 1857 was a year of financial panic in the United States. Thereafter, American ascents were recorded every season except during the Civil War years of 1863-64 and Franco-Prussian War of 1870-71. After each of these periods, however, there was an influx of pent up demand. Increasing numbers of Americans made the ascent in 1865 and 1872, those in the former year obviously being undeterred by the highly publicized

---

57. Further information on Stone can be found in the ALPINE JOURNAL; XXXIII-453 and XXXIV-344.

58. Colgate (1854-1919) was the grandson of William, a soap maker who emigrated from England in 1795 and later endowed Madison University of Hamilton, NY, which thereupon changed its name appropriately.
This Morse (1841-1926) graduated from Union Theological Seminary in 1867.

accident following the first ascent of the Matterhorn.

Dr. Benjamin Lincoln Ball (1820-1859) seems to have been the first American to make an ascent of a snow peak in the Alps, other than Mont Blanc. He had been in Asia in 1848-50 and was on his way home when he crossed the Bernina Alps and climbed the peak now called the Torrenthorn. Ball was soon to leave his name on a rocky crag near the summit of New Hampshire's Mount Washington, where he spent two stormy nights without shelter in the summer of 1855 before rescuers found him. He achieved further notoriety a year later by having himself lowered into a cave on New Hampshire's Mount Willard, known as "the Devil's Den" where he found some small bones and the remains of an eagle's nest – but no devil.

The first American to become a statistic in the Alps was William Oxnard Moseley a participant in the 438th ascent of the Matterhorn. On 14 July, 1879, after completing the ascent, the 30-year-old Bostonian doctor and medical administrator had insisted on descending the lower portion of the standard route, unroped and against his guides' advice. Moseley slipped and fell 2,000 feet to his death. He was not an inexperienced climber, having ascended Mont Blanc five years earlier, but the evidence shows he was impetuous and the inevitable was bound to happen.

Other Americans were more successful at the game. Most notable was the expatriate clergyman, William Augustus Brevoort Coolidge, often with his aunt Meta, and their dog, Tschingel. He was to be widely honored for his alpine accomplishments, by the alpine societies of Switzerland, Italy, Great Britain and finally the United States, and he came by such distinction honestly; his grandmother Brevoort had climbed the Faulhorn in 1835.

Many other Americans, more notable in other forms of endeavor, made early ascents in these mountains in the years after the Civil War, and before the national organization of American climbing had been founded. Coolidge (1850-1926) first came to attention with his winter ascent of the Jungfrau in 1874, but achieved global distinction among alpinists during his decade-long tenure as editor of the ALPINE JOURNAL.. In all he made over 1750 ascents in the Alps alone.

The lengthy list of early American ascents also includes that of Henry Mather Warren of Philadelphia, a Wesleyan graduate who was later the first person to carry a collapsible, sectional boat across the Chilkoot Pass for use on Lake Labarge and the Yukon River during the Klondike gold rush. Warren (1853-1942) was already a lawyer, but was to become a writer and world traveler. Like thousands of others, he has gone to the Klondike; but when news reached him of the formation of Theodore Roosevelt's Rough Riders, he went "out" to join. By the time he got back to the "lower 48" though, it was too late; the terribly one-sided war was already over.

On 4 August, 1881, five years after the AMC had held its organizational meetings, and long before starting his meteoric political career, Theodore Roosevelt climbed the Matterhorn, having already climbed Pilatus and the Jungfrau, the latter with future AAC President Harry Pierce Nichols. By 1906 Roosevelt was a world famous outdoor figure and became one of the early Honorary Members of The American Alpine Club. David Starr Jordan (1851-1931), naturalist and educator, who became president of Indiana University in 1885 and of Stanford University after 1891, followed Roosevelt up the Matterhorn 10 days later.

Others active in the Alps prior to the 20th century included William Williams, the New York lawyer who later made a valiant attempt on Alaska's Mount Saint Elias [See page 30 and AAJ VI-407], who ascended the Monte Rosa via the Gorner Gletscher from Zermatt at age 13. Abbott Lawrence Lowell (1856-1943), a famous runner and cousin of the notable alpinist and gentleman meteorologist, Abbott Lawrence Rotch, and later president of Harvard, did so in 1890. Lowell was the younger brother of Percival (1885-1916) the astronomer who died in office as president of the Appalachian Mountain Club. Rotch (1861-1912) who built and endowed the famous Blue Hill Meteorological Observatory south of Boston, was even more attuned to the sport. He became a founding member of The American Alpine Club, and made five visits to the crest of Mont Blanc, mostly however, to look in on the various scientific observatories that had been placed there.

Finally, rounding out the early international presence of Americans, the Workmans, William Hunter and Fanny Bullock, natives of Worcester, Massachusetts, climbed Mont Blanc, the Matterhorn, the Zinal Rothorn and several peaks in the Tyrol in the 1890s, as warmups to their further and grander exploits in the Himalaya and Karakoram.

AMERICAN ALPINE CLUB

THE Committee on Organization of the American Alpine Club has carefully reviewed the comments that have been submitted to it regarding the proposed Constitution and By-laws.

In view of the general endorsement which the prepared draft of laws, etc., has received, the Committee finds it unnecessary to make in it other than verbal alterations, except to establish the two paragraphs:

1. The present seat or home of the Club shall be Philadelphia.
2. There shall be a life-membership fee of $50.

To facilitate the official organization of the Club and make possible the obtaining of a charter at an early day, the Committee on Organization has taken upon itself the consideration of the election of officers for the first year, leaving for the first general meeting the official acceptance of the By-laws as proposed.

Acting under the recommendation of a Committee on Nominations, the Committee respectfully submits to the members of the Club the following names for officers for the term of office extending to December, 1903.

A general membership list is herewith enclosed. Members are requested to send their ballots, with the names voted for marked or checked thereon, at the earliest day to the Chairman of the Committee on Organization

Respectfully,

THE COMMITTEE ON ORGANIZATION A. A. C.,
ANGELO HEILPRIN, *Chairman.*

ACADEMY OF NATURAL SCIENCES, PHILADELPHIA.

March 15th 1902.

VI – FOUNDING
APPALACHIAN MOUNTAIN ROOTS
Fay

*M*ountaineering is still in its infancy in the United States," wrote Edward Coleman, the expatriate English artist, for the ALPINE JOURNAL in August, 1877, nine years after his successful ascent of Washington state's Mount Baker. He went on:

. . . The absorbing pursuit of money, the strangely practical character of the American mind, so averse to anything merely visionary, are quite sufficient to account for the absence of that passion des montagnes which is so often to be met with in older communities. At the same time there are symptoms of a change; the clubs formed of late years in Europe, on the model of the Alpine Club, have at length found an echo in the Far West, and one has been formed at Denver, Colorado, which is a healthy sign, and a proof of a growing love of mountains in that section of the community [The Rocky Mountain Club had been formed in 1875, but lasted only a few years]. "

Coleman continued for another dozen pages, recounting the history of American alpinism as he knew it at the time, concluding his article with a recitation of the "*...principal mountains of the Northern Pacific coast, commencing North and going South:*

Alaska

Mount	Latitude	Height
St. Elias	60 ° 20'	19,500 feet ± 400
Cook	60 ° 15'	16,000 "
Vancouver	60 ° 13'	13,100 "
Fairweather	58 ° 54'	15,500 " ± 150
Crillon	58 ° 40'	15,900 " ± 500
La Perouse	58 ° 34'	11,300 "

British Columbia

Brown	54 ° 15'	16,000 feet ?
Hooker	54 ° 15'	15,700 " ?
Murchison	51 ° 50'	15,789 " ?

Washington Territory

Baker	48 ° 48'	10,814 feet

An unknown mountain to the South-east of Mount Baker [Glacier Pk.]

Rainier (Regnier)	46 ° 48'	12,330 "

St. Helen's	46° 11'	9,550	"
Adams	46° 12'	13,258	"

Oregon

Hood	45° 10'	11,225 feet	
Jefferson	44° 35'		
Three Sisters	44° 5'		10,500 "
Diamond Peak	43° 27'	10,000 "	
Scott's Peak	43° 4'		
Pit, or McLoughlin	42° 31'	10,500 "	

California

Shasta	41° 50'	14,440 feet

The latitudes given vary with different authorities and maps. Vancouver and Humboldt vary with each other. The above figures are, however, sufficiently near to identify the different mountains on the maps. "[1]

Apparently unknown to Coleman was the founding of the Appalachian Mountain Club, which had occurred 18 months before his article appeared. Members of that club were soon strongly in evidence in Europe.

Coleman was also a bit premature in his damnation of Americans as being principally involved in the *"search for money."* While this pursuit has without doubt affected a number of individuals, it has also bred an enormous amount of philanthropy. The Federal Income tax (adopted in 1909) has, without doubt, been a great incentive toward private munificence, but the largess of Andrew Carnegie and numerous others predated this landmark of taxation. The mountaineering organizations of North America have all benefitted greatly from the private philanthropy of their members. In later years, the Marshall Plan, of 1947, has been widely regarded, particularly among its recipients in Europe, as the greatest example of unfettered national generosity in human history.

An alpine conference was held at Paris in September, 1878, courtesy of the newly founded Club Alpin Francais, and three AMC representatives attended: Philip Cogswell, George Hammond and the distinguished Thomas

---

59. ALPINE JOURNAL, VIII-233 & 385.

Mount Jefferson and the remaining high peaks of Oregon were not named by Vancouver but rather derive from subsequent settlers half a century later.

Dr. John McLoughlin (1784-1857) was the humanitarian factor of the Hudsons Bay Company at Fort Vancouver who was later proclaimed as the `Father of Oregon.'

The name `Pit' was derived from the traps dug by local Indians for trapping game near the local streams.

Sterry Hunt (1826-1892), a native of Norwich, Connecticut, who had been with the U. S. Geological Survey for 25 years before joining the faculty of the Massachusetts Institute of Technology as professor of mineralogy. The next year, at a late August conference in Geneva, AMC president Charles Robert Cross (1848-1921) an MIT physicist specializing in electrical engineering, was himself in attendance. In 1881, at a meeting sponsored by the Club Alpino Italiano near Milan, AMC Recording Secretary Henck[2] was the representative. The principal spokesman for the CAI was Carlo Fanchiotti, who discussed at some length a problem that was even then beginning to become important to lovers of the mountains and their scenery – *the work and results of a committee on the planting of mountain slopes.*
. .

At a further meeting sponsored by the Club Alpino Italiano in Turin, in July, 1884, Augustus Elwin Scott (1838-1886), barrister from Salem and State Senator of Massachusetts, and Lucius Lee Hubbard, state geologist of Michigan, were the AMC delegates. Hubbard (1849-1933) was also the author of several non-scientific books. Three years later, Gardner Maynard Jones, librarian, also of Salem, Massachusetts, attended a follow-up meeting held in Rome. Jones (1850-1941) was elected treasurer of the AMC in 1885 and served as its president in 1893. At the time of this meeting, Msgr. Achille Ratti, later Pope Pius XI, was making one of his more interesting ascents of the Gran Paradiso.

And so things went, with the scientific and erudite leadership of the AMC, largely headquartered at the then Boston campus of MIT, providing a worldwide presence for American mountaineering. They did so with class, for throughout its first half century AMC presidents were unanimously men of great prominence in their fields, listed in WHO'S WHO, on the faculty of Harvard, Tufts or MIT, distinguished researchers, professors and clergymen. And they did so with foresight, too. During the first generation of its existence, the AMC built more than 300 miles of trails, mostly in the White Mountains of New Hampshire, with all distance and altitude measurements given in metric terms. But in time, the emphasis of the AMC on science, to the seeming detriment of more strictly mountaineering matters, stimulated a reaction by some of its members, as was noted by one of its most promising younger climbers.

The 27-year-old Boston attorney Philip Stanley Abbot, only a few months before he fell to his death on Mt. Lefroy in the summer of 1895, near

---

60. John Benjamin Henck (1854-1945), then professor of engineering at MIT, was spending the summer in Europe anyway – at the expense of the Bell System which employed him to help establish some of Bell's patents on the continent.

the pass which now bears his name and in one of North America's most publicized mountaineering fatalities, wrote a long letter to his friend and contemporary Charles Sproull Thompson (1869-1921) the Illinois Central Railroad freight agent in St. Paul. The recipient also had first ascents to his credit in Canada and has left his name on the difficult Thompson Pass in the Canadian Rockies. Abbot urged the formation of an "Alpine Section" within the AMC, of which the expressed object was *"to encourage expert climbing of a distinctively alpine character."*

In considering the characteristics desirable for membership, Abbot had also written to Professor Fay:

. . . Such experience as would enable one to become a member of a party in the Canadian Rocky Mountains which should climb without guides and do original work of medium difficulty. The practical use of the section will not be so much an appeal to vanity as the facilitating of getting properly qualified companions for climbing work. Although glacier work is the proper and normal test, we cannot apply it absolutely because there is considerable climbing in this country which is almost first rate and involves no glaciers. Therefore, I think we ought to commute glacier work for a somewhat greater amount of exploration in rock mountains such as the Sierras and the Rockies, giving special credit here to the ability to plan and lead.

I do not care if the section numbers only half a dozen at first. If we hold its standards up, we shall be the best, and indeed the only thing of its kind in the country and we shall grow as fast as the taste for mountaineering grows. . .

Abbot was justified in his pessimism regarding the number of persons that might become part of the section. It was never to grow beyond seven. Such types of alpine adventure took a serious setback with his death and his message languished. Yet, his optimism lived on in the minds of his friends and on 1 January, 1898, the AMC Council finally went on record:

MINUTES

On invitation of the Council Prof. C. E. Fay was invited to explain the plan of organization of the Alpine Section. On motion of Mr. [William Crowninshield] *Endicott it was voted that the report of the Committee on Alpine Section be accepted and adopted. The report in question is this: -*

To the Council of the Appalachian Mountain Club,

Gentlemen: -

The Committee appointed by the President under vote of December last to take charge of the organization of a Section to be known as the "Alpine Section" met with full numbers on January 1, 1898, and, after due deliberation, deemed it expedient to give effect to the vote of the Council by constituting themselves said Alpine Section whom they hereby request your honorable body to recognize as such and with the following By Laws: -

Art. I.   This organization shall be called the Alpine Section of the Appalachian Mountain Club.

Art. II.   Its object shall be to encourage expert climbing of a distinctively alpine character, and in particular among the mountains of North America.

Art. III. Its management shall be vested in an Executive Committee of four persons, to be chosen one annually by ballot by the members of the Section for terms of four years each. The executive officer of this Committee shall be its Secretary, who shall also act as Treasurer, who shall be elected annually by the members of the Executive Committee from their own number. The annual elections shall be held in January, but elections to fill unexpired terms may be held at any time.

Provided, that, in January 1898 the Section shall elect members of the Executive Committee for terms severally of four, three and two years and of one year, their respective successors to be elected for the full term of four years; and that for the year 1898 and until their successors shall be elected the Committee submitting this report shall be the Executive Committee of the Section.

Art. IV.   The Section shall elect its members from among the members of the Appalachian Mountain Club whose experience may render them eligible. Elections shall be made by ballot upon recommendation by a majority of the Executive Committee to whom the Candidate's record shall have been submitted in writing. Three adverse ballots shall prevent an election.

Art. V.   The expenses of the Section shall be met by an annual fee of one dollar, ($1.00) assessed upon its members; and whenever this payment is made to the Treasurer of the Appalachian Mountain Club, it shall be held by him - as also all other sums in his hand intended for the benefit of the Section - subject to demand of its Secretary.

Art. VI.   The Section shall have the power to drop any person from its membership for cause by a majority vote to that effect, due notice having previously been sent to the member against whom such action is contemplated.

We would further announce that, in case of the recognition of the Section as above and the approval by the Council of Art. III of the foregoing draft of ByLaws, Mr. Charles S. Thompson of Chicago, Ill., will thereby become Secretary of the Alpine Section for the year 1898.

Respectfully submitted,

[signed]   *Charles E. Fay*
                  Charles S. Thompson

Arthur Michael
Charles L. Noyes
Members of the Committee of the Council"[3]

Notwithstanding the failure of vast numbers to flock to the banner thus raised, by 1901, the seed of genuine alpinism had indeed germinated west of the Atlantic. Far-ranging Appalachians, frequently under the leadership of the first and foremost of these authors, had carried out many climbing forays in the Canadian Alps; casually in the early 1890's, and more industriously after 1897, following the creation of the Alpine Section.

Two other events of this period deserve mention as part of the background for this growth of interest. The first was the visit to the Canadian Rockies in 1897 of a party of prominent English climbers led by George Percival Baker (1856-1951), a wealthy manufacturer and amateur botanist who was accompanied by the first professional guide to work in North America, Peter Sarbach (1849-1930) of St. Niklaus (near Zermatt). This one event put the stamp of acceptance on the extensive district as an arena fully suitable for serious mountaineering and emphasized to everyone the fact that North Americans need not cross the ocean to climb challenging peaks.

A second influence that operated to the same end was the publication in 1896 of the elegantly illustrated book, CAMPING IN THE CANADIAN ROCKIES, the earliest of its type in this field, by Walter Dwight Wilcox (1869-1949) an original member of the AAC who became the Club's secretary in 1920. In 1894, with Samuel Evans Stokes Allen, the first to map the Lake Louise area, and Louis Fox Frissell,[4] Wilcox had accomplished the ascent of Mount Temple, the initial ascent of a peak above 11,000 feet in Canada. Wilcox's photographs also presented graphic evidence of the grandeur and extent of

---

61. From pages 153 and 154 of the Appalachian Mountain Club Minute Book, normally kept in the copper plate hand of its longtime recording secretary, Rosewell Bigelow Lawrence. On this occasion, however, the minutes were written by John Ritchie, Jr, 'Secretary pro-tem,' a noted astronomer and conchologist.

Michael (1853-1942) was a professor of organic chemistry at Tufts College.

Rev. Charles Lathrop Noyes (1851-1923), born in India of missionary parents, was Councillor of Exploration for the AMC.

62. Allen (1874-1945), Yale '94, was a frequent contributor to the ALPINE JOURNAL and APPALACHIA, a member of the Royal Geographical Society and an avid alpinist. His parents disapproved of their son's interests to such a degree that he became insane and was confined for the greater part of his life.

Frissell (1872-1943), Yale '95, became a distinguished physician in New York and was professor of clinical medicine at Columbia's College of Physicians and Surgeons.

the alpine territory available. Ten years later, the newly formed Alpine Club of Canada elected Wilcox an Honourary Member, largely on the strength of his writings about these ventures.

However, Professor Fay, the senior of these authors, writing in the 13th Annual Recreation Number of THE OUTLOOK, in an article entitled, *Mountain Climbing as an Organized Sport* was not sanguine. One could gather that he regarded true mountaineering as a thing of the past. The new "Switzerland" in Canada was:

. . . too remote to be availed of, save by a few. . . [As for the Alps, they were so hackneyed that] *the British Alpine Club has developed a marked proclivity for exploration in the unknown portions of the earth, so that to be a mere climber confers only a secondary distinction among its members. . . The Alpine Club idea has undergone a manifold development. Even in England, the land of precedent, it is... no longer quite the same. There has arisen a reaching out after prizes that reluctant nature has hitherto kept concealed in the uttermost parts of the earth [where] the joy of first discovery is held superior to that of winning the laurels of a first ascent.*

Rather wistfully Fay regretted : . . *that the future will not witness a large return to genuine alpinism, worthy as it is of being fostered and helpful as it might become to society and the state. . .*

In the light of hindsight, these observations may seem puzzling. *The joy of first discovery* is often inseparable from a first ascent, not some abstract entity apart from it. And both, in their attainment, almost invariably involve the practice of genuine mountaineering. Be this as it may, the AAC's first president's pessimism proved to be hopelessly overstated. Since new climbs, as the term was understood in those days, seemed almost exhausted, true mountaineering was doomed to fall by the wayside for lack of chance to practice it. Repetition of old climbs would not suffice because for the more inquisitive they have become matters of rote. Such seems to have been Fay's line of thought, yet it can hardly be accepted as a satisfactory explanation of his mood, for at the time he wrote the highest peaks in almost every area of the world except Europe had yet to be climbed – let alone attempted.

One should look a little farther, bearing in mind that the confessor of these gloomy views was destined, within the year, to assume the presidency of the infant American Alpine Club and to dedicate much of the rest of his long life to promoting its success. This paradox may be resolved, the other authors believe, by recalling that when Fay penned those lines, no one could have foreseen how, in the future, many clubs (yet unformed) were to popularize serious climbing and bring it within reach of the ordinary mortal. Such a thing had hitherto not happened. When pack-trains and comfortable camps were available at the very base of great peaks in places like the Canadian Rockies, the earlier bugbears of suitable companions, experienced guides, and costly access vanished almost overnight. Anyone who wished was free to indulge in the sport, under ideal training conditions and no longer at prohibitive expense. Across the continent, this changed the whole picture for the individual alpine aspirant. Once this concept of mountaineering access became established, results built up like snowballs. Everywhere, "graduates" trained others and then plunged into the wilderness, particularly among the mountains of the North American west, to seek the prizes which "reluctant nature" had provided there with such a lavish hand.

However, despite his momentary pessimism, Fay did not falter in his underlying devotion to mountaineering, summing up his article in words prophetic of the Outward Bound movement of a half-century later and touching on the fundamental social justification for an activity with such inherent objective risks:

". . . Its contempt of hardships, its acceptance of a certain element of personal danger to be averted by judgement and coolness, its alluring invitation to conquest in which the heart need not harden as it exultantly strengthens in tenacity of purpose, render it [mountaineering] *not only the king of sports for strenuous man, but the one theoretically the best adapted to develop fearless leaders."*[5]

Fay, despite his long record of interest in alpinism had seriously misjudged its future and succumbed to a belief common among British climbers of that era who felt that once the great alpine peaks had been scaled there would be no future for mountaineering and the sport would die out. In fact, however, the ascent of the great peaks, as subsequent history has shown not only in the Alps, represented not the past so much as the prologue for increased interest and activity.

* * *

Across the Atlantic in 1903, the ALPINE JOURNAL, (which had not known of the infant AMC 25 years earlier when edited by the distinguished Douglas William Freshfield, who became one of the new Club's first Honorary Members) under the editorship of George Yeld was quick to notice the newly announced American Alpine Club. In that interim, of course, many things had changed and the American presence in European mountaineering, as well as in all other elements of human affairs, was

---

63. Fay's views appeared in the 7 June, 1902, issue on pages 377 to 384. In that period, this magazine was among the leading journals of intellectual thought; after his term as President, Theodore Roosevelt enjoyed a long relationship with THE OUTLOOK as a contributing editor.

increasingly visible. An American, Coolidge, had even served as editor of the ALPINE JOURNAL and subsequently became a figure of enormous presence in the Oberland Alps. On page 341 of the February issue, the following notice appeared:

AN AMERICAN ALPINE CLUB. -- We are glad to be able to announce the formation of an American Alpine Club, of which Dr. Charles Fay is the first President. Its objects are defined as the scientific exploration and study of the higher mountain elevations and of the regions lying within or about the Arctic or Antarctic circles; the cultivation of mountain craft; the promotion and dissemination of knowledge regarding the regions above indicated.[6] Persons eligible for membership are those who have made the ascent of one or more mountain elevations which are considered 'acceptable' to the Board of Directors (no mountain will be allowed in this category which does not attain an altitude 2,000 ft. above the snow-line of its region); those who have conducted explorations in the Arctic or Antarctic tracts, or contributed substantially to a knowledge of the natural phenomena of those regions and of the regions of high mountain elevations; those who are engaged in the special study of (recent) glacial phenomena. Ladies are eligible for membership. Five honorary members – namely, H. R. H. the Duke of the Abruzzi, Sir W. M. Conway, Mr. Douglas W. Freshfield, General A. W. Greely, and Rear-Admiral G. W. Melville – have been appointed by the 'Board of Directors.' The Secretary is Mr. H. G. Bryant, 2013 Walnut Street, Philadelphia.

A dozen pages further down, one learns why the British had become so much more enlightened about their American cousins: a further notice included the fact that Professor Fay was an Honorary Member of The Alpine Club, a distinction he very richly deserved. The ALPINE JOURNAL notice concluded: "...the Club should have a prosperous and useful career before it."

These announcements were the outgrowth of a call issued by Angelo Heilprin, a vulcanologist and noted arctic authority, for a meeting to be held on 9 May, 1901, in Philadelphia *to consider the formation of an alpine society.* Following that initial gathering, a report was circulated to those whose names had been suggested by the people who had attended, stating: *"A meeting for the organization of an American Alpine Club was held in the room of the Geographical Society of Philadelphia, 1520 Chestnut St, on Thursday afternoon, May 9, 1901. At that time the following names were enrolled for membership in the association: Edwin Swift Balch, Esq.,*

---

64. As will be seen below, much of the language in this note has been carried forward unchanged into the basic principles of The American Alpine Club.

Thomas Willing Balch, Esq.,
Capt. Amos Bonsall,   Kane Arctic Expedition,
Herbert L. Bridgman, Esq.,   Sec'y Peary Arctic Club,
Henry G. Bryant, Esq.,
Dr. Frederick A. Cook,   Gerlache Arctic Expedition,
Prof. Chas. E. Fay, Tufts College,
Prof. Angelo Heilprin,
Thomas R. Hill,
Prof. Harry Fielding Reid,   Johns Hopkins University,
Prof. Israel C. Russell,   University of Michigan,
George Vaux, Jr., Esq.
The objects of the association are briefly stated in the paragraphs following, as well as the conditions which at this time are thought desirable to control membership.

The Committee on Organization believe that the general work and purposes of an American Alpine Club, as here outlined, will appeal to you; they accordingly invite you to join the association in the list of original members or founders, the number of which shall be limited to those members whose names appear enrolled before the execution of these By-Laws.

It has been recommended that the annual dues should not exceed Five Dollars.

Respectfully,
Committee on Organization   Edwin Swift Balch,
*   Harry Fielding Reid,*
*   Angelo Heilprin, Chairman,*[7]

All the persons named above became dues-paying members (at $5 per year) of the Club – with one exception – T. W. Balch. Not all of them stayed, however; E. S. Balch and T. R. Hill, along with several others, resigned their memberships in 1904 after the election to Honorary Membership of Robert Peary. But this controversy was in the future; the "alpine society" was in business. Enclosed with its report, the founders furnished a statement of the objects and qualifications pertinent to the new

---

65. Both the Balch brothers were lawyers. Edwin (1856-1927) served as president of the Geographical Society of Philadelphia and became a strong supporter of Dr. Cook, culminating his efforts with a 1914 work, MOUNT MCKINLEY AND MOUNTAIN CLIMBER'S PROOFS. Thomas (1866-1927) wrote extensively on various alpine topics including several works on Alaska and the then currently virulent controversy over its boundary with Canada.

Hill (1864-1923), nephew of the noted naturalist, Raphael Pumpelly, was a geologist and later an insurance executive.

organization. They closely resembled those of the predecessor club domiciled in London. Though amended slightly and with some minor changes in emphasis, these fundamental principles have remained intact.

AMERICAN ALPINE CLUB

OBJECTS:
The Scientific Exploration and Study of the Higher Mountain Elevations and of the regions lying within or about the Arctic and Antarctic Circles.
The Cultivation of the Mountain Craft.
The Promotion and Dissemination of Knowledge regarding the regions above indicated.

PERSONS ELIGIBLE FOR MEMBERSHIP:
Those who have made the ascent of a mountain elevation which is considered "acceptable" to the Board of Directors; no mountain will be allowed in this category which does not attain an altitude 2,000 feet above the snow-line of its region.
Those who have conducted explorations in the Arctic or Antarctic tracts, or contributed substantially to a knowledge of the natural phenomena of those regions and of the regions of high mountain elevations.
Those who are engaged in the special study of (recent) glacial phenomena."

On 15 March, 1902, the self-appointed `Committee on Organization of The American Alpine Club reported, over the address of the Philadelphia Academy of Natural Sciences, that it had
. . .carefully reviewed the comments that have been submitted to it regarding the proposed Constitution and By-Laws.
In view of the general endorsement with the prepared draft of laws, etc., has received, the Committee finds it unnecessary to make in it other than verbal alterations, except to establish two paragraphs:
1. The present seat or home of the Club shall be Philadelphia.
2. There shall be a life-membership fee of $50.
To facilitate the official organization of the Club and make possible the obtaining of a charter at an early day, the Committee on Organization has taken upon itself the consideration of the election of officers for the first year, leaving for the first general meeting the official acceptance of the By-laws as proposed.

Acting under the recommendation of a Committee on Nominations, the Committee respectfully submits to the members of the Club the following names for officers for the term of office extending to December, 1903.

President   Chas. E. Fay,

Vice-Presidents (two to be elected)   Angelo Heilprin,
*   George Davidson,*

Secretary   Henry G. Bryant,

Treasurer[8]   Wm. S. Vaux, Jr.

Councillors (four to be elected) Harry Fielding Reid,
*   John Muir,*
*   Israel C. Russell,*
*   Harry P. Nichols."*

A general membership list is herewith enclosed. Members are requested to send their ballots with the names voted for marked or checked thereon, at the earliest day to the Chairman of the Committee on Organization

Respectfully,

THE COMMITTEE ON ORGANIZATION, A. A. C.

Angelo Heilprin, Chairman.

---

66. The original printed notice contained the name of **George** Vaux, Jr, but it was crossed out and the name of his brother was substituted in longhand. George, however, did serve as treasurer in due course, after the death of William in 1908.

VII – THE SOCIAL ASPECT OF ALPINISM
Palmer

Much of this chapter appeared originally in the AMERICAN ALPINE JOURNAL, V-175

D r. Thorington has demonstrated (in Chapter V) that prior to the last decade of the 19th century, other than those living abroad or traveling there for other reasons, few Americans went to the Alps for climbing. Prior to 1870 there was minimal American tradition or presence in any major mountain area and the Alpine climbs by Americans were mainly confined to Mont Blanc (from the French side) and usually as a onetime venture. During the last quarter of the century, however, as their nation's economic prosperity grew, Americans became more catholic in taste, climbing generally throughout the Alps. Nevertheless, the number of their recorded ascents remained trivial compared to those made by Europeans. Obviously, distance and cost had much to do with this for Americans had also become increasingly active in the recreational use of their own mountains. However, there were few organizations in North America through which interest in alpinism could be maintained and even fewer publications in which climbing information could be found.

To set this part of our narrative in perspective, one should note the situation as it was a century ago. Interest in mountaineering for recreation was concentrated along the Atlantic and Pacific coasts. The Appalachian Mountain Club was 25 years old and had rendered great service to mountain-oriented people particularly by "opening up" and defining the mountain areas of the Northeast and engaging in recurrent ventures farther afield. For almost a decade the Sierra Club had energetically pioneered the Sierra Nevada. The Mazamas had organized climbs among the Cascades for half a dozen years, though in Seattle, the Mountaineers had yet to be set off from their parent in Portland. But all these clubs were not then primarily alpine organizations as the term is presently understood. Still less did their existence mean that Americans as a people were alpine-minded, for the expeditions of Kane, Melville, Greely, Peary, Cook and others had received wide publicity and the perils of polar ice with its months of privation, dark and cold – if either topic was considered at all – were vastly more real to the man in the street than those of glacial ice or rocky cliff.

As for winter sports, the now forgotten ski-trains that became a big feature of railroads operating out of Boston and New York in the years prior to World War II had yet to be heard of, and recreational snow-shoers were even then apt to be looked at askance. Not the wildest of imaginations, at the turn of the 19th century, visualized the future customary weekend automobile dash off to the hill country, or a ski area, or to polish off an already started new rock climb. Had they stopped to consider it, senior alpinists of that period might have been severely shaken by the thought that the inventions of the Duryea brothers, and their successors and competitors, would do more for the training of climbers than the sturdiest cayuse. Indeed, this narrative's junior authors made some of their first sustained ventures into extended high-angle climbing areas with the unfailing cooperation of a 1932 Chevrolet coupe.

*   *

The first purely social gathering of the newly formed American Alpine Club took place at the Colonial Hotel in Washington on 2 January, 1903. Eighteen members and various guests were on hand. Preliminaries as to the organization's aims, methods and eligibility had been settled, a constitution and bylaws printed and a governing board of officers and councilors were in office. The menu showed the members' dinner (at a cost of $4) to be well worth attending in its own right:

Blue Points

SAUTERNE

Cream of Chicken, Beaufort

Celery   Radishes   Olives

Medallion of Striped Bass, Rochelaise

Potatoes Duchesse

Terrapin, Maryland

Saratoga Potatoes

CLARET

Filet of Beef a la Richelieu

French Peas

Punch de Maraschino

Quail Roti au Cresson

Lettuce Salad

Fancy Ices   Assorted Cakes

Roquefort Cheese

Coffee

Distinctive features for an alpine society of that day were the reception of polar explorers and glaciologists on a parity with mountaineers and the admission of females fully equal to males. The Club, however, had to wait until the 15th presidency [that of John Case] for a woman [Elizabeth Cowles] to sit among its councillors and almost a century to elect its first woman president [Alison Osius]. The prominence of Arctic interest in the early years is shown by the presence among the enrolled members of names like Amos Bonsall (1830-1915), that can readily be found in any good biographical reference. Included in this category were Herbert Lawrence Bridgman (1844-1924), General Adolphus Washington Greely (1844-1935), Thomas Roby Hill (1864-1923), Admiral George Wallace Melville (1841-1912), Commander Robert Edwin Peary (1856-1920), Josephine Diebitsch Peary (1863-1955), Donald Baxter Macmillan (1875-1968), Angelo Heilprin, Henry Grier Bryant (1859-1932), later to serve as AAC president, and Frederick Albert Cook (1865-1940). A decade later, at the annual dinner of 1912, Peary, Ernest Shackleton and Vilhjalmur Stefansson were present together and at one time half of the Club's 12 Honorary Members were arctic explorers.

At that initial gathering polar exploration was decidedly more in evidence than alpinism. Assembled was what certainly at the time was perhaps the most remarkable gathering of polar explorers that could be found in any country. Afterwards it was accurately stated that the meeting represented the largest amount of Arctic suffering that could have been brought together at any table. One carefully anonymous wag opined that Greely, dining alone – if not on or with any of his former companions – could have met this description, unassisted.

In looking back, it is worthy of note that Professor Heilprin, himself, would barely qualify as a mountaineer by present standards. He was primarily a scientist, to whom mountains, as significant manifestations of nature, were objects for study rather than challenges to human prowess. His chief climbs were the four principal volcanoes of Mexico, which he ascended in 1890 during the course of a three weeks' visit. Heilprin knew his business, though. A year after those Mexican ascents, Josiah Thomas Scovell, a 50-year-old Indiana professor of botany, took levels along the railway grade from tidewater at Vera Cruz to Chalchicomula at 8,314 feet. In company with Otto Bunsen, he then carried spirit levels to a 1,500 foot-long baseline high on Orizaba (Citlalpetl) and thence triangulated the summit. The mean of his results was 18,314 feet, leaving – in the words of the editor of the American Geographical Society BULLETIN in its issue of 31 December, 1892 – . . . *little reason to doubt the conclusion that Orizaba is the highest mountain in Mexico, and possibly, in North America.* A century later, the official calculation of its altitude was 5555m, or 18,226 feet, while Heilprin, with the far less sophisticated instruments of his day, had determined it to be 18,205 feet. In that period it is obvious that the altitudes of both Denali and Mount Logan, the two highest points of North America were sufficiently unknown that the ALPINE JOURNAL (Vol XVIII p 68) of 1894 speaks of Mount Saint Elias as the second highest point, *"for the Mexican peak overtops it by about 300 ft."*

In 1906, the founder of The American Alpine Club attained the top of 1350m Mont Pelee in Martinique (his fifth ascent of it) and descended into its smoking crater, ascertaining that the unique tower which had been extruded previously was a solid block of rock – a tidbit of geological trivia on which four subsequent generations of college students were weaned. Few such students, however, are made aware of the person who made this study. Heilprin's significant bravery in this scientific pursuit made him the undisputed authority on the 1902 Pelee disaster.

Ten years earlier the principal framer of the American national organization of alpinism had commanded the Peary Relief Expedition to Greenland, where the Heilprin Glacier still bears his name. For five years he served as president of the Geographical Society of Philadelphia and for some time was professor of geology in the Academy of Natural Sciences. Culminating his career, an obituary resolution passed by the Club at the meeting of 30 December, 1907, specifically designated Professor Heilprin as . . .the founder of this organization. . . stating further that . . . *it was owing to his initiative and sustained interest more than to any other one factor* [our emphasis] *that this organization was instituted in 1902.* Professor Heilprin's devotion to the Club was unremitting and he attended four of the five dinners held prior to his death, during all which time he held the office of eastern vice-president.

A further tribute of respect read:
"The present successful status of the club is largely due to the high aims, liberal policy and efficient standards advocated by him from the outset. In his fieldwork in Mexico, Greenland and Martinique, he exhibited the greatest enthusiasm and perseverance as a student, scientist and explorer and at the same time endeared himself to his associates by his modest demeanor and genial disposition. He was a sincere and gifted student of nature and one whose name will always be associated with the early history of this club."

*   *   *

Almost a year after that initial Washington gathering, on the afternoon of 31 December, 1903, the first regular business meeting of the active members was held in New York City. The original officers and councilors were elected for another year, thus following the British pattern and establishing the tradition of a three-year term for Club officers. The publication of a series of monographs on the mountains of America was authorized. In time, this resolution took the form of three (now quite rare) large-format, illustrated, soft-cover publications:

I   –   THE HIGH SIERRA OF CALIFORNIA, by geologist Joseph Nisbet

LeConte;

II – THE CANADIAN ROCKY MOUNTAINS, by philologist Charles Ernest Fay;

III.-- MOUNTAIN EXPLORATION IN ALASKA, by geologist Alfred Hulse Brooks.

The second annual dinner occurred that evening in the rooms of the Aldine Association; 28 members and guests attended.[9] The menu was graced with "salad a la Goodsir" and "Mt. McKinley pemmican," President Fay having finally accomplished the first ascent of 3562m Mt. Goodsir, in the Canadian Rockies, during the preceding summer and Dr. Cook, who was present, having attempted Alaska's Mt. McKinley from the west.

It may be gathered from the above that the birth of an "alpine society" was not a spontaneous movement of a nationwide group of climbers to band themselves together. Rather was it a tentative effort by a limited and exclusive few to discover whether leading personalities in the fields adopted by the Club would wish to gather annually and thus constitute themselves a nucleus around which serious mountaineers and explorers from across the nation could rally when they desired or it became necessary. The general pattern of activity held in view – then and henceforth – was that typified by The Alpine Club [London], not to duplicate the place of or compete with other societies already in existence in the country but to include all persons who had a sustained and creditable interest in the various forms of serious alpinism.

In consequence, the early annual gatherings were small and informal in nature. In the morning there was a meeting of the Council to pass on nominations and to formulate Club policies. The directors would lunch together, then join in the afternoon open session of active members. Routine reports and business having been disposed of, papers and talks germane to the purposes of the Club were given. The remainder of the time was spent in social enjoyment -- a pattern that was to be altered only by the continuous expansion of attendance as the years progressed. The evening dinners were of similar character but distinguished by more elaborate addresses descriptive of outstanding feats of exploration or climbing in all parts of the world. Postprandial pleasantries were by no means the least enjoyable features of these affairs. For the first decades of the Club's existence accounts of these sessions, in the form of printed leaflets, were subsequently sent to the entire membership.

---

67. Most Club members of a century later would be surprised to meet in such a venue. The Aldine Association is an assemblage of erudite scholars of classical literature that took its name from Aldus Manutius (1450-1515) and Italian printer and scholar.

Growth during the first decade was slow. By 1911 there were a total of 80 members – only 35 more than at the first annual meeting in 1903. No particular reasons can be assigned for this slow rate of growth, unless it was the comparative obscurity – coupled with a generous measure of genteel snobbishness – in which the organization then operated and the fact that no membership drive had been undertaken. There was no dearth of climbing, but for many members, the pull of the Alps was sufficiently strong that American peaks and cliffs tended to be ignored in preference to the more developed areas in Europe. The American style of climbing, as it developed, tended – like other aspects of American society – to be individualized rather than communal.

Analysis of the Club's 1911 register indicates that fewer than a quarter of the names had performed recent ascents. Perhaps their collective maturity had something to do with the unfavorable and inaccurate image of stodginess from which the organization continued to suffer for many subsequent years in the minds of many. At any rate, the members' spirit did not abate, even if their meetings often reflected more of the joys of past climbing than anticipation of future ascents. Nevertheless it is an interesting tribute to their common enthusiasm the same small group of people undertook days' long railway journeys year after year, some from across the continent, to attend these meetings and thus nourish the life of the organization.

The AAC's fifth annual meeting was held in New York on 7 January, 1907, at the quarters of the Explorers Club. Notice was taken of the recent death of a distinguished founding member of the club and of its directorate, Professor Israel Russell. He had been a conspicuous figure in the mountaineering world, having carried out in 1890 and 1891, two audacious assaults on Mount Saint Elias with mining engineer, Mark Brickell Karr (1860-1917), on the second of which they reached an elevation of 4420m. In Filippi's narrative of the ultimate conquest of that mountain in 1897, cordial tribute is paid to his *"tenacious and rash courage"* and to the help which his explorations had been to the successful Italian party. Russell furnished a notable example of the prodigies that could be accomplished by enterprise, persistence, contempt for hardship and by reliance on common sense to offset lack of technical experience.

At the dinner, Commander Peary, Dr. Cook, Captain Robert Abram Bartlett (the only one present who never became a member of the AAC), Professor Herschel Clifford Parker (1867-1944), a professor of physics at Columbia, and the budding nature artist, Belmore Browne (1880-1954), were present with 27 other members and guests. Vice-President Heilprin presided for part of the evening in his last appearance before the Club. Dr. Cook repeated his barefaced fabrications about his ascent of Mt. McKinley the previous year. This, of course, was before any public challenge had been made to his claims, so the report of the meeting contained no hint of criticism. But some of the amazing (at least for that day) incidents related, such as passing the night in a snow igloo at 16,000 ft (4877m) and in a niche cut in a 60-degree ice slope with only a tiny stove for warmth, caused many a raised eyebrow in the audience. Three years later, when the truth became inescapably clear, his membership was not so quietly terminated. Though there have been a number of controversial and noisy resignations in the history of the AAC – as in many other alpine societies (to some of which reference will be made below) – Dr. Cook's remains the only expulsion in the Club's history. The message was that it was understandable – in an association of non-conformists (if not egotists) – to engage in a little self-glorification, but it was wrong to get caught in outright fraud.

During those first years of the AAC, the Workmans, Fannie Bullock and William Hunter, were extraordinarily active in exploring the Himalaya and Karakoram areas. In 1898 they had organized the first American expedition to an 8000 meter peak – Kangchenjunga. But – in the first reported case of the soon-to-be-chronic problems with native porters – were forced to turn back before reaching the mountain. In the Karakoram, a record altitude for camps at 6492m and a record altitude for women at 7070m were established. However, their very activity became the cause of controversy after the reported ascent of the north peak of Huascaran in the Peruvian Andes in 1908, by Annie Smith Peck (1850-1935), a school mistress from Providence and also a Club member. Her account had given rise to exaggerated reports respecting its altitude, some placing it as high as 7925m.

By the time of the Baltimore meeting of 1909, the Club officers had taken action to clarify this divisive matter by appointing a committee of unimpeachable qualifications to examine and report on the question. Subsequently, an expedition was dispatched to South America, financed by Mrs. Workman, to triangulate the peak on which Annie might just have beaten her record. Between the lines of these actions it was not hard to discern the jealous but well-financed hand of the patrician lady from Worcester, whose father had been the governor of Massachusetts.

Meantime, the small gathering at the Hotel Belvedere on 2 January, 1909, did not stint on either good food or good company. Their guests of honor were Professor Albrecht Penck,[10] the world authority on geomorphology then visiting at Columbia, and local philanthropist General

68. Penck (1858-1945) was professor of geography at the University of Vienna – 1885-1906, then at Berlin until his retirement in 1926. He was also noted for his studies of the stratigraphy of the Bavarian Alps.

Lawrason Riggs of Johns Hopkins University. The menu was even better than before:

Lynnhaven Bays

Celery   Olives   Almonds   Bon Bons

Clear Green Turtle

MADEIRA

Bay Mackerel Sauté Meuniere

Cucumbers   Potatoes Bernhardt

Filet Mignon, Bearnaise

French String Beans

Punch Baltimore

Roast Royal Squab, Guava Jelly

Smithfield Ham and Asparagus Vinaigrette

Cream in Form

Assorted Cakes

Camembert

SAUTERNE

Apollinaris

Demi Tasse

Cigars

Two years later, in 1911, the select committee on the altitude of Huascaran (consisting of Professors E. C. Pickering, the astronomer; Reid, the geologist; and Rotch, the meteorologist) rendered its report, accepting the results of the special triangulation; i.e. 6648m for the north peak and 6761m for the south. Mrs. Workman had gotten her money's worth. The latter peak was first climbed by a German party 24 years later.

In this decade, two gatherings of exceptional brilliance deserve fuller mention. The first was a special dinner tendered to an Italian nobleman on 28 May, 1907, at the Hotel Astor in New York. Luigi Amadeo of Savoia-Aosta (1873-1933) had come to the United States as commander of a small flotilla of Italian Navy vessels sent to represent that country at the Jamestown Tercentenary Exposition.[11] At this dinner, Admiral Peary met for the first time his once momentarily successful rival for the prestige of "Farthest North." Both made brief speeches. Then Chairman Bridgman read an address that had been beautifully engrossed on parchment in large

---

69. The Duke, one of the legendary figures of alpinism, was to command most of the Italian Navy during the first years of World War I. His death of cancer occurred while engaged in philanthropic work near the African village of Mogadishu, the scene some 60 years later of an ill-fated United Nations action by the 10th Mountain Division of the United States Army.

old-English letters of red, white and green, and bound in seal leather lined with silk:

"The American Alpine Club welcomes to America H. R. H. Prince Luigi Amadeo di Savoia, Duke of the Abruzzi, and congratulates him on his memorable achievements within the Arctic Circle and at the Equator since his conquest of our own Mount Saint Elias.

The Club gladly records its appreciation of this latest visit of His Royal Highness to the United States, which will renew and strengthen the cordial and historic friendship between his country and ours, for it will never fail to remember that to his countrymen we owe the discovery and name of America.

May long life and happiness attend Your Highness."

Professor Fay wrote a lengthy report on the dinner for APPALACHIA, [Vol. XI-254] in which he noted:

. . . Over the Broadway entrance of the hotel, at an early hour, the mingled folds of the Italian and American flags gave notice to the public of the coming function, while in the beautiful smaller ball-room covers were laid in sumptuous style for the thirty members and guests who had signified their purpose to be present. Besides the flags of the two countries on the wall at the rear of the head table, a profusion of palms almost entirely concealed the remaining lower walls of the room. The table itself was adorned with three large banks of Jacqueminot roses within connecting festoons of smilax, and, with the exquisite service, presented a rarely beautiful appearance. . .

Two years later, the Eighth Annual Dinner in Boston was considered to have set a new high-water mark for these affairs. Whether science, as exemplified by the eminence of those seated at the president's table, or mountaineering as represented by the company generally, be taken as the criterion, the occasion was an impressive testimonial to the position which the Club had attained in its comparatively brief existence. The guests of honor were Dr. David Starr Jordan (1851-1931), now president of Stanford University, and the renowned glacial geologist, Professor Thomas Chrowder Chamberlin (1843-1928). These men were respectively the incoming and outgoing presidents of the American Association for the Advancement of Science. Also at the dinner were Dr. William Morris Davis (1850-1934), meteorologist, geologist and president of the Harvard Travelers Club; Dr. Harry Walter Tyler (1863-1938), historian, scientist and president of the Appalachian Mountain Club; Professor Arthur Philemon Coleman (1852-1939), geologist of the University of Toronto then president of the Geological Society of America and Professor William Hittell Sherzer (1860-1932) geologist and glaciologist of Michigan.

Reference was made by the presiding officer, Vice-President Fay, to the great successes of the year by two of the Club's Honorary Members, the attainment of the North Pole by Commander Peary and the highest mountain ascent made to that time, by the Duke of the Abruzzi on 7493m Bride Peak. Brief addresses were made by Professor Chamberlin, President Jordan, Judge Harrington Putnam (1851-1937)[12] and Professors Ernest William Brown (1866-1938) and Edward Charles Pickering (1846-1919), both astronomers, the latter having also been the first president of the AMC. Dr. Coleman then favored the company with an illustrated account of his two attempts to climb Mount Robson. Dora Keen completed the program with an illustrated talk on the southern Andes.[13] This was one of the few occasions in its history when a photograph was taken of the entire assemblage.

A year later, at the Club's Ninth Annual Dinner, held on 31 December, 1910, at the Hotel Manhattan in New York, it was obvious that the gastronomic enjoyment had in no way diminished during the decade. The printed menu (at the same cost as previously but without wine) listed:

Cape Cod Oyster Cocktails
Clear Mock Turtle
Celery   Olives   Salted Almonds
Kingfish Saute Meuniere
Cucumbers
Tenderloin of Beef, Mushrooms Farcie
Potatoes Fondante
French String Beans
Sorbet au Kirsch
Roast Squab sur Canape
Salad Manhattan
Fancy Ice Cream
Cheese   Coffee

Another topic of great contemporary interest were the several attempts

---

70. The Club's third elected president, a justice of the New York Supreme Court, was born in Shrewsbury, Massachusetts, the son of Charles Adams Varnum Putnam and Ellen Triphosia Harrington. His relationship to the Club's 23rd president was definite, but very distant.

71. Miss Keen (1871-1963) married George W. Handy (1881-1982) of Philadelphia in 1916. She was a Bryn Mawr graduate (1896), joined the AAC in 1907 and was widely regarded as an authority on the then recent spectacular events of the Kenai Peninsula. She died in her sleep in Hong Kong.

on Mount McKinley by Club members. In 1903, Dr. Cook[14] had investigated the westerly side, and in 1906 claimed to have attained the top from the east. The storm of controversy which this provoked raged on for four years and did not really wane until the Parker-Browne expedition of 1910 brought back cogent proofs of Cook's mendacity. Those, however, who read Robert Dunn's THE SHAMELESS DIARY OF AN EXPLORER, a small but terribly damning book published in New York in 1907, by a member of Cook's expedition, were aware of the falsehood three years earlier. Compounding and clouding that matter was the further controversy surrounding Dr. Cook's claims regarding the attainment of the North Pole. Indeed, it was the McKinley fabrication that led more directly to the undoing of Cook's North Pole claim. With the benefit of sufficient hindsight, it is obvious that had Cook not resorted to the first fabrication, his other very valid contributions to exploration and alpinism would have brought him justifiably great acclaim and perhaps credit for the first attainment of the elusive pole. There is, of course, no stationary landmark among the shifting ice of the polar sea; in those days the spot could only be determined by precise mathematical calculation – an arithmetic exercise that can be done as easily backward from the desired result as forward from the observation. Nor should it be overlooked that, in his final dash for the pole, Peary had deliberately left Bob Bartlett behind – the only other man in the party who was competent at celestial navigation. Interestingly, two of the Club's Honorary Members were drawn into the public discussion on attainment of the elusive Pole. General Greely was quoted as believing Cook's version of his activities and Admiral Melville stood fast by his naval confrere, Peary.

Since this controversy continues to simmer in certain quarters there is little need to further evaluate any of the claims pertinent to Dr. Cook (and some other less publicized alpinists) save to point out a sensible moral for claiming a first ascent:

BUILD A GOOD CAIRN
TAKE A GOOD PHOTOGRAPH ON TOP
OR LIVE A GOOD LIFE
On one of these grounds the verdict of posterity will be rendered.

But – as is more fully developed in the following chapter – the attempts

---

72. Cook (1865-1940) a surgeon by training, became widely honored for his explorations.

to attain the summit of North America's highest peak became a notable topic in its own right and has received wide attention over the years – starting with the mountain's sighting by Captain George Vancouver in 1794.

Meantime, the social aspects of America's "alpine society" continued in good form. Its 11th Annual Meeting was again held at the Hotel Manhattan in New York. On 27 December, 1912, 43 members enjoyed a fine dinner:

Cape Cod Oysters

Petite Marmite

Olives   Celery   Salted Nuts

Striped Bass Joinville

Cucumbers

Filet Mignon

Peas   Fresh Mushrooms

Potatoes Rissoles

Curacao Punch

Breast of Chicken Chasseur

Salad Imperial

Fancy Forms Ice Cream

Assorted Cakes

Coffee

and then heard from three guests of honor: the expatriate Englishman, James A. Cook of the Swiss Alpine Club, and two distinguished polar explorers, Sir Ernest Shackleton and Vilhjalmur Stefansson.

VIII – TO THE TOP OF THE CONTINENT
Putnam

This was the title used by Dr. Frederick Cook for his 1908 opus on the "first ascent" of Mt. McKinley. While Cook's subsequent activities (including a 1923 conviction for mail fraud for which he served six years in federal jail) embroiled him in larger and more public controversy, the questions raised about his actions in Alaska caused a much longer-lasting stir among the smaller but testier group of alpinists.

For a fuller account of the early record of exploration and climbing on Denali, one should consult the 1967 work by Dr. Terris Moore, MT. MCKINLEY – THE PIONEER CLIMBS published by the University of Alaska Press.

By the late 18th century their reports indicated that Russian traders were aware of the "bolshoe (great)" mountains of the Alaskan interior, though – their interest being centered on pelagic furs – they were never motivated to visit or seek descriptions of them. However, on 6 May, 1794, Captain George Vancouver returned to Alaskan waters from his third over-winter visit to Hawaii, looked northwards from Knik Arm of Cook Inlet and noted in his journal that the upland terrain:

. . . between the west and northwest were not very remote; and even in that quarter the country might be considered as moderately elevated, bounded by distant stupendous mountains covered with snow, and apparently detached from each other. [Along] the coast of North West America …lofty summits formed in many instances the bases only of still more stupendous detached mountains. . .

After the American purchase of Alaska early in 1867, explorers and traders began to learn more about the mountains, but it was not until mid-1896 that the highest point received a written name, that of the man nominated on 18 June to be Republican candidate for the 25th president of the United States. This unfortunate choice of names was instigated by William Dickey, who wrote an article on the region that was published in Charles Dana's NEW YORK SUN. Dickey had visited the area but was apparently unaware of the long-standing native name for the "Great One" – Denali. William McKinley, a veteran of the Civil War, had spent most of his subsequent career in elective office and defeated silver-loving William Jennings Bryan twice for the presidency.[15] Two years later, Robert Muldrow, who left his name on a later well traveled glacier, and George

---

73. These explorations are discussed in ALPINA AMERICANA, #3. Eldridge (1854-1905) became much better known as an authority on the extensive coal deposits of Montana.

Homans Eldridge (1854-1905) of the U. S. Geological Survey, calculated the peak's height at the remarkably accurate 20,300 feet. In 1902, Alfred Brooks and his assistant David Raeburn actually traversed its northwest slopes.

In 1933, The American Alpine Club's incumbent president, Henry Schwab, summed up the early history of climbing on the Great One. His account began with the story of Alaska's famous Judge James Wickersham in May, 1903:

. . . Judge Wickersham and four men ascended the Kantishna [river] from Fairbanks and attacked Mount McKinley by the Peters glacier on the west, being defeated by the cliffs of the North Peak. Shortly thereafter Frederick Cook with three companions approached by pack-train from Cook's Inlet, crossed the range southwest of the mountain and made an attack from near that point, being defeated at an elevation of 8,000 feet. They then continued around northeastward to the Peters Glacier where they found the Judge's camp site. An attempt from here was likewise futile. . .[76]

Dr. Frederick Albert Cook's first written account of his activities in the area stated that in his opinion the most practicable route to the summit would be *"by the glacier that comes from the gap between the north and south summits, which glacier can only be reached from the Muldrow glacier,"* and came back in 1906 to make another attempt.

To continue Schwab's narrative:

. . . Starting in May, Prof. Herschel Parker, Belmore Browne, Dr. Frederick A. Cook and W. R. Russell, with the photographer Walter Miller and the packers Fred Printz and Edward Barrille, went up the Sushitna and its tributary the Yentna by launch, thence across to the headwaters of the Tokositna by pack-train. No feasible route up Mount McKinley could be located however, and the party returned to Cook's Inlet where it broke up. Shortly thereafter Doctor Cook went off with the packer Barrill to the Tokositna and the glacier at its head which he named the Ruth Glacier [after his step-daughter, Ruth Hunt]. *On his return a few weeks later he announced that they had ascended Mount McKinley."*

Then the fun began. Parker and Browne were highly skeptical of this claim and sure they knew better. So were many others, but Cook was now off on his 14-month, isolated Arctic venture before this hoax could be fully

74. AMERICAN ALPINE JOURNAL, II-121.

Henry Baldwin de Villiers Schwab (1887-1935), AAJ II-384.

Wickersham (1857-1939), then the Federal District Court judge for Alaska, was later the Alaskan delegate to Congress for several terms and wrote the BIBLIOGRAPHY OF ALASKAN LITERATURE - 1724-1924.

exposed. Alaskans familiar with the area were among the most skeptical and some of them, Thomas Lloyd, Charles McGonogill, William Taylor and Peter Anderson, collectively known thereafter as "the sourdoughs," set out by dog-team from Fairbanks in midwinter of 1910 to see for themselves. From a camp on Cache Creek they reached the Muldrow Glacier via what is now known as McGonigal Pass and by late in March had carried their camp to an elevation of 12,000 feet near the head of the glacier, where Lloyd remained. On 10 April, Taylor, Anderson and McGonogill ascended the ridge, unroped, carrying a 14-foot pole, in one of the most extraordinary feats of alpinism on record, and erected their flagstaff on the somewhat lower North summit, but the one which can be seen from Fairbanks.

There were skeptics of this ascent, too, but London-born Archdeacon Hudson Stuck, a man whose word no one could doubt, stated at the AAC Annual Meeting on 27 December, 1913, that when he reached the South summit three years after the sourdough ascent, their pole could still be clearly seen.[77] In the meantime, Professor Parker, with Browne and several others had made two attempts on the mountain, one later in 1910 and another in 1912. The first time they ran into difficulties at 10,230 feet on the southwest ridge and on their second attempt ran out of food. On their first trip, however, they succeeded in duplicating, at a vastly lower altitude, the supposed summit photograph that Dr. Cook had published. Very soon thereafter, the not-so-good doctor was dropped from WHO'S WHO and expelled from The American Alpine Club.

Schwab resumed his Denali saga:

. . . *Although Mount McKinley* [north peak] *had been conquered, there remained the necessity of someone standing upon the highest point before an actual first ascent could be claimed. On March 17th, 1913, Archdeacon Hudson Stuck, Harry P. Karstens, Robert G. Tatum, the half-breed Walter Harper* [whose father, Arthur, had come from Ireland], *and an Indian boy started from Nenana with dog sleds for the Cache Creek base camp where they arrived on April 10th. Freighting to the head of the Muldrow Glacier took them until May 9th. The great northeast* [now Karstens] *ridge was found to be so riven and shattered by the earthquake of the year previous, that it required three weeks of step-cutting before they could establish camp at the gateway to the 'Grand Basin,' which point they called 'Parker Pass.' Further camps were made in the Grand Basin: on June 3rd at 16,500 feet; on June 5th at 17,500 feet; and on June 6th at 18,000 feet. From the latter*

---

75. Stuck (1863-1920) had served his church in Dallas for 10 years before assignment to the Yukon in 1904. He was the author of five books on arctic topics. His diocesan superior was the Rt. Rev. Peter Trimble Rowe, Anglican bishop of Alaska.

the South and highest summit of Mount McKinley was ascended on June 7th by Stuck, Karstens, Tatum and Harper, the party being favored with clear weather and good conditions[78]

* * *

At the winter meeting of 1912, the congratulations of the Club were extended to Messrs. Parker, Palmer and Browne, and to Miss Keen, for their documented successes in conquering Mts. McKinley, Sir Sandford and Blackburn, during the past summer. That evening Dora Keen told of taking her pack dogs up sharp ridges and weathering storms in snow caves. Other speakers on this occasion were Sir Ernest Shackleton, Vilhjalmur Stefansson, Admiral Peary, Herschel Parker and Belmore Browne.

During those years it was appropriate that Justice Putnam, fortuitously an "official referee" by appointment of the United States Supreme Court, presided over The American Alpine Club for the youthful organization was the focal group for much of the subsequent controversy over the alleged accomplishments of Dr. Cook. Though that argument continued to swirl vigorously in June of 1911, the judge stayed sufficiently above the furor to tender a dinner in New York to honor John Muir, where 17 members gathered to pay their respects to the Club's recent "president in absentia," the only occasion on which the noted conservationist met personally with a Club gathering. After dinner, Muir gave a speech dealing with his early career and extensive explorations in the Sierra Nevada. It is worthy of more than parenthetic note that the AAC's second president [from 1908-1911] was already widely regarded as the nation's – and perhaps the world's – environmental conscience, a status that only increased with time.

About a year later, Judge Putnam again entertained the nearby members at a special dinner, this time to honor Henry Fairbanks Montagnier (1877-1933), the distinguished and scholarly expatriate American mountaineer whose then residence near San Remo on the Ligurian coast of Italy had precluded his attendance at any Club gathering. Montagnier, whose maternal grandfather had also been an alpinist [see Chapter V] had ascended more than 70 summits in the Alps. His impressive personal library of alpine literature numbered in excess of 4,000 volumes, many of which he donated to the Club during his lifetime and another 500 of which came later from his estate. In gratitude for his final generosity, the Club's council voted that this valuable book collection should henceforth be known as THE MONTAGNIER

---

76. Students of Alaska Range toponymy will recognize the derivation of a number of modern place names in the preceding lines. But with Cook's public discomfiture a large number of the names he had applied to features in the vicinity of Denali were dropped from usage.

MEMORIAL LIBRARY.

Five years after this dinner, in 1917, the Club was able to return him a small favor. The Italian government had abruptly ordered him to leave the country on the suspicion that he was a spy. At that time, the Montagnier, whose maternal ancestry was French and who was known as an authority on the literature of Mont Blanc [See AAJ II-234] made his home near the foothills of the Alps where some of his solitary rambles took him near the mountain frontiers of allied France and neutral Switzerland. However, his possession of numerous detailed topographic maps of the peaks just did not look right to a nervous government. After the disastrous Battle of Caporetto [now Kobarid] the previous spring, the Italian government felt that it had a lot to be nervous about.[79]

Montagnier had been forced to break up his home and remove his bulky library to Switzerland – a matter of no little difficulty under wartime conditions. He reported this discouraging affair to his American friends and at their request the Department of State made representations to Rome on his behalf. In time, the whole affair turned out to be a monument to bureaucratic idiocy. But three years later, when Montagnier attended the International Congress of Alpinism at Monaco (a meeting that ultimately gave rise to the present world body of alpinism, the UIAA) he was a representative of the AAC and the Alpine Club, not the Club Alpino Italiano.

Visualizing the great future of alpinism in North America, Judge Putnam continually urged the expansion of Club membership, extending it to be more representative of the entire country and sport. At the same time he was attentive to other circumstances and showed a grasp of the bigger and traditional fellowship of alpinism. When Rudolph Taugwalder, a noted guide from Zermatt, became crippled by frostbite and lost most of his hands as a result of his heroism with Annie Peck on Huascaran in 1908, Putnam led a subscription on Taugwalder's behalf. In conjunction with Benjamin Frank Seaver, the Club's treasurer, he continued for many years to solicit aid for this worthy but unfortunate guide.[80]

In 1914, the AAC's second president died. John Muir had been on its council from the beginning, though he had attended but one of its then exclusively East Coast meetings. He did, however, have a massive presence among the climbers of the Sierra Nevada and Alaska and cast a shadow that

---

77. Students of historical or military trivia will note that Erwin Rommel (1891-1944), who achieved greater distinction a generation later, commanded the infantry company that made the initial disastrous fracture in the Italian lines.

78. See AMERICAN ALPINE JOURNAL, I-213, for more on Seaver.

still influences AAC policy towards exploitive restraint in approaching the world's wilderness and alpine areas. At the 1916 annual meeting of the AAC, Professor Henry Fairfield Osborn (1857-1935) the distinguished paleontologist and president of the American Museum of Natural History, gave a personal remembrance of Muir:

"He exemplified tenderness, idealism and indomitable personal force – the majesty of the human soul in overcoming difficulties. In the wilderness he was a superman. He held that the works of nature are the works of God. Writing was exceedingly arduous for him and was probably the hardest work he did. He owed much of his power of description to his study of Milton, Carlyle and the Bible; and could recite much of the latter from memory.

"One day, on an Alaska-bound steamer, he was pointing out the beauties of the scenery and telling of his travels to an interested group of passengers. A man who could not understand such enthusiasm for nature interrupted; `Pardon me, Mr. Muir, this is all very well, but how do you make your living?' Temporarily nonplussed by the irrelevance of the question, Muir withheld a reply, but one of the ladies present turned to the questioner to ask what his own calling might be. To the amazement of everyone, it turned out that he was a horse-car manufacturer from Boston. A few days later, the same man again joined a group to which Muir was talking, and inquired; `Is that a bit of snow up there, or is it a glacier?' Muir's eyes twinkled as he replied; `Yes, it is a glacier, and I wonder how the poor thing makes a living way up there'."

Mention of the Montagnier library, above, anticipates the order of events. The original offer was received in the summer of 1911 and had been officially accepted a year before the dinner in honor of the donor. But there were much more far-reaching consequences for the AAC possessed no quarters for properly housing so many books, nor, as an unincorporated entity, could it legally accept them. Thus, over the next few years, several possibilities were explored. Finally, during the presidency of Henry Grier Bryant[81] and at a meeting on 8 January, 1916, in New York, a formal incorporation was consummated – appropriately enough – under the laws of Pennsylvania.

The charter's critical provisions have stood the test of time and read as follows:

1. The name of the intended corporation is
        THE AMERICAN ALPINE CLUB

---

79. A Philadelphia lawyer, Bryant (1859-1932) was a collaborator with "Chief Engineer" Melville in the determination of Arctic Ocean drift patterns. See AAJ II-108

2. *The purposes for which the said corporation is formed are as follows:*

• *The scientific exploration and study of high mountain elevations and of the regions lying within or about the Arctic and Antarctic Circles*

• *The cultivation of the mountain craft*

• *The promotion and dissemination of knowledge regarding the regions above indicated*

• *It shall for its primary work undertake the study of the high mountains of the world, gathering in the facts and observing phenomena pertaining to them, and shall publish a series of illustrated publications of these mountains for the purpose of presenting a complete description of the alpine mountains of the world*

3. *The business of the corporation is to be transacted in the City of Philadelphia, State of Pennsylvania, or at such other place or places as the Board of Directors may designate from time to time*

4. *The corporation shall have perpetual succession by its corporate name*

5. *The yearly income of the corporation shall be without limit*

6. *The said corporation shall have no capital stock. The names and residences of the subscribers are as follows: HENRY G. BRYANT, 2013 WALNUT STREET, PHILADELPHIA, PA.; GEORGE VAUX, JR., BRYN MAWR, PA.; J. HENRY SCATTERGOOD, VILLA NOVA, PA.; J. WILLIAM WHITE, 1810 RITTENHOUSE SQUARE, PHILADELPHIA, PA; THOMAS DEWITT CUYLER, PHILADELPHIA, PA.*

7. *The number of directors is fixed at nine, and the names and residences of those who are chosen directors for the first year are as follows: HENRY G. BRYANT, 2013 WALNUT STREET, PHILADELPHIA, PA.; HARRY FIELDING REID, 608 CATHEDRAL STREET, BALTIMORE, MD.; RODNEY l. GLISAN, 612 SPALDING BLDG., PORTLAND, ORE.; HOWARD PALMER, NEW LONDON, CONN.; ALLSTON BURR, 60 STATE STREET, BOSTON, MASS.; LEWIS L. DELAFIELD, 20 EXCHANGE PLACE, NEW YORK CITY; EDWARD C. PICKERING, CAMBRIDGE, MASS.; HARRINGTON PUTNAM, 404 WASHINGTON AVE., BROOKLYN, N.Y.; J. HENRY SCATTERGOOD, VILLA NOVA, PA.*

Witness Our Hands and Seals this twenty-second day of November, A. D. 1915.

In anticipation of owning the remainder of the Montagnier collection the Club concluded a contract with the New York Public Library, and the first act of the membership was its ratification. The initially received books were then deposited as a loan collection in a special room that was also open to the public. An excellent lecture hall and conference room were also made available for the members' use. The public library on Fifth Avenue between 41st and 42nd Streets thus became the de facto headquarters for America's "alpine society" for the next 13 years – until 1929, and proved to be a valuable stimulus for its growth. A small endowment was raised, initially totaling $1,025, the income from which was earmarked for the acquisition of new volumes. Seventeen members, besides President Bryant, contributed to this fund.

In later years, and with later gifts, the largest of which, to this date, have come from Dr. Thorington, Arkel Erb, Henry Hall, Horst von Hennig, Dr. and Mrs. Beckett Howorth, Nicholas Clinch and John Boyle, the Club was able to open several branch libraries with its numerous duplicate volumes. The other locations were at the Malibu Public Library, the Mountaineers Clubhouse, Teton County (Wyoming) Public Library, and Yosemite National Park. But with completion of the move of the Club's main facility to Golden, Colorado in 1993, by far the largest "branch" remained temporarily in New York.

At about the same time, the AAC decided to sponsor a project for the creation of an association of mountaineering clubs of North America. Invitations issued to 18 such groups brought a most gratifying response and the concept was formally begun on 31 May, 1916. The AAC's librarian, Leroy Jeffers, who initiated the idea, was appointed its general secretary and his office in the Public Library became its headquarters. The aim was to act as a clearinghouse for information to and from the constituent clubs, and a small but concise bulletin of news and statistics was distributed to them regularly thereafter until the energetic secretary lost his life in a private airplane accident.

In those 10 years, the consortium grew to include 71 organizations with a combined membership in excess of 100,000 persons. The community of interest, in addition to out-of-doors and climbing activities generally, lay in the preservation of natural scenery and the development of recreational activity in the national parks and forests.[82] As a sideline to the main activity, Jeffers compiled the AAC's collection of mountain photographs, which reached more than 4,000 views before his death.

At the meeting of 30 December, 1916, Mr. Bryant's term concluded and Professor Fay was elected for his third term as the AAC's chief executive, this incumbency covering the war years of 1917-19. Bryant had completed

---

80. For more on Jeffers (1878-1926) see the ALPINA Section of APPALACHIA XVI-540.

The association included the British Columbia Mountaineering Club and the first Kootenay Mountain Club, but not the somewhat more chauvinistic Alpine Club of Canada.

15 years of continuous service on the Club's board, the first nine years as its secretary and then three years as vice-president. Fortunately, American mountaineering was not to be deprived of his unique knowledge for he remained as a director for another six years. In his private capacity as a lawyer, he had carried almost single-handedly the difficult and `pro bono' legal research and detailed arrangements for the club's formal incorporation.

In more informal moments, Bryant liked to tell of his meeting with the AAC's first Honorary Member, the celebrated Duke of the Abruzzi, while Bryant was returning from a fruitless attempt on the southwest ridge of Mount Saint Elias – the line that was later used in the first American ascent of this peak. After a terrible night spent among the mosquitoes in his last camp on the shore near the Malaspina Glacier, the Duke was then resting on his borrowed yacht, *Agie*, at anchor off Yakutat. Bryant's party had been the first to cross the full width of this massive, piedmont glacier. However, he did not wish to pass by on his way home, when they were so near, without tendering his congratulations upon the Duke's successful ascent. The two parties had been in the field simultaneously, but on different sides of the mountain. Bryant made his way aboard and was shown into the cabin. There he saw the Duke, who spoke quite good English, reclining on a locker, clad in flannel trousers and sweater *"so disfigured by venomous bites as to be about unrecognizable."* He saw Bryant and said, *"Mr. Bryant, I have conquaired zee Mt. St. Elias, but ze mosquitoes, zay have conquaired me!"*

The Annual Meeting of 29 December, 1917, was held in Boston, but was much smaller than usual. Even the secretary, Major Robert Hollister Chapman,[83] was kept away by wartime duties. Resolutions of amity and allied solidarity had been communicated to the British and Canadian clubs the previous year, and now similar messages were proposed for transmission to the French and Italian Clubs. Professor Fay congratulated those present on their successful continuance during this trying period and offered words for the resolution:

"As fellow alpinists we are proud of their record of achievement. . . on the icy mountain barriers where alpinism has demonstrated its value in preparing armies for action above the snow-line. To this fraternal greeting, we would join the assurance... of our unshaken conviction of the successful issue of the cause of civilization. Our hearts are with you, our hands are joined with yours in a grasp more fraternal than ever before."

---

81. Like many another alpinist, Chapman (1869-1920) was an employee of the U. S. G. S. after 1890 and did much exploration in the Canadian Rockies and Selkirks from 1910 to 1915. See APPALACHIA XV-106 & 235.

The AAC had little formal part in aiding the military effort of World War I, but two dozen years later, in another global conflict, most AAC officials and many members of the nation's regional mountaineering clubs were actively involved in the planning, equipping, training and leading in combat of the only formally constituted mountain troops among the Allied forces arrayed against Hitler, Mussolini and Hirohito.[84] But, in that first World War, the combat feats of Italian Alpini and Austrian Kaiser-Jaeger units in the Dolomite and Julian Alps were among the most heroic in military and mountaineering history. [See AAJ V-250 for TERROR ROCK by H. Adams Carter, a brief account of but one incident in this fascinating sidebar to the main conflict areas of World War I]. In the Dolomite Mountains of northeast Italy the trenches took on the form of tunnels and gains were measured as frequently in the vertical dimension as in the horizontal.

At the dinner following the 1917 meeting, the Club's strong initial focus on arctic activities was given renewed prominence when Admiral Robert Peary gave a stirring and prophetic address on the importance of the United States securing command of the air. And in a concluding talk, Donald Baxter MacMillan spoke of his journey in search of Crocker Land and of finding relics of the expeditions led in the 1850's by the Philadelphia explorer, Dr. Elisha Kent Kane (1820-1857), the surgeon for the two expeditions outfitted by Philadelphian Henry Grinnell in the 1850s to search for traces of Sir John Franklin.

There was no formal membership meeting of the AAC for 1918, but a council meeting was held in March, 1919, and a full meeting of the membership was held in New York on 3 January, 1920. At that time, the Club elected another lawyer, New Yorker Lewis Livingston Delafield as the fifth person to hold the office of president.[85] The evening program included a report by Arthur Tate on his 1919 climbs in the Wind River Range of Wyoming, Leroy Jeffers' account of his first ascent of the northeast peak of Mount Moran in the Tetons; and one of these authors described two first ascents that he had made in the Tonquin Valley of the Canadian Rockies with Robert Chapman and 25-year-old Allen Carpé.[86]

A few days after the meeting, Secretary Chapman died from

---

82. In 1990, in preparation for celebrating the golden anniversary of the establishment of mountain infantry units within the United States Army, the Club commissioned the writing of GREEN COGNAC, a narrative of the 10th Mountain Division's formation and activities.

83. For more on Delafield, see AAJ V-405.

84. See AMERICAN ALPINE JOURNAL XV-453 for more on Tate.
See AMERICAN ALPINE JOURNAL I-511 for details of Carpé's death on Mount McKinley.

complications of the influenza epidemic then sweeping the world. For many years a member of the U. S. Geological Survey and one-time Superintendent of Glacier National Park, his name was thereafter briefly applied to a peak in that domain. However, Howard Palmer applied his name with greater durability to a striking and isolated summit in the Selkirk Range near the apex of the Big Bend of the Columbia. The crisis for the AAC, in having its official records, all in the personal custody of the secretary, suddenly unavailable, was eased by the willingness of Walter Dwight Wilcox, then living in Washington, to take charge of the situation. The files were enough to fill a taxicab and were thus transferred to the Wilcox residence, where they remained for the next six years under his efficient custody.

NOMINATIONS

FOR

Officers and Councillors

A. A. C.

President.

CHAS. E. FAY.

Vice-Presidents.
(Two to be elected.)

ANGELO HEILPRIN,

GEORGE DAVIDSON.

Secretary.

HENRY G. BRYANT.

Treasurer.

~~GEORGE~~ VAUX, JR.

Councillors.
(Four to be elected.)

HARRY FIELDING REID,

JOHN MUIR,

ISRAEL C. RUSSELL

HARRY P. NICHOLS.

The "great peak of the Mexican Mountains" *Lt. Z. Pike, photo*

I

Montée de M. de Saussure sur la Cime du Mont Blanc en 1785

"A dangerous position" on the Finsteraarhorn in 1822

Jean Louis Rudolphe Agassiz (1807-1873) paleontologist and initiator of modern
glacier theory

Arnold Henry Guyot (1807-1884) geographer and geologist

Anglo-American climbing party at Lake Louise in 1897; C. S. Thompson and C. E. Fay at left

The Duke of the Abruzzi's guides on Mount Saint Elias in 1897—A. Maquinaz, G. Petigax, L. Croux, and A. Pellisier

The Vaux family's reference boulder near the snout of the Victoria Glacier in 1903

Talung Peak, prior to its ascent by the Workman expedition

Edward Whymper, honorary member, a year before his death

The Workmans, Fanny Bullock & William Hunter, in a civilized environment

Angel's landing at Zion National Park, in 1919

John Muir, AAC's 3rd President, among the big trees later flooded in Hetch Hetchy Valley

Arthur Oliver Wheeler & Thomas George Longstaff after a grizzly bear hunt near Bugaboo Pass in 1910

Mount Sir Sandford in 1910, before its ascent by Palmer, Holway, Feuz and Aemmer

Henry Grier Bryant, 4th president of The American Alpine Club, in 1913

The Grand Teton, before it was climbed

Henry Fairbanks Montagnier, donor of The American Alpine Club's library

Stephen Tyng Mather, 1st Director of National Park Service

John Barrymore, as an American climber, on the Brévent in 1921

On the platform at Glacier Station in 1922—Dr. A. J. Gilmour,
Howard Palmer, E. W. D. Holway

Howard Palmer & Alan Carpe after their 1923 trip to the mountains at the head of Maligne Lake

An early version of Chateau Lake Louise, before the "great fire" of 1924

On the summit of the Strahlhorn in 1925. Dr. Thorington (center) with his two guides

Andy Taylor, riverboat captain, scout, alpinist and "all-around good fellow"

Nephew of the founder of the Club Alpino Italiano, Vittorio Sella,
mountain photographer par excellence, in 1927

A ROYAL MOUNTAIN CLIMBER. Albert, King of the Belgians (with the cap), on one of his winter hikes in the Dolomites. He is one of the best mountain climbers among royalty. *Associated Press*

Albert, King of the Belgians (right rear) with his guides on a climb in the Dolomites

Belmore Browne, alpinist and artist, at work

Captain Albert Henry MacCarthy (USN ret) at his home near
Wilmer, BC

Early AAC involvement with Guide Certification—Eugene Jack, Fritz Wiessner,
C. E. Schurman & Richard Klinge at Mt. Rainier—1937

Dr. Ladd's "Old Firehouse" at 113 East 90th Street in New York

The junior author of this book—as president of The American Alpine Club in 1975

IX – THE OTHER MOUNTAIN CLUBS
OF AMERICA
Kauffman & Putnam

In compiling the following chapters, the authors cited initially received much assistance from other contributors, including but not limited to: Nicholas B. Clinch; James P. McCarthy, and T. C. Price Zimmermann.

The first of what could be called a formal club of alpine climbers was a typically British invention, organized by a number of patrician Englishmen in 1857. However, other nations soon followed and within 20 years there were national "alpine" societies in every major nation of Europe, and the word itself had moved into the dictionary as well as the encyclopedia. By 1916, when one of these authors undertook to research the subject, the climbing club virus had spread to Africa (both north and south), India, and Japan as well as all across North America. By the time of this present compilation such clubs have become well established across Asia and South America – even in Oceania, and the International Union of Alpine Societies (UIAA), of which The American Alpine Club was a founding member, included some 88 member associations, world-wide.

However, Virginia's colorful colonial governor, Lt. Gen. Sir Alexander Spotswood (1676-1740),[87] seems to have been the first to decide on the format for many a mountaineering society, when he created the Tramontane Order after a four-week trek from Williamsburg across the Blue Ridge Mountains in 1716. The primary condition for admission seems to have been the ability to drink to His Majesty's health on the summit of Mount George, which was followed by the right to wear the order's insignia:

Sic Jurat Transcendere Montes.[88]

It is worthy of more than passing note that many subsequent climbers have found to their regret that drinking to anyone's health on a summit can easily lead to swearing and a loss of judgement when crossing mountains. Sadly, the overthrow of the colonial regime pertinent to this King George's

---

85. Born in Tangier, Spotswood served the celebrated Duke of Marlborough and was appointed governor of Virginia in 1710. A believer in westward expansion, after his term expired in 1722 he stayed on in the colonies as deputy postmaster general – an office later held by Benjamin Franklin. His name is on the Virginia landscape.

86. "Thus he Swore to Cross over the Mountains."

great grandson worked an equal hardship on his mountain; it is presently known more democratically as Brown's Mountain.

The record of formation of North American mountaineering societies is far from complete, for smaller and splinter groups come and go with regularity. However, the Boston-based Appalachian Mountain Club (AMC), of which there has been considerable mention above, has clearly established the Western Hemisphere record for longevity. But it does not represent the earliest attempt to establish a club based on more modern mountaineering criteria, rather than an unwise display of loyalty to King George. The Alpine Club of Williamstown (Massachusetts) was formed in 1863, largely due to the enthusiasm of the Reverend Albert Hopkins (1807-1872), professor of mathematics and astronomy at Williams College. Never a large group, it was barely alpine in its activities and waned with its patron's demise. The White Mountain Club was formed in Portland (Maine) 10 years later and maintained a vigorous existence for another decade before being largely absorbed into the growing AMC.

Thus it is reasonable to state that the AMC, with its nucleus of MIT-based scientists, represents the core and source of organized North American alpinism. These authors very understandably subscribe to that opinion for all of us have maintained some form of membership in or relationship to the AMC – indeed, one of these authors chaired its organizational meeting in 1876 and three of us have been elected Honorary Members. In 1889 the AMC published the first book on mountaineering in Colorado [Frederick Hastings Chapin's MOUNTAINEERING IN COLORADO, 168 pages of information mostly about the peaks in the vicinity of Estes Park]. The AMC has published numerous other guidebooks, mostly pertinent to the New England area, and in more recent years has engaged in an extensive publications program.

With the completion of the Canadian Pacific Railway in 1886 began the influx of American climbers to the even more spectacular terrain of the Canadian Rockies. Over the next generation, AMC members averaged two first ascents a year in Canadian mountains, and APPALACHIA, for many years the only climbing journal in North America, carried as many articles on that region. Until the Montagnier collection was given to the AAC, the AMC library, in Boston, was the primary mountaineering reference source on the continent – a condition which has changed very much in the last generation. With the subsequent accretion of several major donations as well as many minor gifts, The American Alpine Club's library in Golden, Colorado, is now the world's finest such in English language literature even exceeding that of the Munich-based Deutscher AlpenVerein in its totality.

Though it stimulated the pursuit of alpinism in many distant areas, the

AMC stood steadfastly by its Northeastern roots and (with occasional abortive and unremunerative forays into distant projects) continued its role with commendable persistence and glory. Its White Mountain Guidebook is the longest running such endeavor in North America, the first edition appearing in 1907, only five years after The American Alpine Club's formation. Its journal, APPALACHIA, now published semi-annually, was the editorial creature of the AAC's first president for its initial 40 years, and also served as the primary organ for AAC membership communications until 1929, the entire span of the national club's first generation. Perhaps even more noteworthy from an historical viewpoint, in the years prior to the establishment of the AAC, the AMC list of honorary members and the criteria set for its own elected leaders were global standards for scholarship and achievement that have seldom been matched and never exceeded [See Appendix A].

In a pattern repeated across the country,[89] a number of more localized outdoor groups have grown up in the shadow of the larger AMC, mostly with increasingly specialized geographic areas of concern. These range from the small but fiercely independent Randolph Mountain Club, since 1910 firmly perched amid its own shelters and trails on the northern fringe of New Hampshire's Presidential Range, to the almost equally old but more widespread Green and Adirondack Mountain Clubs with far larger, but still easily identified, spheres of primary concern.

Collegiate climbing and outdoor groups also came to abound in the Northeast from early in the 20th century. These ranged outward from the Dartmouth Outing Club, the nation's first such, to the Harvard Mountaineering Club [1924], which latter became the breeding place for two generations of leadership in the national organization.

* * *

In 1892 Californians awoke to the glorious possibilities of climbing in their state and the San Francisco-based Sierra Club is the result. The endeavor was genuinely pioneering work, for their were precious few trails in the nearby mountains other than to areas of mining desolation, and public sentiment had to be generated. The following year, that club's BULLETIN was started, a publication which has (with a change of name, content and format) been continued intermittently with ever increasing beauty. In 1901 the Sierra Club took its first large party into the nearby mountains, a process continued for three generations – a few earthquake and certain war years excepted.

---

87. For example, in 1920, the Mountaineers listed two dozen minor or local clubs within the State of Washington, with which they maintained contact.

Owing much of its origin and momentum to the energy of Scots-born John Muir, the Sierra Club developed an early emphasis on mountain ecology and conservation. This profound and often conflicting bifurcation sometimes led to internal dispute such as how to reconcile the true instinct for conservation with the concentrated trail damage done by lengthy pack trains. With time, the Sierra Club evolved more and more toward conservation as its primary reason for existence, rather than the exploitive "opening up the mountains" philosophy that initially dominated the older AMC. However, Sierran leadership and membership have furnished a large portion of those Americans actively interested in the pursuit of alpinism, and many other alpinists have likewise vigorously supported Sierra Club conservation goals.

Among the most appropriate of the Sierra Club's legacies are those pertinent its founder (who also served as its president until his death in 1914). The first such was the Muir Lodge, built by the Southern California section on the slopes of Mount Wilson. Another was the Muir Trail, along the crest of the Sierra from Yosemite Valley to Mount Whitney, passing en route the summit of 4272m Mount Muir. A third was the Muir Woods just north of San Francisco. All these memorials commemorate the world's most famous voice of environmental consciousness – a voice that echoes ever louder in the proceedings of many of the world's alpine societies. But, with the passage of time, some of its inherent complexities and conflicts caused the Sierra Club to evolve from a group caring for and enjoying the mountains to the world's environmental watchdogs.

*   *   *

Two years after the birth of the Sierra Club, the Mazamas sprang into existence in a most dramatic manner. On 19 July, 1894, 155 men and 38 women climbed Mount Hood. It was by no means the first such climb (as noted in Chapter I), but it does stand as some sort of early record for a mass ascent. On the summit (more or less) the regional club was organized with Rev. Earl Morse Wilbur as temporary chairman. The first president was Will Steel,[90] soon to become supervisor of the Crater Lake National Park. This group was, to some extent, an outgrowth of the earlier but short lived Oregon Alpine Club, formed in 1887, of which Steel was the first chairman

---

88. William Gladstone Steel (1854-1934), later a founding member of The American Alpine Club, was a real estate developer, urban transit entrepreneur, and an early and strong advocate of the national park system in the United States - Crater Lake in particular. Steel, author of the authoritative MOUNTAINS OF OREGON, was a cousin of Dr. William Sargent Ladd, the distinguished physician who was also a generous supporter and leader of The American Alpine Club.

of exploration and former United States Senator Henry Winslow Corbett (1827-1903), the first president.

The word "mazama" has been alleged to mean "mountain goat" and be of Mexican derivation; thus to become a member of that club one had to demonstrate an ability to climb where mountain goats go. Of greater authenticity in geological parlance, the word refers to the erstwhile volcanic peak, Mount Mazama, of which the 10 kilometers-wide, Crater Lake is the modern residuum. Several cubic kilometers of the mountain itself were blown away in an explosion of enormous force some 6000 years ago, depositing orange colored ash across a wide expanse of the present states of Oregon and Washington, and born by the prevailing westerly winds into much of Idaho and Montana, even into the southern parts of British Columbia and Alberta.

Members of that Club have followed those winds with considerable mountaineering success, but have tended to concentrate their climbing on the remaining volcanic summits of the Cascade Range – Mount Adams was their collective goal in 1895, Mount Rainier in 1897 and Mount Saint Helens in 1898. Subsequent years saw similar large scale ascents of Glacier Peak, Mount Jefferson, the Three Sisters and Mount Shasta.

The next major alpine society to be formed in North America was Canadian. Originally suggested by Professor Fay as a semi-autonomous division of the AAC, its existence as a fully independent national entity was vigorously promoted by Elizabeth Parker, then a writer for a Winnipeg newspaper. She rapidly enlisted the support of Arthur Oliver Wheeler (1860-1945), a native of Kilkenny in Ireland, who had already surveyed most of the high points of the Canadian Rockies and Selkirks. With a strong assist from the Canadian Pacific Railway, which had an understandable interest in developing tourism of all sorts in its bailiwick, the Alpine Club of Canada burst with a flourishing start in 1906 and published its first journal the very next year.

The Canadian Pacific had started offering the services of Swiss guides to its hotel patrons in 1899, stimulated in no small measure by the death of Philip Abbot and the strongly phrased written advice to its president of the English-born San Francisco surgeon, Joshua Harrison Stallard (1821-1899). The railway now subsidized the new alpine club by offering special rates for those attending its annual camps and providing the services of its Swiss guides at no charge. These camps have been held (a few war years excepted) annually since 1907 at some of the most scenic locations in the Western Hemisphere, of which the mountains of western Canada possess more than an average share. For many years the ACC maintained the office of 'American vice-president,' as a token of its interest in a wider presence, and a good number of its members have always resided south of the border.

Also in Canada, in 1907, the British Columbia Mountaineering Club was organized with an emphasis on exploration of the Coast Mountains. While this latter club was initially very active, even with its own clubhouse on Grouse Mountain near Vancouver, in time it gradually merged into the larger national group. However, the concept of separate identities remained in Canada, both in the east and the west. Sixty years later, the Kootenay Mountaineering Club was to re-crystalize around alpinists that lived in southeastern British Columbia. And in the genre of bi-lingualism that swept Canadian officialdom in the same era, the Fédération Quebecoise de la Montagne took root in Montreal.

In Seattle, the year 1907 also marked the initiation of the Mountaineers as an independent club, separate from its parent Mazamas. Founded largely under the impetus of Asahel Curtis, one of the best of mountain photographers, its first president was yet another geologist, Professor Henry Landes (1867-1936) of the University of Washington. The guiding spirit of the Mountaineers, however, soon materialized in the form of historian Edmond Stephen Meany (1862-1955) the de facto founder of the University of Washington. The Mountaineers were simply but aptly named, providing the by now usual fare of summer encampments for a number of years, but then aiding in the formation of a cooperative store for climbing equipment that has since evolved into one of the nation's best known suppliers – Recreational Equipment, Inc – and entering upon the publication of mountaineering literature with considerable vigor and success.

In the mountain heartland of the continent there was a Rocky Mountain Club established as early as 1875, which included a distinguished lineup of members: Frederick Vandiveer Hayden (1829-1887), [surveyor of the Rocky Mountains 1872-1879; promoter of Yellowstone National Park, 1872; and founder of the U. S. Geological Survey], Albert Bierstadt (1830-1902), landscape artist of the Hudson River school, Cyrus West Field (1819-1892), famed for his Atlantic cable, and James Bayard Taylor (1825-1878), poet and author. Despite its distinguished initial membership, this club, unfortunately, died with its founders but was succeeded in 1912 by another Denver-based entity, the Colorado Mountain Club. This second entry, at least partly due to the vigor of its founder, James Grafton Rogers, became a more permanent part of the alpine landscape from whose membership later came four more presidents of the national organization – John Lathrop Jerome Hart, Robert Wallace Craig, Glenn Edward Porzak, and Alison Keith Osius.

The contagion of organization spread to Utah in 1913, with the formation of the Timpanogos Club, named for the most prominent peak of the Wasatch Range. In 1914, the virus spread to the very non-alpine terrain of Chicago when the Prairie Club, now in its sixth year, joined the Coloradans for their summer camp. In later years, the Iowa Mountaineers, under the leadership of Sylvanus John Ebert, became a very prominent part of the North American mountaineering scene.

And on New Year's Eve, at the close of 1914, one hundred members of the Trail and Mountain Club of Hawaii, camped overnight at 6,500 feet in the spectacular crater of Haleakala on the island of Maui. Organized American mountaineering had finally reached from sea to beyond the shining sea. But its history was as ancient as any in the world, for under date of Saturday, 26 January, 1793, one of the earlier executives to overwinter in Hawaii, Admiral George Vancouver, took time out from his discussion of the activities (and degree of submission to Britannic majesty) of King `Tamaahmaah' to note some of his men's activities in his journal:

"Their object had been to gain the summit of Mowna Roa, which they had not been able to effect in the direction they had attempted; but they had reached the top of another mountain, which though not so lofty as Mowna Roa or Mowna Kaah, is yet very conspicuous and is known to the natives as Worroray. This mountain rises near the western extremity of the [big] *island. "*

CHARTER
OF
The American Alpine Club

IN THE COURT OF COMMON PLEAS Nº 4, FOR
THE COUNTY OF PHILADELPHIA, SEPTEMBER TERM 1915, Nº 4165.
TO THE HONORABLE THE JUDGES OF SAID COURT.

AGREEABLY

to the provisions of the Act of the General Assembly of Pennsylvania, entitled "An Act to provide for the Incorporation and Regulation of certain Corporations," approved the 29th day of April, A.D. 1874, and the several supplements thereto, the undersigned all of whom are citizens of Pennsylvania, have associated themselves together for the purposes and upon the terms and by the name hereinafter set forth, and to the end that they may be duly incorporated according to law hereby certify:

1. THE name of the intended corporation is

◁ THE AMERICAN ALPINE CLUB ▷

2. THE purposes for which the said corporation is formed are as follows: The scientific exploration and study of high mountain elevations and of the regions lying within or about the Arctic and Antarctic Circles, the cultivation of the mountain craft, the promotion and dissemination of knowledge regarding the regions above indicated. It shall for its primary work undertake the study of the high mountains of all America, gathering in the facts and phenomena pertaining to them, and shall publish a series of illustrated monographs of these mountains for the purpose of presenting a complete description of the alpine mountains of the Western Hemisphere.

3. THE business of the corporation is to be transacted in the City of Philadelphia, State of Pennsylvania.

4. THE corporation shall have perpetual succession by its corporate name.

5. THE yearly income of the corporation from other sources than real estate shall not exceed the sum of Twenty Thousand Dollars.

6. THE said corporation shall have no capital stock. The names and residences of the subscribers are as follows:

Henry G. Bryant, 2013 Walnut Street, Phila., Pa.— George Vaux, Jr., Bryn Mawr, Pennsylvania—
J. Henry Scattergood, Villa Nova, Pennsylvania.
J. William White, 1810 Rittenhouse Square, Philad.— Thomas De Witt Cuyler, Philadelphia, Pa.—

7. THE number of directors is fixed at eight, and the names and residences of those who are chosen directors for the first year are as follows:

Henry G. Bryant, 2013 Walnut Street, Philadelphia, Pa.— Henry Fielding Reid, 610 Cathedral Street, Baltimore, Md.
Rodney L. Glisan, the Spalding Bldg., Portland, Ore.— Howard Palmer, New London, Conn.
Allston Burr, 60 State Street, Boston, Mass.
Lewis L. Delafield, 20 Exchange Place, New York City— Edward C. Pickering, Cambridge, Mass.
Harrington Putnam, 404 Washington Ave., Brooklyn, N.Y.— J. Henry Scattergood, Villa Nova, Pennsylvania.

8. THE corporation has no capital stock.

WITNESS OUR HANDS AND SEALS this twenty second day of November A.D. 1915.

Henry G. Bryant ● Geo. Vaux Jr. ● J. Henry Scattergood ● J William White ● Thomas De Witt Cuyler ●

✳ DECREE ✳

AND NOW this twenty fourth day of December A.D. 1915, the above and foregoing Charter and Certificate of Incorporation having been presented to this Court, accompanied by due proof or publication of the notice of this application, as required by the Act of Assembly and rule of Court in such case made and provided, and I certify that I have examined and perused the said instrument and have found the same to be in proper form and within the purposes named in the first class specified in Section Second of the Act of the General Assembly of the Commonwealth of Pennsylvania, entitled "An Act to provide for the Incorporation and Regulation of certain Corporations," approved the twenty-ninth day of April A.D. 1874, and its supplements, and the same appears to be lawful and not injurious to the community. I do hereby, on motion of

P.F. ROTHERMEL 3RD. ESQ.

on behalf of the Petitioners, order and decree that the said Charter be and the same is here by approved, and upon the recording of the same and of this order the subscribers hereto and their associates and successors shall be a corporation by the name of

✳ "THE AMERICAN ALPINE CLUB." ✳

for the purposes and upon the terms therein stated.

Chas. Y. Audenried
President JUDGE

X – MOMENTOUS EVENTS
Palmer

The original of much of this chapter can be found in AMERICAN ALPINE JOURNAL *V-163.*

Mid-summer of 1921 witnessed the most publicized fatality in North American mountaineering to that date – and less than 20 miles from the scene of Abbot's death in 1895. The event caused a furor somewhat akin to that in England when a member of the peerage was killed following the first ascent of the Matterhorn. Dr. Winthrop Ellsworth Stone, 59 year-old president of Purdue University fell to his death on 17 July while climbing the south face of 3310m Mount Eon, south of Mount Assiniboine in the Canadian Rockies. Stone was relatively new to serious alpinism, though not inexperienced; he and his second wife, Margaret, were near the top of the mountain and Stone had climbed a steep chimney to the summit area then unroped in order to complete the ascent over the loose, sedimentary rocks in this vicinity.[91] Mrs. Stone had been belaying from a sheltered ledge some distance below him and only witnessed his body falling. Though unharmed, she was thinly clothed and also felt unable to get down to timber alone. Thus she spent the next seven days stranded on the exposed mountainside without food, until rescuers arrived.

A massive rescue effort was mounted after the couple failed to return to camp when expected and Mrs. Stone was finally located by Rudolph Aemmer, one of the five Swiss guides then employed by the Canadian Pacific Railway, and Ebenezer (Bill) Peyto, a celebrated local woodsman, poacher and packer. Aemmer carried her down the mountain and after two days managed to reach a comfortable camp and medical attention. While she recovered fully, the then unique enormity of the rescue and body recovery process attracted wide attention and several well-to-do alpinists raised a substantial fund for the recompense of the participants. Further, a highly complimentary resolution of thanks was drawn up by the AAC and forwarded to the several individuals involved. These were: guides Conrad Kain and Edward Feuz, Jr, Constable Charles Pounden of the RCMP, as well as Aemmer and Peyto – who had especially distinguished themselves in the effort and had unselfishly left their regular employment to render aid.

---

89. Stone, New Hampshire-born, was the older brother of the distinguished jurist and future U. S. Supreme Court Chief Justice, Harlan Fiske Stone, and had been divorced from his first wife, Victoria, several year earlier. The widow continued as a member of the AAC for another decade, but was resident in New York, not Indiana.

Assisting in the rescue effort were: a sometime amateur alpinist, Lennox Hubbard Lindsay; the local outfitter, Ralph Rink; and Stone's son by his first marriage, Richard.[92]

Sixty years later, through the instigation and generosity of Andrew John Kauffman, who had known some of those rescuers, and aided by the input of several other concerned alpinists, the AAC established its David A. Sowles Memorial Award:

. . . *to be conferred from time to time on mountaineers who have distinguished themselves, with unselfish devotion at personal risk or sacrifice or at sacrifice of a major objective, in going to the assistance of fellow climbers imperiled in the mountains.*

This citation is named for David Ambler Sowles, who lost his life in an electrical storm on the Weisshorn, 4 August, 1963, at age 30; [see AAJ XIV-159].

On a considerably more upbeat note, at the AAC's Annual Meeting in Boston on 7 January, 1922, President Delafield stated the *"most noteworthy achievement of the club during the past year has been the publication by two of its members of A CLIMBER'S GUIDE TO THE ROCKY MOUNTAINS OF CANADA. "* This work, the first alpine climbers' guidebook for any region in North America, had been initiated by Dr. Thorington who presented a manuscript to the Club for completion and publication. Howard Palmer was the rewrite man for the first edition, but Thorington completed four subsequent revisions alone before co-opting Putnam as his successor in 1966. This pioneering literary venture came out in the fall of 1921 and has since passed through seven editions, expanded tenfold in size, been divided into two volumes, engaged the services of four other editors, latterly included the participation of the Alpine Club of Canada. Prophetic of its future success, the meeting accorded the authors a rising vote of thanks.

The publication of the Club's first guidebook was not its first literary endeavor; as the three numbers of the ALPINA AMERICANA series had been initiated a decade earlier and were to be followed over the course of the next

---

90. For more on Aemmer (1883-1973) see THE GUIDING SPIRIT, Revelstoke, 1986.

Peyto (1868-1943) who had gone west with the CPR. was a fixture with the annual camps of the Alpine Club of Canada.

Kain (1883-1934) was the subject of an autobiography (written with considerable help from Dr. Thorington) entitled WHERE THE CLOUDS CAN GO, that has since gone through three editions.

Charles Edward Pounden was 21 years of age at the time. A native of Montreal and with but two years of service, he stayed with the NorthWest Mounted Police for another nine years.

An excellent contemporary account of this rescue can be found in CAJ XII-14.

generations by a series of guidebooks, position papers, and scientific treatises. The Club's JOURNAL, initiated in 1929, has since become the world's standard annual reference work and its annual Safety Committee's annual report, initiated in 1949 – ACCIDENTS IN NORTH AMERICAN MOUNTAINEERING – become required reading for all budding alpinists and teachers of the sport.

When the Club's 20th annual meeting was held in Philadelphia on 29 December, 1922, President Delafield was able to note in his retirement speech that in the season just past, 45-year-old Arthur Tate had made the first ascent of Wyoming's highest summit, Gannett Peak (4207m) in the Wind River Range. Furthermore, Club members Winona Bailey, of Seattle, and Laurie Renshaw Frazeur, of Chicago, two of the more adventurous women of their day, had attained all four summits of snow-clad Mount Olympus (2817m) in Greece, becoming the first women known to do so since various gods and demigods of ancient mythology.

Until this time, attendance at the annual dinners of the national organization had averaged about 40, and membership had increased by a mere half-dozen per year. But, in the mid 1920's the attendance at annual dinners more than doubled and the rate of membership increase jumped dramatically. While still vigorously maintaining its standards of accomplishment for joining, at the end of 1926 AAC membership now stood at 152, over half of whom – 98 – attended the annual meeting and dinner.

Much of this increase could be credited to the prestige and energy of the AAC's sixth president who had been one of its original councilors, the Reverend Harry Pierce Nichols, "Uncle Harry" to a generation of younger mountain-oriented people from the East Coast to the West. He was the last of the founding members to serve as president, and had retired from his lengthy rectorship of Holy Trinity Church in New York to live among the hills of New Hampshire, where he continued his vigorous life. Dr. Nichols spanned a lot of mountaineering history; He had climbed with Theodore Roosevelt in the Alps (while the two men were in their early twenties) and in his latter years with a series of budding climbers in New Hampshire's White Mountains. At age 47, he had preached a sermon at the Glacier House on "The Glory of Aspiration" after returning from a strenuous, three-day series of first ascents in the Selkirk Mountains of western Canada.[93]

---

91. For more on Rev. Nichols (1850-1940), see AAJ IV-278 and JOE DODGE, ONE NEW HAMPSHIRE INSTITUTION, 1986. Dr. Nichols made more 250 ascents of Mount Washington on foot, including one to celebrate his 85th birthday.

   The most famous of these budding climbers was the soon-to-become equally legendary, Joseph Brooks Dodge, "Mayor of Porky Gulch."

In 1923, the Canadian Rockies were still a prime area for exploratory alpinism and 10 AAC members participated in 12 major ascents, of which nine were "firsts." Among these were 3730m North Twin by the young Field brothers (Bill and Fred) with guide Edward Feuz, Jr., the highest summit still remaining unclimbed; and 3658m Mount Clemenceau, the highest major peak in the region of which the first ascent was made by a completely amateur party.[94] In 1924, 16 AAC members participated in 27 "firsts" in Canada and three in the "lower 48," another unprecedented record of alpine accomplishment. This included 3270m Mount Geikie in the Canadian Rockies and 3520m Mt. Titan in the more remote Premier Group of the Cariboo Range in British Columbia. Allen Carpé had originally named the latter peak in recognition of its status relative to its neighbors, but in later years the Canadian Permanent Committee on Geographic Names officially renamed the mountain after the late Prime Minister Sir Wilfrid Laurier. In the autumn of the year 2000, alpinists from around the world recorded their shock and dismay that a nearby peak in this range was ignored in the case of a later and late prime minister, Pierre Elliott Trudeau, in whose honor one of Trudeau's successors, Jean Crétien, proposed to rename Mount Logan.

The climbs mentioned above would not be considered particularly outstanding in the light of later accomplishments in more distant ranges that have been made with the aid of prior experience, aerial photography, improved equipment, helicopter access and different attitudes toward acceptable risk. However, they were regarded as exceptional in their day, and based on the ruling spirit of the times they deserve recollection for their historic significance. No reflection is intended on other ascents not mentioned, for this kind of history is not primarily concerned with the independent activities of various individuals. Yet, as a practical matter, when any mountain activity becomes the subject of a talk before the annual meeting of the national organization, that fact enters into its records. As regards the frequent mention herein of the "Canadian Alps," if these authors should seem partial, it may be understood from the fact that the development of alpinism in that area has, from even before the AAC's formation, been so closely associated with the members of The American Alpine Club as to be an integral part of its history. Moreover, all of these authors have found those mountains to be a major focus of their climbing activities.

Another occasion of unusual interest to mountaineers in that decade was the visit in 1923 of 37-year-old George Herbert Leigh Mallory, then on a

---

92. For more on William Osgood Field, a glaciologist who became an AAC Honorary Member, see AAJ XXXVII-363, and THE GUIDING SPIRIT, op cit.

fund-raising lecture tour of North America. President Nichols and the New York AAC members arranged a dinner in his honor, at which Mallory described the general problems encountered on Mount Everest and particularly of high altitude ascents made both with and without the aid of supplementary oxygen apparatus, then under design by the British alpinist/chemist, George Ingle Finch (1888-1970). Mallory's remarks were fascinating to the audience which was composed wholly of those who had never been exposed to the exalted levels with which the celebrated English schoolmaster had become so familiar. Heart and lung tests made on him, the very morning of his visit, disclosed that he possessed a far greater than average capacity in both these organs. Later that year he was elected an Honorary Member[95] and in 1924 the news of his tragic disappearance on Mount Everest touched with especial poignancy those who had been privileged to meet with him at this dinner. The discovery of his broken and frozen body high on the north face of Mount Everest in 1999 was a nostalgic event for alpinists all over the world.

* * *

The project of an expedition to ascend Mount Logan, the highest peak of Canada and second highest of North America, was formally brought to the AAC's attention in 1923 when the Alpine Club of Canada appointed a special committee to consider the matter. During the ensuing year, the enterprise took on more definite form after a journey to the base of the mountain made in the spring of 1924 by Captain Albert MacCarthy, formerly of the U. S. Navy but now a resident of Wilmer, British Columbia, who had accepted leadership of the project. This expedition was the first in which the AAC officially participated, and its endorsement and sponsorship set a precedent for a galaxy of future expeditions to the world's major mountain ranges, all of a unique or pioneering nature.

Later concepts of supply by air, or helicopter access to a high-level base, were unheard of in those days and the supply problems on Mt. Logan involved far greater effort than had ever pertained to a previous North American mountaineering venture. Estimated costs reached as high as $12,000. To raise such a sum would obviously take more than a localized appeal; success might well require an international financial rapport. Early in 1924, a token appropriation of $1,000 was voted by the AAC, following receipt of the Canadian club's invitation to send representatives on the

---

93. President Harry Nichols had proposed the election of the alpinist Pontiff, Achille Ratti, Pope Pius XI, to Honorary Membership. But, upon learning that His Holiness had declined such an honor from The Alpine Club, *"for reasons of policy"* the matter went no further and Mallory was elected.

expedition, and a special committee was appointed to raise additional money. In due course, individual American Alpine Club members contributed $2,419, matching an almost identical amount from the Alpine Club of Canada, with the balance coming from a wide variety of sources, including $1,000 from The Alpine Club in England.[96] This fund-raising effort was the first of numerous contributions to alpine ventures in which the fine, but anonymous, hand of Henry Hall might be discerned. Those round numbered contributions from various organizations of which he was a member gave away his anonymity to those who understood the process.

In February, 1925, MacCarthy returned to Alaska and spent two more months freighting supplies for the climbing party by dog sled with Andy Taylor. The final party consisted of eight persons, most of whom were members of both the sponsoring clubs – the co-leaders were MacCarthy and Howard Frederick John Lambart. A surveyor, Lambart (1880-1946) was subsequently a revered member of the ACC and served with distinction as the Canadian member of the International Boundary Commission. Other team members were: William Wasborough Foster; Allen Carpé; Norman Henry Read; Robert M. Morgan, Henry S. Hall, Jr, and, of course, Taylor. In a noteworthy gesture, one of the earliest governmental demonstrations of environmental concern relative to alpinism, the Dominion government sent along Hamilton M. Laing as naturalist.[97]

Although the mountain is huge, being one of the largest uplifts in the world, the route of ascent was not technically difficult – a long and tedious march over snowfields with the greatest dangers coming from crevasses, altitude and weather. Several miles of trudging along the 5000m crest of the massif took the party from its northerly end to the summit nearly a dozen miles distant at the southern end. All but two members of the party reached their goal on 25 June, 1925. At the next annual dinner Carpé showed four

---

94. In terms of the relative purchasing power 70 years later, this would represent a sum of about $250,000. In the end the total sum raised was $11,983.40; including $1,449 from the AAC itself, $740 from its New York members, separately, and $500 from the Royal Geographical Society.

95. For more on MacCarthy (1876-1956), see AAJ X(2)-137.
    For more on Hickson (1873-1950) see AAJ X(2)-141.
    For more on Lambart (1880-1946) see CAJ XXIX-284.
    For more on Foster (1875-1954) see AAJ IX(2)-220.
    An engineer by profession, Read (1883-1979) earned his way to a place in WHO'S WHO.
    Laing, 42 years of age at the time, was already an established ornithologist. His 39 page report (with the help of P. A. Taverner and R. M. Anderson) was entitled BIRDS AND MAMMALS OF THE MOUNT LOGAN EXPEDITION, 1925 and published by the National Museum of Canada in Ottawa.

reels of moving pictures which he had taken at elevations of from 14,000 feet to the 19,520 foot (5951m) peak. These films were the more remarkable because on the trip out, after the ascent, the raft on which he and Hall were floating capsized in the turbulent Chitina River, completely soaking everything aboard. In later years Hall loved to regale younger climbers with the story of how he and Carpé had dried out the undeveloped film, inside of a doubled sleeping bag, which was in turn inside their tent, placed in the shade of an ice cliff, and with the benefit of what limited darkness was obtainable on the 62nd parallel only three weeks after the summer solstice.

As might be expected, a report on the successful outcome of the Mount Logan trip occupied most of the next issue of the CANADIAN ALPINE JOURNAL (Vol XV) and dominated the AAC's annual meeting of 9 January, 1926. It had been by far the most financially important project which either national club had so far undertaken. Professor Joseph William Andrew Hickson (1873-1950), professor of psychology at McGill and at the time president of the Alpine Club of Canada, spoke at the dinner. He paid a warm tribute to the work of Captain MacCarthy, in personally exploring a route to the base of the mountain in the spring of 1924 – a 44-day backpacking journey covering 550 miles.

Almost 12 months later, at the annual dinner on 29 December, 1926, Noel Ewart Odell, soon to become a visiting professor of geology at Harvard, was the guest of honor. He spoke of the 1924 Mount Everest Expedition, focusing on its final and tragic phase wherein Mallory and Irvine lost their lives, in one of the most endlessly debated of mountaineering mysteries. As the presiding officer, Howard Palmer was privileged to allude to the speaker's unequaled record for continuous climbing at altitudes within what has come to be described as "the Death Zone," without the benefit of supplementary oxygen.[98] During this decade the work of Sir Joseph Barcroft, Edouard Wyss-Dunant and George Finch in studying high altitude physiology was known only within very limited medical circles. However, Edward Whymper's graphic description of the problems encountered at altitude was available to any mountaineer who chose to read his 1892 book, TRAVELS AMONG THE GREAT ANDES OF THE EQUATOR, a book that details his remarkable ascents of Chimborazo and other exalted volcanic summits of the region.

This same meeting also saw the beginning of a fund-raising effort aimed

---

96. For more on Odell (1890-1987) see AJ-XCIII-309. Though an alpinist of note and a major player on the 1924 Everest Expedition, Odell did not personally establish any significant altitude record. His name, however, is on the American landscape in the form of the leftmost major ice gully of Mount Washington's famous Huntington Ravine.

at establishing a permanent location for the national Club's headquarters in New York City. Subsequently, President Palmer appointed a committee to canvass the membership on this topic. In result, by the end of March 1928, $9,450 had been collected and four years later, at the time of the annual meeting on 30 January, 1930, a grand total of $18,360 appeared to be on hand. Unfortunately, as a result of the worldwide financial collapse that had set in the preceding October, some $6,000 worth of the bonds that had been contributed were found to be worthless. Nevertheless, the Club's board felt it was on strong enough footing to enter into a three-year lease with the Explorers Club for quarters in their new premises on 110th Street. This arrangement lasted close to four years, until 15 November, 1932, when severe financial difficulties beset the Explorers [who had to file for bankruptcy and were forced to sell their building] and the mountaineers were obliged to relocate to other leased premises at 140 East 46th Street. This building was not far from Grand Central Station and for several subsequent years annual meetings were held at the Cosmopolitan Club on East 66th Street.

The AAC was to live at this address for another 15 years. The association with the Explorers Club had been a happy one, and its dissolution was much regretted by both parties. However, in allying with them, the AAC had discontinued its arrangement with the New York Public Library. The new quarters required more space than previously, for the AAC Library had continued to grow over the years since its first acquisition. Most of the important questions dealing with the Club headquarters were settled by the time of the annual meeting on 19 January, 1929, at which Dr. William Sargent Ladd succeeded to the presidency. This meeting also marked the end of 72-year-old Benjamin Seaver's twelve years as treasurer, a length of sentence in that often unpopular office exceeded only by those of two of these authors.

However, the turmoil as to the location of the national headquarters that came during Dr. Ladd's term as president obviously remained very much in his thinking after he left that office. A dozen years later, and acting without any prior commitment from the Club, he began negotiations to acquire a three-story building on East 90th Street that had been the used by a private, insurance-company-operated, fire brigade. These private firms had been quite popular in the late 19th century, existing in many large cities, initially for the security and assistance of their own subscribers, but latterly supported by fire insurance carriers anxious to help reduce their liabilities in the face of occasionally insufficiently responsive public fire departments. This one had been in use until 1943 and was disbanded only as a result of wartime manpower shortages.

* * *

The last few paragraphs above are somewhat out of order, for there was an event on 6 May, 1927, that presaged a greater alteration in the Club's operating procedures that set in with vigor 40 years later. Fourteen members attended the first official American Alpine Club dinner to be held beyond sight (or smell) of the Atlantic Ocean. At the Faculty Club of the University of California Berkeley campus, Francis Peloubert Farquhar, a leading light of the Sierra Club and soon to become a sterling laborer for the AAC, presided over the first of several such gatherings held at his invitation. Farquhar, incidentally, bequeathed his extensive library of mountaineering literature to the university at which he had taught, where it is still held in a special collection.

Another noteworthy event of this period was the founding of THE AMERICAN ALPINE JOURNAL. It came about due to events beyond the Club's control. For 30 years the Club had made use of the certain reserved pages of the Appalachian Mountain Club's semi-annual APPALACHIA, as recounted above. But when the older club encountered personnel difficulties and failed to publish for more than a year, only the lack of an editor of its own held the AAC back the institution of an independent journal. The chance mention of this limiting fact at a council meeting prompted Allen Carpé to volunteer to undertake the first issue, but without any commitment for later ones. The council accepted his offer at once and voted to establish an annual Club periodical. On 24 March, 1928, it appointed an editorial board consisting of Howard Palmer, Helen Isabelle Buck, the Club's volunteer librarian, and Carpé, the latter being chairman. He pushed the matter energetically, shouldering the lion's share of the work, and in the early summer of 1929 the first number was distributed to the members.[99]

The annual publication has continued thenceforth, with supplemental issues appearing occasionally and under a distinguished succession of editors. Palmer acted as such for the succeeding four issues, Thorington took over in 1934 for the next dozen years, Bob Bates and David Robertson co-edited from 1947 through 1955, then Richard Houston took on the task for one year. In 1957 Adams Carter and his wife, Ann, began their noteworthy, 39-year, endurance contest as editor, taking the Club's JOURNAL from its status of just one of many such publications, into the world's most

---

97. Farquhar (1887-1974), a public accountant by profession, was the leading American authority of his day on mountain toponymy.

Miss Buck (1884-1972), one of the leading female athletes of her day, had also been instrumental in the acquisition of the Montagnier Collection, which she tended carefully for 21 years. See AAJ XVIII-543.

complete and sought-after annual mountaineering reference. But that was all in the future; the Club was soon to have other and more demanding business as the world lurched through the Great Depression towards World War II.

*   *   *

During the decade of the 1930s, mountaineering performance was on the American agenda and members of the AAC were in the forefront. Their accomplishments in the Andes, the Caucasus and the Himalaya brought credit to the nation and form the topic of the next chapter. However, in the politics of alpinism, another development had been coming about – the International Union of Alpine Associations, UIAA in its French language acronym.

Alpine Clubs were a big thing in Europe after the original such association had been formed in London in 1857. The first Austrian club was formed in 1862, the Swiss and the Italian clubs in 1863, the German club in 1869 and the French in 1874. International gatherings of leading alpinists began soon afterwards – attended frequently by officials of the Appalachian Mountain Club. The Club Alpin Français hosted conferences in 1876 and 1877; other continental clubs in subsequent years. Interestingly, a common topic of discussion at these meetings was the quality of guide certification, but problems of hut construction, reduced rail fares for alpinists, and study of glacial movements all received attention. And – as early as 1864, in a report of a special committee of the Alpine Club – the necessary strength of a climbing rope was agreed upon. The Alpine Club had been spurred in this process by the famous Matterhorn accident earlier in the year, and the committee's initial recommendation was that the rope [then most frequently of manila hemp] be able to withstand one shock of a free fall of 76 kilograms from a height of three and one half meters. Later UIAA standards, for far stronger fibers, specified a weight of 80 kilograms, a height of five meters and five such shocks.

Periodic conferences ensued – all at other European locales – but were interrupted by the onset of World War I. After that conflict concluded a meeting was convened at Monaco in 1919 that led to a renewal of these periodic gatherings culminating in the "Third International Alpine Congress" at Chamonix from 21 August to 3 September, 1932. It was this gathering that gave birth to the formal existence of the UIAA. Eighteen national clubs, including those of both the United States and Canada, were represented, plus some specialized entities. The following year the AAC participated in the first general assembly of the organization at Cortina d'Ampezzo, but the Canadian club was absent, though a Mexican club took part.

The very Eurocentric domination of the group's initial thinking, plus the dismal state of the world's economy forced a retrenchment in American participation in the UIAA in 1935 and participation was not renewed until Fritz Wiessner, once again a publicly accepted leader of The American Alpine Club, personally instigated a return to full membership in 1968. The major value to American alpinists came from the fact that the multinational trade in mountaineering equipment had given rise to a serious concern on the Club's part as to the quality of the climbing equipment items of foreign manufacture being sold in the United States. While many felt that the testing required for application of the UIAA label was not what they might have wished, it served, at least, as a minimal standard of quality assurance. In subsequent years, American representatives came to participate in almost every aspect of UIAA activities, served continuously on its Executive Committee and hosted periodic commission meetings in the New World, including the General Assembly for 1979, at Pinkham Notch, New Hampshire, and that for 2002, the United Nations-decreed *Year of the Mountains,* in Flagstaff, Arizona.

AMERICAN ALPINE CLUB

A meeting for the organization of an American Alpine Club was held in the room of the Geographical Society of Philadelphia, 1520 Chestnut St., on Thursday afternoon, May 9. *1901.* At that time the following names were enrolled for membership in the association:

Edwin Swift Balch, Esq.,

Thomas Willing Balch, Esq.,

Capt. Amos Bonsall,
Kane Arctic Expedition.

Herbert L. Bridgman, Esq.,
Sec'y. Peary Arctic Club.

Henry G. Bryant, Esq.,

Dr. Frederick A. Cook,
Gerlache Antarctic Expedition.

Prof. Chas. E. Fay,
Tufts College.

Prof. Angelo Heilprin,

Thomas R. Hill,

Prof. Harry Fielding Reid,
Johns Hopkins University.

Prof. Israel C. Russell,
University of Michigan.

George Vaux, Jr., Esq.

The objects of the association are briefly stated in the paragraphs following, as well as the conditions which at this time are thought desirable to control membership.

The Committee on Organization believe that the general work and purposes of an American Alpine Club, as here outlined, will appeal to you; they accordingly invite you to join the association in the list of original members or *founders*, the number of which shall be limited to those members whose names appear enrolled before the execution of the By-Laws.

It has been recommended that the annual dues should not exceed Five Dollars.

Respectfully,

Committee on Organization
{ Edwin Swift Balch,
Harry Fielding Reid,
Angelo Heilprin,
Chairman,
Academy of Natural Sciences, Philadelphia

XI – AFIELD and AT WAR
Putnam & Kauffman

D uring the decade of the 1930s significant numbers of American mountaineers began to make their appearance in the last great earthly bastion of high alpinism – the Himalaya/Karakoram. In earlier decades Americans had done great pioneering climbs in their own Alaskan mountains, setting on their way to worldwide prominence such names as Hudson Stuck, Frederick Cook, Bradford Washburn, Robert Bates, Charles Houston, Adams Carter and Terris Moore. As noted in the preceding chapter, Americans had also been active in the high mountains of South America, in the pioneering footsteps of Annie Peck. But after the end of World War I it was the high peaks along the northern boundary of British India that began to claim priority of attention from alpinists everywhere. The uniquely exalted nature of these summits had become more fully understood as the 19th century drew to a close and, with the advances in communications and transportation that came with the new century, political hindrances aside, they were now attainable goals for those who could afford the time to reach them and the means to pay their way.

Though fringes of this area had been visited by Alexander the Great, Marco Polo and a number of subsequent westerners, it was hardly explored to the satisfaction of non-resident mountaineers and nomenclature was confusing. Thus the Workmans, William Hunter and Fanny Bullock, who pursued most of their explorations in the early years of the 20th century, were regarded as among the pioneering explorers and popularizers of the challenges of the Himalaya and Karakoram Mountains. Not the first, the Workmans followed such legendary British figures as Thomas George Longstaff and Francis Edward Younghusband and the great Swedish explorer, Sven Hedin. The Workmans, however, lectured to many organizations, including the AAC, on their travels, wrote comprehensive narratives of them, and were elected to several Honorary Memberships.

Until the early 1930s, few other Americans had cared – or even tried – to follow their example. In that decade, however, the urge to sample the climbing possibilities offered by these tremendous peaks reached across the Atlantic from Europe. The process was inspired largely by the heroic British attempts on the north side of Mount Everest which, for months at a time, retained front page interest around the world. Also known as Sagarmatha, to the natives seeing its 8848m crest from the south and Chomolungma to those resident to the north, in 1852 this summit was determined to be the highest known point on Earth. Initially recorded merely as "Peak XV," it was renamed in 1865 after Sir George Everest (1790-1866) who had been Surveyor General of India when it was first triangulated from more than 100 miles distant.

In 1932, came the first real signs of awakening on the part of American climbers. That year an American team with Harvard affiliations undertook the study and possible ascent of a mysterious peak in the little known hinterlands of China that was rumored to exceed in elevation, even the vaunted Mount Everest. The recondite Chinese peak's name was Amne Machin but its exact location was uncertain. Its existence, however, was thought sufficiently certain that an attempt on its summit seemed worth the gamble and a large team of climbers undertook the venture, leaving their homes late in 1931.

Upon their arrival in Shanghai the Americans were victimized by a classic type of adventurer who, under the guise of expediting their way through the notoriously corrupt and unresponsive Chinese bureaucracy, absconded with most of the group's funds. Handicapped but undeterred, they were fortunate that one of their number, Jack Theodore Young, though born in the United States, was of full Chinese ancestry. Since he was at least partially able to pass as a native, most of the team, reduced in number by those now penniless, pressed on. After several months of travel, much of it by very primitive means, four of them reached the Konka Gampa Lamasery, located at 3650m in the shadow of the elusive mountain. Continuing their project, the party first mapped the area, then assaulted the peak in traditional Alaskan style, establishing four intermediate camps between the lamasery and their high camp near 22,000 feet (6880m). Finally, on 28 October, 1932, Terris Moore and Richard Burdsall, who had learned about big mountains in Alaska and had been accompanied most of the way by Arthur Emmons and Jack Young, stood on the second highest peak thus far attained by man. Emmons and Burdsall, both surveyors, determined the peak's altitude to be more than a thousand meters lower than Everest, but nevertheless a very respectable 7591m. Upon their return home, the summit and support teams were the mountaineering heroes of the day. [98]

---

98. Most members of this party stayed prominent in American alpinism for another two generations.

See AAJ XIII-461 for more on Emmons, AAJ VIII-507 for more on Burdsall and AAJ XXXVI-317 for more on Moore.

More recent surveys give its altitude as 7587 meters. Kamet, which was climbed earlier the same year, reaches 7745 m.

The story of this expedition is well told in AAJ II-1 and II-135. However, its fuller description can be found in MEN AGAINST THE CLOUDS, by Burdsall and Emmons, London, 1935.

Much earlier that same year two other Americans had been in action a thousand miles across the range on the Indian subcontinent, in that part of Kashmir which is now Pakistani. A nine-person [six Germans[99] and three Austrian] expedition, led by Willi Merkl (1900-1934), began the first of their ultimately ill-fated assaults on 8125m Nanga Parbat. They were aided by the participation and financial resources of two Americans, 30-year-old Elbridge Rand Herron and Elizabeth Knowlton (1895-1989). As in several other attempts on this notorious summit, success eluded the team and tragedy struck when Herron stumbled over a loose stone as he was running down and fell to his death while visiting the second Pyramid of Gizeh on his return home.[100]

Four years later, in the spring of 1936, another group of four Americans, all with considerable experience in the Alps and Alaska, merged with four even more experienced British alpinists to attempt the ascent of Nanda Devi, at 7821m the highest summit that was to remain wholly within the boundary of the subsequently independent India. In the end, the summit team of two British members, Nocl Odell and Harold 'Bill' Tilman, both well known for their previous Himalayan exploits, established another new record for the highest point yet ascended. While the prime organizers of this venture, like so many others before and since, did not personally share in the ultimate accomplishment, the effort took more young Americans to the field of Himalayan action and brought to wider acclaim two personages whose names were to remain in the limelight of American alpinism for more than half a century – Charles Snead Houston and Hubert Adams Carter.[101]

Nevertheless, the great Himalayan 8000 meter peak rush was fairly begun – not merely among Americans, for various British teams had been assaulting the north side of Mount Everest since 1921, since access to the great peaks through Nepal had been denied by the country's ruling prime ministers – a condition that changed dramatically with the return to real

99. One of the Germans was Fritz Wiessner, who took out American citizenship in 1935.

100. This was the first 8000m peak on which Americans actually essayed an attempt.
    For more on Knowlton (1895-1989), see AAJ XXXI-330. See AAJ II-110 for more on Herron. See also Knowlton's book, THE NAKED MOUNTAIN, New York, 1936.

101. This endeavor was well described in AAJ III-1 and the ALPINE JOURNAL, IL-13.
    Houston, an internist and professor of medicine at the University of Vermont, became the world's leading authority on acclimatization and the medical disorders associated with high altitude.
    Carter (1914-1995), a teacher of modern languages at Milton Academy, became an authority on the Andes of Peru, a beloved workhorse of the AAC and honored around the world.

power of King Tribhuvan in 1950. Various German-Austrian parties had been after Nanga Parbat and 8595m Kangchenjunga since 1929; Italians had been on 8612m K2 as early as 1909, and the French has attempted 8068m Hidden Peak and other peaks. Thus, when The American Alpine Club asked the Indian government for permission to attempt K2, even though communications were much slower in those days, the request was granted not only for the summer season of 1938, but also for a follow-up effort in 1939, if such should prove necessary. Alpinists of subsequent generations will rapidly note that exclusive rights to an entire peak, for two years at no charge, is a long lost part of ancient history. However, in those days, the non-mountaineering costs and hazards assumed very different forms from those encountered both 50 years earlier and 50 years later.

With the prime choice for leader, Fritz Wiessner, unable to take time off from his employment in 1938, the first American Karakoram Expedition was rapidly organized by Houston, aided by Robert Hicks Bates, with whom he had shared several earlier Alaskan endurance contests. Their party consisted of some of the most vigorous younger alpinists of the country. Twenty-five-year-old Bill House, a Yale-educated forester; 43-year-old Minya Konka veteran Richard Burdsall; and Paul Petzoldt, a tough Teton mountain guide. The American team was accompanied by the mandatory British transport officer, in this case the exceptionally competent and gallant Lt. Norman Streatfeild, who was to lose his life only two years later during the evacuation of Dunkirk.

The route of ascent, selected after various other approaches proved impractical, was up the ridge named for the leader of the 1909 Italian party, a line that had first been reconnoitered by the illustrious Luigi Amadeo di Savoia-Aosta, the archetypical alpinist Duke of the Abruzzi. But for climbers to get established on its upper portion required negotiating a very difficult step. This task fell to Bill House, the skilled rock climber who, in 1935, had been Wiessner's companion on the first ascent of Mount Waddington and, a few weeks later, on the first free ascent of Wyoming's Devils Tower. After a strenuous day, at an altitude far higher than any at which comparable endeavors had been done before, fixed ropes were placed in the "House Chimney," a route landmark used by every subsequent expedition on the Abruzzi Ridge.

In the end the summit team of Houston and Petzoldt came within an ace of making it, turning back only when the route above seemed assured and because the mores of the day mandated a conservative approach to the risks of altitude and weather associated with their extended support system. On 20 July, 1938, they camped at 24,700 feet (7530m), went about 1,500 feet higher the next day, reaching barely 700m below the summit, and then retreated to their base. Returning home, co-leader Bob Bates reported to the annual meeting of The American Alpine Club that the mountain could definitely be climbed by the now famous Abruzzi Ridge.[102]

One year later, Wiessner was able to take the leadership of a second effort. He had already been to the Himalaya with the German expedition to Nanga Parbat in 1932. Initially, Wiessner was able to recruit a strong party, but then, one by one, the experienced and vigorous members withdrew and Wiessner was left with a team made up largely of two extremes, the rich but incompetent and the young but inexperienced. Had any of Sterling Hendricks, Alfred Lindley, Bestor Robinson or Roger Whitney (all of whom had been asked) been able to join the expedition, its outcome might well have been dramatically different. Once in the field, it became clear that the 1939 team had none of the internal cohesiveness of its predecessor and precious little of its expeditionary experience.

The outcome could have been predicted, and in fact, was. Only Wiessner had the drive, the competence and the physique to do the job, but he was isolated in his "Germanness" at the wrong time and place for such leadership. The tragic outcome of this expedition, with one sahib (Dudley Wolfe) and three brave Sherpas left dead on the mountain, brought on years of name-calling and controversy, largely initiated by the party's internal incompatibility, which had been exacerbated by Wiessner's inability to understand and make allowances for the enormous difference between his own attitude and ability toward the venture and that of his associates. Only Jack Durrance, among those who finally went, had the ability to keep pace with Wiessner, and he was hampered by inadequate footwear. The more experienced deputy leader – at least on paper – Eaton Cromwell, turned out to be a defeatist and a hindrance to the party's success. Even so, Wiessner got closer to the summit than anyone prior to the successful Italian party of 1954.

Understandably insensitive to current American mores, after the expedition's return Wiessner, whose youthful cousin had been killed while climbing in their native Elbesandsteingebirge, was quoted in the press to the effect that in mountaineering – "as in war" – one must expect casualties. While the remark is true, in early 1940 it was perceived as being excessively Teutonic – not a good thing for one of German ancestry to blurt out in public in a nation that was rapidly becoming alarmed by Adolf Hitler. The complete

---

102. A teacher at the prestigious Phillips Exeter Academy, Bates became the second Honorary President of the AAC and a beloved figure to all alpinists. The 1938 American Expedition was the subject of a joint publishing endeavor by its participants entitled FIVE MILES HIGH, New York, 1939.

story of this ill-fated trip is, as was stated by American Consul Edward Groth in his official report to the Secretary of State, quite involved. Nevertheless, it was incompletely written up in a number of accounts, based initially on "facts" supplied of Oliver Eaton Cromwell, the treasurer of the expedition, who left the base camp early and hurried home ahead of the rest of the party. Many subsequent writers, in an attempt at historic revisionism, tended to glorify Wiessner at the expense of Jack Durrance. The truth is very much more complex.[103]

*   *   *

Mountaineering in the war years was devoted to victory. While the last of the Americans straggled home from K2, another group of far-sighted mountaineers at home were already beginning to focus on their place in a revived military preparedness on the part of the American people. Except for its navy, the United States' peacetime armed force was minuscule in 1939, less than one thousandth of what it became five years later. But among the civilian and military leaders of the American government, as the nation fumbled closer to involvement in the European and Asiatic conflicts, were several who foresaw the need to meet armed force with equally competent force in the winter, in the arctic and in the mountains. With its heritage of interest in the arctic, The American Alpine Club became the nation's focal point for cold weather and mountaineering experience.

Meantime, American ski enthusiasts, led by Charles Minot Dole, had heard and read reports of the startling success of Finnish ski troopers in holding back the numerically superior Russian forces in the winter of 1939-40, and began to bombard the War Department with offers of help. On their way to Washington, the skiers found themselves joined by alpinists bent on a similar mission. In the capital the offer was more acceptable because of the willingness of an American Alpine Club member to listen – Secretary of War Henry Lewis Stimson who had returned from semi-retirement for the final public task of his life. By the time of the Japanese attack on Pearl Harbor, the first of the mountain units, the 87th Mountain Infantry Regiment, had already been established and civilian alpinists, among whom were many of the persons mentioned above, were hard at work designing materiel, manuals of survival and technique, and donning uniforms.[104]

---

103. Wiessner (1900-1988) became a hero to a younger generation of American climbers, among which are two of these authors. For the documented story of what happened on the 1939 expedition see K2, THE 1939 TRAGEDY, Seattle, 1992.

104. Dole (1898-1976) had been one of the organizers of the National Ski Patrol.
    Stimson (1867-1950), soon to become an Honorary Member of the AAC, had done considerable climbing in the Alps, and held a long series of public offices. A law partner

The most long-lasting of the civilian efforts was probably that of a Naval Reserve officer, Lt. Cmdr Kenneth Atwood Henderson, a leader in American high-angle alpinism and mountain training, who had been among the first to make serious climbs in the Teton and Wind River Ranges. His 1942 volume, HANDBOOK OF AMERICAN MOUNTAINEERING, published in cooperation with the AAC, was ordered in bulk by the War Department and became the de facto training manual for the 10th Mountain Division and was demobilized to become a civilian stand-by for a dozen years after the war. [105]

By war's end, members of The American Alpine Club held dozens of field grade and line officer positions among the 15,000 men of the 10th Mountain Division and associated units. Several past and future officers of the AAC were prominent in the overall effort and others played active – and highly decorated – roles in the Aleutian and Italian campaigns. The exploits of America's "ski troopers" made good reading for civilians but, due largely to the hidebound attitudes of senior officers against specialized forces and equipment, these exciting units never played a decisive role in winning more than a tiny part of the war.

Activities of alpinists in uniform as well as in civilian support of the war effort occupied much of the agenda for all mountaineering clubs during the war years. In marked contrast to the AAC's "presence" during World War I, when it basically ceased operations, the principal speakers at its annual meetings of 1942 and thereafter dealt with the varied aspects of the military applications of mountaineering in which members were involved. Peripheral programs at these meetings covered lesser episodes during the entire period of American involvement in the war. The AMERICAN ALPINE JOURNAL carried a number of articles, many compiled by Dr. Thorington, our scholarly co-author, detailing other aspects of the same topics, along with committee reports on military support activities, sketches of prior alpine military activity and speculation on future such events. At every turn, and in every way possible, organized American alpinism went to war.

But climbing mountains for the sheer joy of it was not forgotten. The testing of equipment under severe conditions justified an ascent of Mount McKinley – each member of the party wore a different type of footwear – to establish the basic production model for the "Boot, Mountain

---

of the distinguished Elihu Root, he had been Secretary of War for President Taft and Secretary of State for Hoover.

105. Henderson was an occasional councillor of the AAC, and served with distinction as the last thoroughgoing alpinist president of the Appalachian Mountain Club. He was elected to Honorary Membership in both groups.

& Ski, M-1942." "Ski troopers," training among the mountains of Colorado, from a camp located at 9,000 feet in the Pando valley, managed to climb many of the surrounding heights on weekend passes, without having to carry the unit's proverbial "90 pounds of rucksack." In the Aleutians a whole battalion of them marched a dozen tedious miles across the island's lava flows, ash drifts and sinking tundra to climb the 4,000 foot Kiska Volcano, after three members of one company had gone AWOL to make its first ascent.[106] In Italy, once peace had superseded the mud and misery of the final winter campaign, members of the 10th Mountain Division, aided by the liberal and far-sighted attitude of their commanding officer, Major General George Price Hays, went on extended sprees of climbing in the Dolomites, Julian Alps, the Ortler, even to Monte Rosa, while still in uniform.[107]

When the war was over, an unprecedented civilian rush to the mountains of America began. A number of diehard skiers "joined the 52-20 Club" for the winter of 1946. Many of these forerunners to a generation of "ski bums" were enabled to pocket $20 a week for up to one year, without any questions being asked, from a program designed to provide adjustment to civilian unemployment for returning veterans. The war-inspired, but now surplus, climbing and cold weather equipment that flooded retail establishments across the nation for several years was far superior to anything available before the war and its cost was now minimal. This condition enabled thousands of young Americans to take to the mountains with relative financial ease. Once there, they began to participate in and frequent an annually increasing number and variety of ski area developments, more sophisticated clothing and equipment outlets, guide services and other mountain recreational facilities. Across the land from Wildcat Mountain in the Northeast, via Iron Mountain, Aspen and dozens of other lesser known emporia, to California's Squaw Valley, veterans of the 10th Mountain Division and their friends found civilian employment, investment opportunity and much recreational pleasure.

---

106. An account of this venture by one of the participants (then in transit to further combat in Italy) was part of the program for the AAC Annual Meeting of 1944.

107. Besides his enormous popularity with the mountain troopers, Hays (1892-1978), who won the Congressional Medal of Honor in World War I, was again the right man in the right place as the Allied Military Governor in Berlin at the time of the notorious Russian blockade.

See the AAC's 1991 publication, GREEN COGNAC, for a fuller account of the origin and activities of American Mountain Troops.

XII – CHANGING MORES
Kauffman & Putnam

With the end of World War II and the rise of new challenges, many attitudes began to change. Airborne access to mountain ranges became much more common, thus gradually eliminating the horse caravans traditional heretofore in North American mountain ranges. In time, the helicopter would enable an alpinist of sufficient means to have his entire party and equipment deposited right at the base of his intended route. Such ease of access was most commonly used in the wilderness areas of North America but then began to spread elsewhere. Among purists, however, a number of ethical questions began to arise.

The leaders of thought in trying to restrict airborne access – or the use of helicopters in the mountains in place of funiculars or ski tows – were the European alpinists, whose native mountains were already the most "developed" on Earth. In the Alps, cog railways and cable cars already reached many alpine areas, even summits, and were soon built to many more. In such areas, airborne access to the start of a climb was hardly desirable and the leaders of the European mountain clubs repeatedly adopted resolutions condemning such services, little noting their own inconsistence or the inappropriateness of such limitations in other parts of the world. Nowhere was this dichotomy more fully borne out – or more widely and continuously decried – than in the alleged first ascent of Cerro Torre by Cesare Maestri and Toni Egger early in 1959, during the course of which several thousand feet of solely aid climbing was necessary. On a subsequent venture an air compressor was hauled up (and later abandoned on) the cliff face to aid in the drilling of bolt holes. The international outcry against such climbing ethics reverberated for decades.

The first major American expedition after the war, also the first to rely heavily on airborne supply, was that of the Harvard Mountaineering Club to Mount Saint Elias in 1946. Organized by correspondence during the war between Maynard Miller and two of these authors, all past presidents of the Harvard Mountaineering Club, it made extensive use of aerial drops at three locations on the southerly approach to the peak -- the route that had been unsuccessfully attempted 50 years earlier by a less effectively supplied American party. The 1946 expedition thus showed the possibility of avoiding the huge manpower demands of such classics as the Duke's expedition to the same peak. It was also a gathering of future leadership for the AAC – Miller served six years as a Club councillor and was a prime mover in initiating the AAC's Safety Committee of which Dr. Benjamin Greely Ferris then served 25 years as its chairman. The expedition was also remarkably successful, placing seven of its eight participants on the summit of the mountain on the 199th anniversary day of its sighting by Vitus Bering in 1747. Most of the other six participants in this expedition became officers, Honorary Members (or both) of the AAC: collectively, they served three years as president, six as vice-president, 15 as treasurer, and as 18 directors, and (as of this writing) 27 as the Club's delegate to the UIAA. Four of them were also elected to Honorary Membership.

Americans were not without presence in the other major ranges of the world. They returned routinely to the Andes of Chile and Peru, making numerous first ascents of peaks such as Yerupaja and establishing firm friendships with local alpinists in both countries. Some of these trips showed the climbing abilities of such future American climbing luminaries as George Bell, David Harrah, John Ayres, David Michael and Graham Matthews. But, as in the years just before the war, it was the Himalaya/Karakoram area that beckoned most forcefully. In 1953, Houston and Bates led another highly competent group of climbers in a return engagement to K2, unfortunately without the element of success that had attended their first such venture, 15 years earlier. Handicapped by severe weather and the illness from pulmonary edema of one of its members high on the mountain, the team returned with sad news of the death of Arthur Gilkey, but with strong memories of the homogeneity of the team, most members of which – Bell, Craig, Molenaar, and Schoening – were to remain in the forefront of American alpinism for decades to come. That epic retreat, dragging the injured Gilkey on a makeshift sled, was punctuated by a slip on a steep and icy slope in which all members of the party found themselves finally held by the belay of Pete Schoening – one of the legendary events of American mountaineering.

Six Americans had a large part in another expedition, in 1960-1, when 22 participants from various portions of the English-speaking world, were led into the eastern Himalaya by Sir Edmund Hillary. Over a two-year period the party carried on extensive experiments on acclimatization, collected valuable data on solar radiation at altitude along with glaciological and biological information never before analyzed. Of course, they also tried to seek out the elusive Yeti, with no greater success than has attended similar "manhunts" for the Sasquatch before and since. Though turned back on Makalu, the world's fifth highest summit, their successful ascent of Ama Dablam, at well over 7000 meters was a new high point of summitry for Americans.[108]

In 1960, an expedition organized by a newly elected member, Nicholas Bayard Clinch, and led in the field by George Bell, a veteran of several Peruvian trips as well as the 1953 K2 expedition. attained the summit of Masherbrum, which though not in the magic circle of the "elite 14," was a remarkably successful ascent and brought great credit to its organizers. A few years later, in 1966, modern means of access led to the first serious attempt at Antarctic alpinism. In December of that year, Clinch led a group to the base of the Vinson Massif of the Sentinel Mountains, the continent's highest. With all materiel and personnel being delivered by C-130 from naval bases on the coast, and then carried closer to the mountains by motorized toboggans, this marked another significant break-through in alpine logistics. Over the next four weeks the members of this party made the first ascents of a half dozen of the highest summits on the continent. The expedition's outstanding success, coupled with the ongoing congeniality of the party, further established its leader as one of the foremost expedition managers in the world.

In the meantime, in 1963 a major American success was achieved on Mount Everest, by an expedition organized and led by Norman Dyhrenfurth with help from Will Siri. The members of this expedition included a WHO'S WHO of American alpinism and

---

108. An enduring memento of this expedition was the prefabricated "Silver Hut" which was later dismantled and given to the Himalayan Mountaineering Institute.

not only made the first American ascent of this peak but – in a major accomplishment – two of the members, Dr. Tom Hornbein and Willy Unsoeldt ascended the west ridge and then traversed the summit to the South Col.

Clinch had been selected as leader of the Vinson Massif party because of his obvious talents in arranging prior successes in the Karakoram, mainly in organizing the only successful first ascent of an 8000 meter peak by an American party. In 1958, Hidden Peak, also known as Gasherbrum I, remained the only one of the exalted 14 peaks that had not climbed. There were the usual problems associated with obtaining permission from the government of Pakistan, late arrival of some party members, the shipment and transhipment of supplies from freighter to railway to porter, and the almost inevitable porters' strike. But, the planning was adequate for these events and the party was comfortably ensconced at its base camp in adequate time to make their ascent before the possible arrival of the monsoon.

Four further camps were established on the way up the ridge the party named for André Roch, who had investigated this line in 1934. There were none of the technical difficulties that had stymied some parties on K2, only 18 miles away, but there was an extended stretch on the upper reaches of the mountain which, while devoid of serious objective hazard and danger of avalanche, required strenuous labor at exalted altitude and was exposed to the equally serious problem of changing weather without ease of retreat. A couple of feet of snow could bog everything down and leave the summit party stranded above 22,000 feet. But things went well, the higher camps were stocked, the oxygen system utilized and several cordial exchanges enjoyed with an Italian party making an attempt on nearby Gasherbrum IV. On July 5th, 1958, Peter Kittlesby Schoening and Andrew John Kauffman, II, became the first and only Americans to make the successful first ascent of an 8000 meter peak.

* * *

Back in the United States a significant alteration was taking place in the ethics of alpinism. Technical and metallurgical innovation -- much of it undertaken by the blacksmith/climber, John Salathé – had made possible the fabrication and placement of ever thinner pitons into the narrowest of cracks; from this it was only a small further evolution to the carrying of drills to make holes for expansion bolts where not even a line of weakness could be found. At the same time, wider cracks could be conquered by the use of widely flaring pitons (bongs) and in one notable case by the use of stove legs. Invariably these products led to the ascent of previously impossible lines – such as the 1958 ascent of the "Nose" of El Capitan – by use of these artificial aids to climbing. Traditional American alpinists, largely brought up in the school typified by the eminent British climber, Geoffrey Winthrop Young, frowned on this "desecration" of the mountains. Yet the practice of using artificial aid to make ascents grew from its nucleus of "Yosemite" climbers to reach across the country and the world.

Inevitably, a backlash set in. Use of artificial aids by stepping into stirrups hung from a piton, was one thing, hanging ever longer ladders to pitons was an easily understood next step. But, after the "Wall of Early Morning Light" episode and being popular for much of a generation, the use of expansion bolts drilled into an otherwise blank face became regarded as beyond the pale of honor. As quickly as the use of pitons for artificial aid and safety had spread, so did a more recent and decidedly more environmentally friendly device, the "nut," which originated in England. Use of these, and their more sophisticated descendants, including cams – devised by the grand old man of Soviet alpinism, Vitale Abalakov – and "friends", turned a day on the cliffs from one long session of tympany back more nearly into the tranquil experience of a contest with nature that the sport of technical rock climbing – indeed all of mountaineering – had started out to be.

XIII – MOVING WEST
Putnam

In the beginning of alpinism – some 200 years before this writing – climbing difficult mountains was a recreational activity practiced almost entirely by those of considerable means, who could afford the time and expense of distant travel. Even in Great Britain, some of whose mountain areas offer extreme challenges of angle and environment, the tendency to regard "the continent" as the venue for real climbing was so strong that the members of the world's first climbing organization dubbed themselves simply as "Alpine." Only later – toward the close of the 19th century – did the Climbers' Club[109] and the Fell and Rock Society come into existence, whose members were equally athletic but generally of lesser wealth and did their climbing thing on the "gritstone edges" and other crags and fells much closer to home.

Across the Atlantic in the United States, at that time most of the money was in the East – as was, consequently, the means to travel and see the more distant spectacular regions of the world. Thus, while some of the social upper crust thought the White Mountains of northern New England offered adventure and challenge enough, and left their names,[110] as well as those of a half-dozen early American presidents, on the local landscape. Meanwhile a few others, like newspapermen Samuel Bowles, II, and Horace Greeley, crossed the country to see and report the financial and recreational potential of more distant ranges in the American West. Nevertheless, by the turn of the 19th century it was still almost as easy to travel in luxury on Albert Ballin's or Samuel Cunard's liners for 3,000 miles to Europe as it was to take the almost equally costly but less comfortable trip of a similar time

---

109. This organization, in particular, owed its founding to the genius and skill of Oscar Eckenstein, an engineer of Jewish ancestry who was not welcomed into the stodgier Alpine Club. These clubs were soon followed by dozens more.

110. These included such names, well known to subsequent climbers, as those of the reverend Congressman Manasseh Cutler, geologist Joshua Henry Huntington, hotelier Abel Crawford, industrialist Francis Boott, and botanist Edward Tuckerman

and distance by railroad across North America.

However, The American Alpine Club was not started as the creature of only those who looked east to the mountains. The first handbook of the Club in 1903 cataloged the major accomplishments of its members – a form of internal ego enhancement or self-glorification that only ended in 1940. It also showed that two of the Founders bothered to list no climbs or explorations whatever, 13 had climbed only in the American West, 10 had done their climbing in Western Canada, seven were known for their Arctic adventures, five had climbed only in Europe, but only two in Alaska, while four had practiced their avocation in other and more distant regions. As the years went on, and such cragwork and shorter technical rock climbs came to dominate the weekend activities of more city-bound members, this form of alpinism became more recognized, but did not appear at all among the Club's founders in 1902.

More important regarding the focus of the Club was the domicile of its 36 "original" members. The "balance of manpower" was tilted heavily to the East. Nine members lived in Philadelphia, eight in New England, six in New York City, six in the Pacific Northwest, five in California, four in the nation's capital, one each in Illinois, Michigan, Maryland, Texas and Alaska; while two – including one of the nascent club's only two females – had become expatriates from Massachusetts and listed their residences in London. With such a domination of membership domicile it is small wonder that the bulk of the Club's leadership for the first half-century of its existence, came from the "Eastern Establishment."

There were intermittent rumblings, however. With some regularity after World War I, Francis Peloubert Farquhar convened dinners for West Coast members at his home in Berkeley. Not until 1965, however, was a formal Annual Meeting held in other than a major East Coast city – mostly New York, Boston and Philadelphia. But in 1950, a group of younger insurgents, including three who subsequently became Honorary Members, thought a change was more than overdue. After all, the organization had a name to live up to – Club it already was; Alpine, mostly with the capital "A"; but to be truly American it really should span the nation with greater effectiveness. With the help of a few others and the sterling support of Joel Ellis Fisher, then the Club's Treasurer, they petitioned the Club officers to hold an Annual Meeting "in the West." When the request was ignored they decided to "go public" and force the issue. Fisher, whose Wall Street business acumen was substantial and who had been through a number of corporate control battles, undertook to organize a proxy ballot so that the more distant members could be heard on this matter.

With the Annual Meeting set for New York City on 2 December, they sent out a mailing to every member in early September. Soon the replies began to trickle in to Fisher's Fifth Avenue home, and it appeared that victory was in sight. The insurgents, however, had not anticipated the equally strong legal capabilities of the Club's then secretary, Bradley Baldwin Gilman. As rumors of the insurgent's strong support reached the officers, they undertook a "management" proxy and distributed a second ballot – *"hereby revoking any previous proxy."*

On the day of the meeting, while committee reports were being heard by most of the members, a tight group of persons clustered at the rear of the meeting hall in the "Old Firehouse" on East 90th Street. First, both sets of proxies were alphabetized, so that those insurgent supporters whose initial reactions of support had been revoked on further reflection of the statement put out by the officers, could be eliminated. Then, the count began in earnest with the insurgents still maintaining a clear majority, until a breathless late-coming member arrived from the West Coast with 20 more "management" proxies "delivered" by Farquhar. While it still looked good for those who wanted to broaden the Club's membership participation, those present in person were yet to be counted and unfortunately they were almost entirely conservative Easterners – at least in their thinking.

Though the younger "troublemakers" lost (and were promptly replaced on various Club committees) the Club lost even more, for its treasurer was also rusticated. Fisher, who had handled the Club's portfolio as a committee of one, had a personal policy of occasionally taking "fliers" in the stock market with Club funds. If the investment went up, as he had expected, the Club was the winner. If, on the other hand, by year end the stock had gone down, Fisher invariably made the Club whole out of his personal pocket. From this time forward, there was no such angel.

Though the westward move appeared to be momentarily dead, its spirit lived on. When Lawrence Coveney, a man who had done most of his better climbs in the West, became president he carried sufficient prestige that in 1965, on 4 December, an Annual Meeting was called to order in Seattle. Fisher was dead, Kauffman was in Calcutta, but Matthews, Beckey and the youngest of these authors were there to rejoice.

But the Club headquarters was still in New York, where it had officially resided for most of its life. Initially the "office" had been the legal domicile of its secretary or its treasurer in Philadelphia. As was appropriate, given the founder's own city of residence, in the first years of its life communications could be addressed to Secretary Bryant at his office: 2013 Walnut Street; or to Treasurer Wm. S. Vaux, Jr. at 515 Stephen Girard Building,[111] both in Philadelphia. In 1911 the Club was still unincorporated, but with the advent of New York-based Judge Putnam as president, the other active officers were now both Bostonians, Secretary Palmer at 42 Mount Vernon Street[112] and Treasurer Burr at 60 State Street, where they stayed for the next six years.

A third membership handbook was due to be issued in 1917, but American entry into World War I brought many such non-essentials to a stop. When it finally appeared in 1919, toward the close of Professor Fay's final year as president, Secretary Chapman lived at 2029 Q Street in Washington and Treasurer Seaver at 14 Wall Street in New York. With the advent of President Nichols in 1923, the Club had a library (and Leroy Jeffers as librarian) and thus more permanent domicile in New York (along with Treasurer Seaver) at 476 Fifth Avenue; though Secretary Wilcox continued in Washington, at 1526 New Hampshire Avenue. Meantime, the Club had acquired many of the books donated by Mr. Montagnier and arranged for them to be housed in a special – but identifiable – collection in the custody of the New York Public Library on Fifth

---

111. Club records show that in 1904, Vaux moved to Room 807 in the Bailey Building.

112. By 1913, Howard Palmer had removed to New London, where he cared for his family business interests.

Avenue at 43rd Street. This special library, with its slow but positive rate of accretion, stayed there for close to 10 years until the Club made an arrangement for it to be moved to the premises of the Explorers Club. This very compatible arrangement went sour in 1932 when the Explorers became faced with bankruptcy and had to sell their building. The AAC library was evicted, an event which caused the Club to seek regular quarters of its own.

Under the regime of President Palmer, starting in 1926, Secretary Henry B. deV. Schwab took his mail at 8 Bridge Street in New York, but the other addresses carried forward. By 1929 the organization had pretty much solidified in New York with President Ladd, Secretary Underhill and Treasurer Fisher all resident in the Big Apple.[113] With Schwab as president in 1932, the Club office pertained to that of the librarian, now Helen I. Buck – the organization's first paid employee – at 544 Cathedral Parkway in New York, though Secretary Thorington maintained his place of business at 2031 Chestnut Street in Philadelphia and Treasurer Fisher was at 875 Park Avenue in New York.

The Great Depression slowed things down – the AAC even felt constrained to resign from the UIAA, of which it had been a founding member – and by 1940, when the next handbook was published, there was no longer a question as to the official domicile. The American Alpine Club had been incorporated in 1915, and it now maintained its own, even if rented, office and kept its 400 volume library at 140 East 46th Street in New York.

There things stayed until 1948, when ex-President Dr. Ladd, who had chaired an earlier committee to determine an office location, acquired the premises at 113 East 90th Street that had pertained to a now defunct private fire engine company. Having signified his intention of giving the "firehouse" to the Club, a committee was formed in 1947 to raise sufficient capital to cover its maintenance – the real start of the Club's endowment. Secretary Hall, by now a very influential officer, had become adamant that the Club simply could not afford to accept Dr. Ladd's very generous offer, unless it had the endowment necessary to keep the

---

113. Dr. Thorington, in Philadelphia, was the librarian, but the library remained in New York, too.

building in good repair.

This arrangement lasted for the next generation, though increasing numbers of members felt that Bill Ladd's "old firehouse" was an inappropriate location for a national society dealing with mountains. While it was and remains true that most of the world's better known national climbing clubs have their headquarters in major cities [London (or Manchester), Paris, Turin, Bern, Munich, Vienna, Delhi, Moscow, Tokyo, Barcelona, Athens, Islamabad] only the Alpine Club of Canada "lived" in the mountains. In 1973 a questionnaire was circulated to the entire membership, then totaling 992. It asked for an expression of opinion − [1] Stay in New York; [2] Move to Washington; [3] Go to a "central location"; [4] Go to "the mountains;" and several other options. The results were not conclusive for any one of the options offered, and no action was taken at the time. It was clear however, that though no plurality existed for any of the options offered, there was a large consensus that the Club's headquarters belonged elsewhere than in the world's busiest city, a financial metropolis with steep canyons but far from "real" mountains.

Meantime, the Club continued to grow as did its paid staff. Helen Buck was succeeded by Gail Oberlin (until she married President Bates and moved to Exeter, New Hampshire). Then Margot McKee took over with occasional help from Pat Fletcher as librarian. In 1974, with Margot's decision to resign, Franc de la Vega became the club's principal employee, a position which he filled admirably considering the budgetary restraints of that day − until the Club's westward relocation was completed.

Without being actually debated, or entertaining a formal offer for the premises on East 90th Street, this basic understanding permeated all deliberations of the officers and Board for the next several years − dormant until an unrefusable opportunity should present itself, and restrained until then by the decades-long dismal real estate market in New York City. To sell the "old firehouse" and move away would hardly be the fiscally sound thing to do until property values improved. By 1993, New York real estate prices had firmed up substantially and a relocation made more economic sense. A consensus of the Board brought on the unanimous vote that the Club should seek a modern facility in the Denver area −

surely close enough to the mountains and definitely nearer the center of the country.

Though there were nostalgic moments – such as a belated final dinner held near the "old firehouse," implementing this decision and establishing the American Mountaineering Center in Golden, Colorado, became the major focus of two Club presidencies, those of Glen Porzak and Jed Williamson.

XIV – NOT ALL SWEETNESS AND LIGHT
Putnam

It would be unrealistic to always expect everyone to agree on everything – particularly in an organization composed of such socially off-beat and egocentric characters as those who climb mountains for fun. The record of disagreements within the Club is therefore, rather lengthy. To set the tone for the major events chronicled further below, however, we open this chapter by assessing a non-event that occurred at two meetings of the Club's Board in the autumn of 1949.

In those days membership applications were gone over by the entire Board of the Club, a process that often took up over half of its meetings and continued until 1975. A new member had been proposed, one Henry S. Pinkham, whose address was given as being in the small central Massachusetts hill town of Petersham. His proposers were climbers of good repute and significant accomplishment, Harvard graduates, active in many ranges and Club members of several years standing. Pinkham's occupation was stated to be that of custodian and his age was stated to be 39. His climbing record extended over three years and included several first ascents in Canada and Alaska, plus numerous lengthy winter climbs in the mountains of northern New England. He was clearly well qualified by the rules then in effect and the Board passed it without significant debate, directing the Secretary to proceed with the usual formalities for admitting new members.

After the meeting, Secretary Gilman, retreated to his "dascha" in the central Massachusetts hill town of Barre where he transcribed his notes into formal minutes, as was his custom. In the process of so doing, he came across the paper dealing with Pinkham. *"Petersham,"* he thought, *"the next town over, and I've never heard of a climber living there who has this good a record?"* Further reflection caused him to exercise an unusual procedure, not provided for in the By-laws. He held the application aside until he could bring it before the Board a second time, at its December meeting. Something seemed to be highly unusual.

At the December meeting, Gilman brought up the

application again and voiced his concerns. Mountaineering was still a small universe and he had simply never heard of this accomplished a climber living in the next small town over. This caused the Board to read the application more closely, peering intently between the lines for additional information. Suddenly, the light dawned – the climbing record may well have been correct, the age was credible, the address may have been suspicious but it was legal, though the applicant's signature appeared to have been forged. Also of interest was the fact that this applicant had done all his climbing only in the company of his sponsors.

In those days the Club's application form specified that an applicant's age be given *"for the information of the officers, only;"* – an archaic holdover from the days of youthful Brad Washburn's problems with acceptance by President Delafield – but it did not require the age to be given in years. Pinkham's, it was felt, had been given in months. At the same time there arose a dark suspicion as to Pinkham's species. The Club by-laws were (then and now, two major revisions later[114]) silent on the eligibility of non-humans, and while the Board had now become of the opinion that this climber was in fact a four-footed as well as a sure-footed malamute, there seemed no way out of the dilemma but to table the application indefinitely.

Pinkham is, of course, long since deceased. However, it remains self-evident from the routine conversations between and about many long-standing members that canine ancestry has never been an effective bar to membership in The American Alpine Club.

* * *

Following the annual meeting and dinner held at the University Club of Philadelphia on 30 December, 1904, the Board reassembled and the minutes kept by Secretary Bryant reported its final action:

The Secretary moved that the name of Commander R. E. Peary, U.S.A. [sic] *be transferred from the active to the Honorary list of the Club. If* [sic] *appearing that the members of the Board present favored such transfer, the Secretary was requested to obtain the*

---

114. Though the forces of non-discrimination have latterly included a provision forbidding discrimination against sinistrality (left-handedness).

written consent of the two absent members off the Board [Muir and Russell] *and then to notify Commander Peary of his election to Honorary membership.*

At that point in his life, the no-longer-youthful Peary had made five arctic voyages, discovering new lands, some of which later turned out to be non-existent, and enlisted the companionship and support of a number of influential Club members – including Heilprin and Bryant. But, though a persistent explorer, he had yet to establish even a "farthest north." Coincident upon Peary's elevation to Honorary Membership, a relatively large number of resignations occurred, almost a quarter of the Club's total. Whether this was done in protest or not, there are no remaining communications and the minutes are also silent, but there was never a comparable exodus of members in any of the divisive episodes that followed.

Those departing in 1904-05 included the following nine original members:[115]

Edwin Swift Balch, former president of the Geographical Society of Philadelphia;

Bolton Coit Brown, artist and author;

Albert J. Capron, corresponding secretary of the Mazamas;

George Davidson, geodesist and vice-president of the Club;

Thomas Roby Hill, explorer and engineer;

Rev. Charles Lathrop Noyes, AMC Councillor of Exploration;

Charles Sproull Thompson; railroad executive;

Walter Dwight Wilcox, writer (later re-elected);

Edward Weldon Young, MD, vice-president of the Mazamas

There was little public discussion of the matter, though some whispers of it were resurrected a few years later when the Cook-vs-Peary North Pole debate sold thousands of newspapers throughout the world. The much more limited polarization within the Club about Dr. Cook's alleged first ascent of Mt. McKinley came back to public view after the spring of 1909 when the controversy over

---

115. Edwina Fay Fuller (one of the Club's two original female members) had resigned prior to this event.

priority of attainment of the North Pole had been widely bruited in the public press. This matter, too, had occupied much press lineage over more than a year, with all possible authorities and participants being interviewed repeatedly. Precious few members, however, objected to the subsequent expulsion of Dr. Cook in 1910. The Club had also become more of a mountaineering society over the decade of its existence than a polar oriented organization.

Since there remain a few – and well-financed – enthusiasts for Dr. Cook, the echoes of the polar question still reverberate in some quarters and with understandable justice. Anyone competent to perform celestial navigation can do the arithmetic necessary to establish latitude just as well from the observation to the result, forwards as backwards. Cook's Polar claim was unsubstantiated by any independent observations – as was also that of the much older Peary, who had deliberately left out of his final polar dash the only person capable of verifying his claim. However, Cook's false claims with respect to Mount McKinley were more promptly and thoroughly debunked, and therefore more easily accepted and understood by alpinists than the still debatable contention of his overstatements on the polar matter relative to those of Peary. There were only two persons leaving the Club in the wake of Dr. Cook's expulsion: Charles Henry Sholes, a three-term president of the Mazamas and George C. Cantwell, photographer of Seattle.

The more public discomfiture of Annie Smith Peck relative to her claim of having attained the highest altitude reached by a woman began with her ascent of Huascaran Norte in 1908 at age 58. It came to a head at the Club's annual meeting of 1910 when a special committee reported on the altitude of that Andean summit relative to the 23,400 foot altitude secured by Mrs. Workman on Pinnacle Peak in the Himalaya in 1906. Dr. Thorington covered the topic quite well in his commentary on Miss Peck in his 1946 opus, ANNALS OF THE AMERICAN ALPINE CLUB, PART I.

"1908. N. summit of Mt. Huascaran (21,812 ft.; 1ˢᵗ ascent). This was afterward named Cumbra Ana Peck by the Lima Geographical Society.

Miss Peck estimated, without instrumental readings above 19,600 ft., that the N. peak (lower summit) of Mt. Huascaran was probably 24,000 ft. and the highest point in South America. Mrs. Workman, believing that Aconcagua held this position, sent a scientific expedition which determined the elevation of the N. peak to be 21,812 ft. and that of the S. peak 22,182 ft. (This was a matter of personal rivalry since Mrs. Workman, in 1906, had made a new altitude record for women by the ascent of Pinnacle Peak, 23,400ft. In the Himalayas.)"

At the annual meeting of The American Alpine Club, on 2 January, 1909, a committee composed of Professors H. F. Reid, A. L. Rotch, and E. C. Pickering was formed to secure information on Mt. Huascaran: *"concerning which exaggerated reports had been circulated in the press."* At the meeting of 1910, the committee confirmed the altitude as determined by the expedition sent by Mrs. Workman..

"1911, (aet. 61). Two peaks (ca. 21,250 ft; 1ˢᵗ ascents) at the S. E. end of the Coropuna massif (Peru). [Miss Peck's attention had been drawn to this mountain by a statement that it was to be an objective of the Yale Peruvian Expedition, led by H. Bingham (AAC 1914). It was then thought, from Bandolier[116]'s book, that it might be higher than Aconcagua. She attempted to be first on the ground, and claimed to have reached the top, but the Yale Expedition's survey showed that the highest point, 21,703 ft., which Bingham ascended, was the cone at the N. W. end of the massif.]"

Be all that as it may, in 1912 when Annie Peck – whose dues for 1903 and 1904 had been remitted by the Club – was thus found to be in error, she felt constrained to leave the organization and was soon followed by the following seven members:

Claude Ewing Rusk; former president of the Cascadians;
Theodore Seixas Solomons, proposer of John Muir Trail;
John H. Cameron, vice-president of the Mazamas;
Edwin Bingham Copeland, professor of botany;
Frank Bruce Leland, lawyer and banker;
Roger Bigelow Merriman, professor of history;
William Lord Smith, medical doctor.

The last public controversy of consequence that caused members to resign, grew out of the sad and embarrassing results of

---

116. Adolph Francis Bandelier (1840-1914) was well known for his archeological researches in Peru and Bolivia for the 10 years after 1892

the Club's 1939 K2 Expedition. As mentioned above and discussed more fully in the 1992 book, K2 – THE 1939 TRAGEDY, O. Eaton Cromwell was first to return to the United States. For reasons never formally disclosed but which could well be imagined given his own behavior while in the field, he sought to lay all the blame for the fatalities onto the expedition's leader, even going so far as to make a public accusation of murder. Wiessner, whose German ancestry made him a convenient target among the largely Anglophilic membership of the Club as World War II was breaking out, understandably sought to defend himself and was strongly supported by many of the Club's most distinguished members[117] and was also gentleman enough not to make further – and much more appropriate – accusations to counter the wild charges made by Cromwell.

On 27 October 1939, the Club's Council appointed a committee of highly respected members [Joel Ellis Fisher, William Pendleton House, Terris Moore, and Bestor Robinson, under the Chairmanship of Walter Abbott Wood, Jr.] to consider all the facts and report to the Board. A preliminary finding was delivered to the Council under date of 7 December 1939, and a finished report was made available to all the members on 16 March, the following year. This report placed no blame for the unfortunate events but did make a number of suggestions for future expedition personnel and management.

With the circulation of this "whitewash" the acrimony between the antagonists continued and both were invited to resign, for the good of the organization. Cromwell and Wiessner promptly complied – the former returning quietly to membership in 1950. Wiessner went on his way, continuing to climb and sharing his very considerable mountaineering skill with any younger persons who acted interested. Honored by the Alpine Club of Canada and the Deutscher AlpenVerein for his very considerable accomplishments in their countries and welcomed everywhere but in the company of The American Alpine Club's officialdom, he came to loom

---

117. These included, *inter alia*, Joel Ellis Fisher and both Miriam and Robert Underhill. In the late summer of 1939, the NEW YORK TIMES carried four prominent stories on this topic.

embarrassingly as a figure of greater importance in the world of alpinism than the Club itself. It finally fell to the two junior authors of this work to seek a correction to this unfortunate state of affairs, by urging that Wiessner be named an Honorary Member of the Club.

In those days, the election of Honorary Members in The American Alpine Club required the unanimous vote of the entire Board of Directors – a deliberately difficult process. When the campaign began, in the fall of 1965, the process was greatly aided by the presence of Lawrence Coveney as President, James McCarthy as Secretary, and Barry Bishop on the Council, all of whom were long-time climbing friends of Wiessner and enthusiastic supporters of the idea. Their advice from the inside made the process of gathering letters of support easier, for the outside "campaign managers" then knew precisely whom to target and how best to counter their residual reluctance.

The Council met in March and voted – by a bare majority – for the proposal. By the time of the June Council meeting there were only two holdouts – Henry Hall and Bradley Gilman (with the latter saying privately that he did so only because he did not wish the Club's greatest benefactor to feel embarrassed by having him isolated as a minority of one). Armed with that knowledge, the managers concentrated on methods of "reaching" Hall.

Knowing of his staunch political faith in Massachusetts's then senior senator, Leverett Saltonstall, and also having contact with a fellow climber who was employed in the Senator's Washington office, it was asked if that worthy would care to enter an encomium for the distinguished German-American alpinist in the CONGRESSIONAL RECORD as an "Extension of Remarks." When the answer came back in the affirmative, such a document was promptly presented with the request that the Senator's office send a copy of the resulting page to Mr. Hall.

At the October meeting of the Council in 1966, the vote was finally unanimous and when this election occurred, Cromwell promptly resigned – again.[118] Greater losses occurred when Roy

---

118. He was also somewhat distressed financially – as a result of neglecting certain legal tidinesses required for his marital rearrangements.

Thorington declared that this act had *"caused his oldest friend to resign from the Club"*, then removed the Club from his will and took back from the Club House and museum a number of artifacts he had placed there on semi-permanent loan. Soon afterwards, the Club's decades-long benefactor, Henry Hall, deleted the organization from a substantial place in his will. But the intellectual integrity of the Club was advanced and in time it became realized that the Club's prior condition of heavy dependence on the financial largess of only one member was hardly a healthy condition.

XV – THE SCIENTIFIC STUDY OF MOUNTAIN ELEVATIONS
Putnam

There are two major branches of the geological sciences that are of particular interest to mountaineers; Orogeny, which deals with the making of mountains [the *genesis* of the *oros*] and Geomorphology, which deals with the shaping – and final erosion – of them. It belongs to the alpinists of Canada to claim the world's greatest authority on orogeny, John Tuzo Wilson (1908-1993), whose theories on continental drift today enjoy almost universal acceptance as the tectonic mechanism behind most mountain-building processes. It belongs to the alpinists of Germany to claim Albrecht Penck (1858-1945), widely regarded in his lifetime as the world authority on the erosive sciences broadly grouped under the heading of geomorphology [the *logos* of the *morphos* of *Gaea*]. Wilson, for whose mother, Henrietta Tuzo (1880-1955) is named the seventh of the "Ten Peaks" above Moraine Lake in the Canadian Rockies, carried forward the 1857 work of the British paleontologist, Sir Richard Owen, and that postulated in 1912 by the German geophysicist, Alfred Lothar Wegener. Penck, then director of the Berlin Institute of Geography, who addressed the Club at its seventh annual meeting on: *THE HIGH MORAL ATTRIBUTES OF ALPINISTS*.

Besides having been founded by members of the scientific and cultural elite of the United States, as the attendance records of its meetings indicates, The American Alpine Club became a periodic gathering point for other and later scientists. High among these was the eminent Canadian geologist, mountaineer and explorer, Arthur Philemon Coleman (1852-1939), who was elected to Honorary Membership five years after his election to the presidency of the Geological Society of America and during the period when he was serving as Dean of Arts at the University of Toronto. But the list of founders also included such as Abbott Lawrence Rotch, whose privately funded meteorological station on Blue Hill was the source of much new information in that science. George Davidson was the leading geodesist of his day, and numerous other eminent scientists participated both in the governance and the literary works of the Club.

While building mountains is an enormously slow process by human standards, the processes of erosion are much quicker – vastly more spectacular – and thus more easily appreciated, giving mountains the exciting shapes and inspiring terrain that have stimulated the human imagination from earliest times. Sheer altitude – as in the expanses of Tibet, most of which lies at a height above sea level greater than all but a few points of the United States – does not make for mountains, which, by Merriam/Webster's definition is: *"any part of a land mass which projects significantly above its surroundings."* Thus, the Club has also been a welcome home for those who have cared for the study of glaciers. Professor Heilprin was one such, but there have been others – a small few having been signaled out for Honorary Membership.

The Vaux family of Philadelphia – Mary Vaux Walcott (1860-1940), George Vaux, Jr.(1863-1927), and William Vaux, Jr. (1872-1908) – were the first, and still regarded as among the foremost, in American students of the behavior of glaciers. They came from a prominent place in American politics, philanthropy and penology – Roberts (1786-1836) devoted his life to public causes in his native Philadelphia and his son, Richard (1816-1895) continued the tradition of public service in Congress and as governor of Pennsylvania's prisons. Starting in 1872, sometimes together and often accompanied by other scientists, the members of the Vaux fifth generation in the New World undertook periodic measurements of several Canadian glaciers. After the opening of the Canadian Pacific Railway, their primary focus was on the Illecillewaet (sometimes in CPR literature called the "Great") Glacier, near the Glacier House, of which they commenced a detailed and almost annual study in 1887. Though their meticulous studies[119] were thereafter primarily of that glacier, they also regularly investigated and documented the nearby Asulkan, and in the Rockies, the Victoria, Wenkchemna, Bow and Yoho Glaciers.

The Vaux siblings' reports formed the basis for longer term

---

119. Their first report in the mountaineering world appeared as a lecture before the Appalachian Mountain Club on 14 February, 1900 and was printed in APPALACHIA, IX-156.

studies carried on mostly by Canadian scientists to the present day. However, the members of this family were far more than dilettante scientists, Mary, who operated a model dairy farm, became wife in 1916 to Charles Doolittle Walcott, director of the Smithsonian Institute and in 1924 was appointed to the Board of Indian Commissioners. George, a lawyer by training, was a founding member of the Alpine Club of Canada, Inspector for the Pennsylvania State Penitentiaries and chairman of the Board of Indian Commissioners from 1906 until his death. William, who died at the early age of 36, was an architect by training and a widely cited authority on construction materials.

The study of ice movement on the open ocean was done – the hard way – by Admiral Melville and General Greely in their separate, but nearly contemporaneous ventures towards the North Pole. Melville later cooperated with Heilprin, Bryant and others in a program to study the currents of the Arctic Ocean by logging the paths taken by various barrels and buoys after their release into the waters of the Northeast Passage. The study of ice movement in the form of mountain glaciers became the life work of two other distinguished members of The American Alpine Club.

Scion of one of America's most famous families, William Osgood Field (1904–1994) made his mark as an alpinist with several first ascents in the Canadian Rockies to celebrate his 20th birthday. As an undergraduate at Harvard he majored in geology and in 1940 became a full-time research associate with the American Geographical Society in New York. His researches were primarily among the coastal glaciers of Alaska. He soon joined the AGS board of trustees and served as that Society's director of research and exploration for many years. In the 1950s he became head of the World Data Center for Glaciology and organized the international photographic repository for this science. In 1975, his culminating and authoritative work, MOUNTAIN GLACIERS OF THE NORTHERN HEMISPHERE, was published by the Cold Regions Research and Engineering Laboratory of the United States Army.

Time was when Bill Field, along with many Club members, heard about Hannibal's crossing of the Alps with a score of elephants but never a mention of encountering snow. Time was when we also learned that Leif Ericsson established a new settlement that he reported was in a "green" land. And then we learned that it was a change of climatic conditions which drove Huns, Goths, Visigoths and Vandals from mid-Asia to the destruction of the Roman Empire. At another time we heard of a more recent period that astronomers called the "Maunder Minimum" and historians had taken to labeling "the Little Ice Age."

In our own time alpinists have noted the disheartening and almost unanimous dwindling – even outright disappearance – of mountain glaciers and our journals and guidebooks have been replete with documentation on this sad topic. For many decades and for many people who knew of Bill Field's interest, there was an all but mandatory routine to photograph the snoutal evidence of alpine glacier recession – preferably from one continual vantage point – and send such pictures to him at the AGS in New York. But only a few of us tried to attain a deeper understanding of the phenomena that were causing the recession we found so universally evident. Often we preferred to deny the worldwide nature of the process, seeking "evidence" in occasional and isolated glacial surges as proof that the process of global warming was neither total nor irrevocable.

On more considered reflection, these relatively minor advances were generally found to be the result of earthquake shakings in the catchment areas of a few glaciers that brought bulges, as in a python's meal, down their length to appear at the snout decades after their causes were forgotten. Only when mankind began to consult the records of several lines of research did we catch fleeting glimpses of the causes behind what had made many routes on alpine peaks so much more tedious and difficult than when they were first ascended more than a century earlier. Historians then told us about the number of weeks in which the arctic ice pack could be seen from the hills of Iceland. These dates had been duly recorded in parish church records from the year of first colonization in 881 AD and contained informative data on climate, as the table below indicates.

PERIOD	NUMBER of WEEKS SEEN
881 – 1010	0 – 4
1011 – 1211	0 – 5
1212 – 1387	6 – 9

1388 – 1586	2 – 3
1587 – 1798	6 – 22
1799 – 1879	7 – 40
1880 – 1964	9 – 13

Other clerics got into the act. In 1126 the Holy See in Rome had established a new bishopric to supervise the two dozen parishes, Augustinian monastery and Benedictine convent that had materialized over the prior century in Ericsson's "green" land. But in 1410, the last shepherd of the cathedral at Gardar rendered his final report to Rome. The Little Ice Age with its increasingly cold winters and shortened growing seasons had wiped out the dairy-based economy of the once green land. Pope Alexander VI noted its sad fate in a papal bull of 1492; and in his famous division of the world, four years later, he thought so little of that forgotten outpost of the known world that he gave the once "green" land to neither Spaniard nor Portuguese.

In the latter part of the 19th century it became a favorite armchair sport of intellectually inclined alpinists to speculate on the pass used by Hannibal for his famous crossing of the Alps in 218 BC. Notable British scholars of alpinism like Sir Gavin DeBeer and Douglas Freshfield debated the topic in profuse volumes, quoting insofar as possible at great length from the secondhand evidence offered by Livy (d. 17 AD) from the original account of Polybius (written about 146 BC). Other writings mentioned that, in contrast to the climatically induced migrations of the 5th and 6th centuries of the Christian Era, by 1273 Marco Polo found "a hundred monasteries," a flourishing silk industry and a library with 2,500 volumes in the central Gobi Desert city of Etzina. But that locality was not heard from again until 1909 when the Russian explorer, Peter Kuzlov, found only the shifting sands of a desert covering most of the famous library.

In the North American continent the historical record of logs kept by early traders and factors discloses a remarkable change in the maritime accessibility of Hudsons Bay from the time the first ships sent out by the English Company of Adventurers began trading there in the middle of the 17th century, to the much longer season of open water that is routine today. Not only is the shallow water of the great bay more open, but its coastline has migrated many hundred of meters out to sea as the land has risen from under the weight of four kilometers or more of ice. For over a hundred years, vacationers visiting New England's White Mountains would regularly visit – all summer long – the ice cave formations in lichenologist Professor Tuckerman's Ravine. But no winter's accumulation has lasted through the summer there since the "abnormally" cool and wet year of 1927.

Even more empirically, North Americans are blessed with three national parks bearing the name "Glacier." The oldest, in British Columbia, was established in 1886 at the behest of the Canadian Pacific Railway, where the scenic attraction for which the company named its "Glacier House," swept down to an altitude of 4,800 feet, barely 200 vertical feet above the station platform. A century later, the original rationale for the park had melted back to the skyline, an altitude some 3,000 feet higher. The park in Montana, designated in 1910 and a featured part of the Great Northern Railroad's "See America First" advertising campaign, once had dozens of what students of geology were informed were "wall" glaciers. Now that park has barely enough permanent ice to meet the summer cocktail demand of any one of a dozen major North American cities once covered by ice. And the famous Bay in Alaska, a national monument since 1925 and studied as far back as 1879 by John Muir, shows no sign whatever of the tidewater ice to which it owes its name.

Bill Field was an acknowledged leader among those who sought to document both the process and the causes of these distressing developments. He sought answers. Is this unwelcome change due to the currently politically fashionable, fossil fueled, greenhouse effect – a condition which the National Academy of Sciences has found to be the case? Or has the Sun simply become hotter? Are we already receiving advance warmth from the Andromeda Nebula, coming towards our Milky Way and Sun at 300km/second? Maybe the record of Pleistocene and Holocene changes in glaciation derives from cosmic collisions or activities on a slightly lesser scale than that which closed the Cretaceous and eliminated dinosaurs? Perhaps we should look to varied output of the Earth's volcanic areas? Or is our fate in a combination of even more obscure hands?

Historical geologists long ago noted that periods of glaciation have occurred several times in the history of the Earth. From the dimness of the Pre-Cambrian, and the better preserved Permian, the evidence is striking and found in many parts of the world. These scientists have also told us that the even more widely available evidence from the Pleistocene shows four major periods of 'continental' glaciation that were, in the words of one of Field's favorite mentors, Harvard's late professor Kirk Bryan, *"worldwide and synchronous."* Many of the current major population centers of North America and Europe were covered by the Pleistocene ice – places where the heat of summer now causes millions to swelter and run from one fossil-fuel powered, air conditioned building to another.

Meteorologists, like the Club's founding member Abbott Lawrence Rotch, also got into the act to report some shifts. Despite the relative youthfulness of standardized weather recording stations, a few recent trends have thus been documented. In the almost 200 years, from 1780 to 1970, that accurate and consistent weather recordings were taken at New Haven, Connecticut,[120] the average temperature in the latest 12-year sunspot cycle was one Celsius degree higher than in the earliest such period, but the average annual precipitation was 20 percent less. Other earth scientists, like Wilson, told us that the world's continents have drifted about on the globe, crashing into each other from time to time, like amusement park buggies in slow motion.[121] Geophysicists then told us that the Earth's polar axes were not always where we find them these days and some even observed that our orbit around the Sun has another set of variations. It was thus rather small potatoes when they disturbed our confidence in the status quo with the disquieting news that the Atlantic Ocean was getting wider all the time.

---

120. Not appreciating the value of consistent long-term weather records, Congressional budget cutters did the unthinkable in 1970 and closed the New Haven station, North America's oldest.

121. Late in 1999, the Club's Honorary Member, the distinguished alpinist, curator and cartographer, Bradford Washburn, startled the world with his precise determination that Mount Everest was still rising – at a rate of several centimeters per year and moving northward at 60 millimeters per year.

Astronomers, such as The American Alpine Club's founding members Douglass and Pickering, weighed in as the debate turned cosmic and their input became decisive. Not only does the North Star wander around the heavens, but the heavens themselves are in constant motion, with galaxies rushing about a speeds far faster than Superman. They told us that our Sun is a middle-aged, middle-sized star, with remarkably reliable energy output. It is located in a suburban part of our Milky Way galaxy and that our nearest neighbor is only some four light years away – just around the corner, astronomically speaking. They told us the Earth is slowing in its rotation (by about one second per century) and predicted that some day – fortunately some considerable time away – it will assume a posture like that of planet Mercury with only one face to the Sun.

Astronomers have also told us that to the well known inevitables of *death* and *taxes*, we should add *change*. Our Sun, the global standard and focus of life throughout human history, has its good years and its bad. Its energy output is enhanced by sunspots, and reduced in times of quiet. Thus, when Bill Field helped bring together the various disciplines of knowledge related to glaciers, there turned out to be a very close coordination between the astronomically determined "Maunder Minimum" of sunspot activity and the historian's onset of the "Little Ice Age."

While employed at Percival Lowell's observatory in Flagstaff, in an attempt to correlate changes in the Earth's climate with variations in solar radiation, Douglass unintentionally invented the science of dendrochronology. By taking core samples from the trunks of mature trees, he was able to count the "good' years and the "bad." Unfortunately, his studies in this vein did not produce the hoped-for correlation, but they did lead to a recognition that the process of comparing annual growth rings could lead to very accurate dating of when beams for ancient buildings were cut, with the result that a new science was created.

The final word on the cyclical nature of climate came from Milutin Milankovitch, a Serbian alpinist and mathematician who brought all the cycles of solar fluctuation into the same equation with variations in the obliquity of Earth's ecliptic and the ellipticity of its annual orbit around the Sun. His calculations showed that

Earth's climate is affected by several interwoven cycles that result in a periodicity of close to 1100 years from high to high. Hannibal crossed the Alps near one such "high" and Ericsson reached Greenland near the next. The Roman Empire fell to the invaders during a "low" and the "Little Ice Age" occurred as a result of the next.

Bill Field's leading position in this movement brought him the International Glaciological Society's Seligman Crystal and a half dozen other scientific societies, at home and abroad, gave him their most treasured citations, including The American Alpine Club's Honorary Membership in 1976. He had worked closely with the late Gerald Seligman, Europe's foremost man of ice, in determining the processes by which glaciers evolve from gently drifting mountain snows to the crushing forces that grind rocks to powder, uproot forests and change the face of the Earth. Field left this Earth as its climate approached the apex of another "high." His beloved glaciers are thus, for the moment, in tough shape. But he would have urged us to have faith.

Among Field's more immediate disciples was the Club's sometime councillor, the leader of the 1946 Mount Saint Elias Expedition, Maynard Malcolm Miller. His 50-plus-year directorship of the Juneau Icefield Research Project, has carried the documentation of glacial behavior a step further. An enormous range of tree rings counts demonstrated the extent of Alaskan valley glaciers in areas that are now heavily forested. The destruction of seaside Tlingit villages by advancing glaciers has been tied closely to sunspot cycles; the cores taken from the depths of the Icefield's catchment basin now record the rate at which planet Earth has been bombarded in the past by other than the simple actinic rays that cause sunburn.

The processes whereby mountain lovers accumulate valuable knowledge for all of mankind, based on mountain-related research, goes on with undiminished vigor.

PROCEEDINGS OF THE CLUB

SECRETARY'S ANNUAL REPORT, 1928

The past year has been a remarkable one in the history of the Club.

Dr. Nichol's presidency brought about an awakening of wider interest in the Club and the infusion of much new blood. Under President Palmer, an aggressive program of betterment and expansion has been in progress.

Our own Club Room, opened today for the first time, marks the beginning of a new era in the Club's life. It fills a long-felt want. These quarters where members can use our books in comfort and meet each other in a home-like atmosphere, while in addition they can enjoy many of the privileges of the Explorers' Club, should be a source of satisfaction and pride.

Another major ambition presently to be realized, is the establishment of our own American Alpine Club Journal. It will contain climbing articles by members, together with the official notices, minutes of meetings, etc. There will therefore be no further separate issues of the Secretary's Annual Circular Letter. Arrangements with "Appalachia" have been discontinued. Whether further issues of "Alpina Americana" will be published occasionally in the future remains to be decided.

The present membership of the Club is 192, of which 11 are Honorary. During the year Messrs. Mumm and Cuntz died, one member resigned and one was dropped. Against this Capt. J. P. Farrar was elected to Honorary Membership and 23 Active Members were added.

The usual amount of climbing was done in Canada and the United States, and several splendid ascents were made in the Alps. I venture to say that the enthusiasm of our membership for the sport and the average skill of our climbers in the field have never been higher.

More pleasure and benefit than ever before may be derived from membership. The Club today stands on the threshold of a new and greater life of usefulness, influence and prestige.

HENRY B. DEV. SCHWAB, Secretary.

— From American Alpine Journal, Volume 1, No. 1, 1929.

XVI – EXCLUSIVENESS OR INCLUSIVENESS
Putnam

At the time of its founding, The American Alpine Club followed very closely to the pattern and policies of its British ancestor – The Alpine Club. Members had to have completed a highly creditable record of accomplishment in high altitude or high latitude activity, in related sciences *"...or the equivalent."* This final phrase in the membership qualification guidelines stood for two thirds of the Club's first century and was the means whereby the Board could in good conscience elect painters of mountain scenery, writers on mountain topics and dealers in alpine literature. To this clause the Club owed the presence on its roster of distinguished members, names such as those of Allen Herbert Bent (one of these authors), Belmore Browne, James Ramsay Ullman, Leroy D. Cross, and Glen Dawson, persons whose actual mountaineering accomplishments at their times of election were relatively minor (except in the case of Browne) but whose knowledge of and contributions to the study of mountaineering art and literature were vast.

But from soon after its inception until the mid-1980s, a sustained record of high altitude, high latitude, and/or high-angle attainments were the basic criteria for membership. In this attitude, the AAC resembled very much The Alpine Club [London] or the French equivalent, Le Group d'Haute Montagne. We felt among ourselves that it was an honor simply to be elected into this society and that fact alone was reason enough to belong. Membership meant that a person had "arrived" in alpinism.

Around the world, however, between the World Wars things were obviously changing. Mountaineering was becoming ever more a sport of the masses, not the elite. The alpine clubs of Switzerland, Italy, Spain, France, Austria and Germany – even Slovenia and Montenegro – numbered in the tens and hundreds of thousands. Only in the United States and slightly less so in Canada did the original British pattern of exclusivity persist. But in Britain, the masses had emerged so that in the 1930s The Alpine Club, while not diminishing its membership criteria, gave support to the formation of a council of other British groups interested in climbing. This was crystallized in 1944 with the official founding of the British Mountaineering Council, made up initially of 25 separate organizations and headed by the world renowned Geoffrey Winthrop Young.

At that period, the relative vastness of the United States, and the immensity of public lands to all parts of which access was almost completely unrestricted, had not brought to public awareness the necessity for communal effort to protect access and the expressions of individualism that mark climbers out from the crowd of the body politic. Americans, despite the antiquity of exploration and "roughing it" that were inherent in our national culture, had an unanticipated awakening coming. And strangely enough, the process was due to one of our own. It was John Muir, the AAC's second president, who founded the conservation movement in America that soon spread worldwide – in great part under American impetus.

In immediate post World War II America, while most climbers wanted merely the freedom to "do their thing," only a few of them were far-sighted enough to respect the rights of others in the future to find the same wildness and freedom from the intrusion of civilization that had been enjoyed by those first on the scene. This "undersight" soon brought on a discussion – still in progress – about the merits of driving pitons, placing bolts, cutting trails, building huts, paving roads, etc. that soon reached the ears and minds of more than just the actually very small percentage of the population that was intimately concerned with – and had real knowledge of – the mountain environment.

While climbers, of their own, largely gave up the use of pitons, collectively they remained less concerned about the use of expansion bolts to make an otherwise impossible climb, or the momentary defacement of scenery caused by garish smears of chalk. When non-climbers – and then the managers of public lands – began to wonder, to ask questions, to place restrictions, to seek proof of ability and insurance, and finally to demand payments for entry, the role of America's only nationwide organization concerned with climbers, was forced to change. The nation's many regional climbing organizations ranging from the "Appies" of the Northeast to the Arizona Mountain Club of the Southwest, were clearly unable to bring forth an united position on issues of nationwide concern. The founders of The American Alpine Club had imagined – and even so stated – that their nascent organization might of necessity become a rallying point for future collective necessity, but they had never actually been faced with such an problem. By the mid-1980s it was clear that external pressures were forcing the issue. If the Club did not rise to the occasion, all American climbers – now and later – would be the losers.

Thus, the barriers to membership of *"significant alpine accomplishment"* were tossed to the winds, and The American Alpine Club opened its rolls to all who cared for the mountains, in any manner, for it now needed to include a much greater body of support, both financially and in personnel, to take on the greater challenges of the future.

XVII – CHANGING FACES
The Leadership of The American Alpine Club
Putnam

This final chapter offers a brief biographical note on those who have served as president of The American Alpine Club, thus providing the primary guiding tone to the organization during their terms of office. One can note, by comparing these names with those in Appendix A, that unlike The Alpine Club [London], the AAC does not necessarily consider election to its presidency to be an honor equivalent to that of its Honorary Membership. Indeed, once the election has occurred this author has long felt that the office carries more onus than honor.

Founder

Angelo Heilprin (1853-1907) was brought to the United States from the wine-making center of Satoralja-Ujhely in northeastern Hungary, at the age of three. Thereafter, he lived most of his life in Philadelphia, where he became curator of the Academy of Natural Sciences. As well as being a fine painter, he had to his credit several learned papers on arctic zoology and was leader of the Peary Relief Expedition of 1892. After 1890, he held a chair of geography at Yale University. He also became an authority on arctic glaciers (one is named for him) and invertebrate paleontology.

Professor Heilprin sent out the call for the meeting of 9 May, 1901, at the Geographical Society of Philadelphia to discuss the establishment of an "alpine society." After the formation of The American Alpine Club, he was elected vice-president along with the British-born geodesist, George Davidson.

Subsequent to the violent eruption of Mont Pelee on 8 May, 1902, Heilprin was the only scientific investigator who dared to enter the floor of the volcano and determine the nature of the huge monolith that was slowly extruded from the throat of the resultant caldera. While there, he made four ascents of the still-active volcano

Following his premature death on 17 July, 1907, of a fever contracted while in furthering his scientific studies in Venezuela, the minutes of The American Alpine Club noted him as the organization's founder.

147

1902-1907, 1917-1919

Charles Ernest Fay (1846-1931) was affiliated, throughout his long and productive life, with Tufts University in Medford, Massachusetts, where he was a Professor of Modern Languages and dean of its Graduate School.

His association with organized alpinism began with the founding meeting of the Appalachian Mountain Club in 1876, over which he presided. He later served four separate terms as that club's president and after 1897 as chairman of its "Alpine Section." He was editor of APPALACHIA for 40 years beginning in1879, and edited The American Alpine Club's first three publications – ALPINA AMERICANA, of which he wrote the second monograph in 1911.

Dr. Fay was the American agent for the Duke of the Abruzzi's expedition that made the first ascent of Mount Saint Elias in 1897. He was elected to honourary membership in The Alpine Club and was the original honourary member of the Alpine Club of Canada.

An authority on the mountains of western Canada, where his annual visits took on an element of a state event, his name is on the first of the Ten Peaks above Moraine Lake, and on the earliest mountain hut built by the Alpine Club of Canada.

Professor Fay was unique in being not only the first president of The American Alpine Club, but also our second and our sixth – a distinction which makes him exceptional among our elected leaders.

1908-1910

John Muir (1838-1914) was born in Dunbar, Scotland, and at age 10 moved to the United States, where he received his college degree in geology from the University of Wisconsin.

Setting out on foot for the West, Muir was soon recognized universally as **THE** voice of the conservation movement in the United States – and after his death, has been acclaimed worldwide as the patron and founder of wise and sustainable use of natural resources.

Muir is primarily associated with the Sierra Nevada – though he visited many other mountain areas – and with the Sierra Club, which carries forward his conservationist legacy to this day.

As the first president of The American Alpine Club represented the eastern section of the country, Muir represented the west. As the Club's first president represented the literary, social and

148

climbing aspects of mountaineering, Muir represented the companion motivation of all alpinists to preserve, protect and perpetuate the wild and beautiful heritage that we enjoy as only temporary visitors and custodians.

Muir was honored for his unceasing labors during his lifetime with degrees from Harvard and Yale, as well as from those universities closer to him – Wisconsin and California. He has been honored in death by having his name placed on more natural features of the American landscape than any other human being.

1911-1913

The Honorable Harrington Putnam (1851-1937), a justice of the New.York Supreme Court from 1909 to 1921, was born in Shrewsbury, Massachusetts.

Though he climbed Mount Fuji, the Breithorn, Mt. Shasta and Mt. Whitney, Putnam was primarily a walker. At age 60, when he was due to open court in Riverhead on a Monday morning, he walked most of the length of Long Island over the weekend, having held court in Brooklyn until late on Friday.

During Judge Putnam's tenure, he was called on to handle the delicate matter of expelling Dr. Frederick Cook from AAC membership. On a more positive note, he also presided at a celebratory dinner held in New York in 1907 to honor the Duke of the Abruzzi, who was touring the eastern United States as commodore of a visiting Italian naval force at the time of the Jamestown tercentennial.

The question of a permanent legal home (other than the residence of the secretary) for The American Alpine Club arose during Judge Putnam's presidency and at the annual meeting on 30 December, 1911, in Philadelphia, the first formal steps were taken toward being able to accept the generous offer of the expatriate alpinist, Henry Fairbanks Montagnier, to give his immense personal library to the Club.

1914-1916

Henry Grier Bryant (1859-1932), a graduate of Princeton College and resident of Philadelphia, was the Club's secretary until 1911, and then served as vice-president under Judge

Putnam. For many years between 1897 and 1931, he was also president of the Geographical Society of Philadelphia.

With the AAC's first Honorary Member, Admiral George Wallace Melville, he conducted experiments with floating drift casks, to determine the patterns and speeds of currents in the Arctic Ocean.

During his term of office, Mr. Bryant arranged the formal incorporation of The American Alpine Club, under the laws of the Commonwealth of Pennsylvania, so that it could hold legal title to property. In addition to performing the necessary legal work for the acceptance of the Montagnier collection, he also gave his own extensive collection of mountain literature to the Club.

Mr. Bryant was a frequent visitor to the "Canadian Alps" and his name can be found on Bryant Creek in the Rockies. In 1903, his name was also placed – by Dr. Cook – on a small group of peaks between Mt. Dall and Mt. Russell near Denali.

˙ Mr. Bryant wrote extensively on arctic topics and on his mountain climbing activities in such diverse and out-of-the-way places as Labrador and Java.

1920-1922

Lewis Livingston Delafield (1863-1944) was always a New Yorker, though educated at private scholastic institutions in Switzerland, St. Paul's School in New Hampshire, Harvard College and returning home finally to Columbia Law School.

While an avid outdoorsman from early youth, his record of actual alpinism was relatively minor – he did not take up this activity until the age of 44, and became a member of the Club four years later. As with many early members of The American Alpine Club, he maintained an active interest in polar matters and served as counsel for the Peary Arctic Club.

During Mr. Delafield's presidency, however, arrangements were begun for the first climbing expedition to receive the Club's formal sponsorship – that to Canada's Mount Logan. He led that trip's fund raising effort, which finally totaled almost $12,000 and included donations from all over the world.

During his presidency, the first major British expeditions were also undertaken seeking to make the ascent of Mount Everest via an approach from India around the mountain through Tibet. Americans

150

first heard of the Rongbuk monastery and were shown the first moving pictures of actual climbing in very high altitudes at the AAC's annual meeting early in 1922.

1923-1925

The Reverend Harry Pierce Nichols (1850-1940) was an original member of The American Alpine Club and served as a director: 1902-10; 1920-22 and 1926-28. During the years 1923-25 he was the sixth person elected as the Club's president. A native of Salem, Massachusetts, he was ordained a priest of the Protestant Episcopal Church in 1877 and served a variety of parishes, culminating with Holy Trinity Church of New York City from 1899 until his retirement to North Conway, New Hampshire, in 1922.

During his term as president he urged the election of Achille Ratti, Pope Pius XI, as an Honorary Member but, because His Holiness felt constrained to decline all such honors, the board elected George Leigh Mallory instead, as the latter was about to return for a further attempt on Mount Everest. During his term as president, the Club's total membership rose from 126 to 144, after noting the deaths of Honorary Members George Leigh Mallory, Dr. Jules Jacot-Guillarmod, Mrs. Fanny Bullock Workman and Rev. W. A. B. Coolidge; and regular members Rev. Hudson Stuck, Herbert Lawrence Bridgman, Alden Sampson and Allen Herbert Bent.

A very popular mountaineer of great persistence and skill, Dr. Nichols celebrated his 80th birthday by making his 250th pedestrian ascent of Mount Washington.

In 1893 he set out from on the Glacier House for an ascent of Mount Fox. Upon his return he preached to the assembled guests on "The Glory of Aspiration."

1926-1928

Howard Palmer (1883-1944) was born, lived, and died in southeastern Connecticut. For more then 30 years after 1911, he served as a councillor or officer of The American Alpine Club. Though a Harvard-trained lawyer, most of his business career was in managing the mattress manufacturing firm started by his father and uncle.

While his first major climbs were of the higher volcanic peaks in the western United States in 1907, thereafter Palmer became inextricably associated with the exploration of the Selkirk Mountains of British Columbia, where his name is on the land and a river and where he made a number of major first ascents.

A frequent patron of the Glacier House, he wrote numerous articles for many publications, but his scholarly 1914 volume, MOUNTAINEERING AND EXPLORATION IN THE SELKIRKS, remains one of the classic pieces of alpine literature. Its thoroughness and abundant appendices have made it a model and a challenge for subsequent authors. Palmer's explorations in the mountains of western Canada were frequently in the company of two Club members and professors of botany at the University of Minnesota – Edward Willett Dorland Holway and Frederick King Butters.

With the collaboration of Dr. Thorington, in 1921 Palmer compiled The American Alpine Club's first guidebook, that to the Rocky Mountains of Canada, which has gone through numerous revisions and later editions.

1929-1931

Dr. William Sargent Ladd (1887-1949) remains notable among The American Alpine Club's presidents for two very important actions:

The participation in the founding of the Union International des Associations d'Alpinism (UIAA), and the gift of our first permanent domicile – "the old firehouse" at 113 East 90th Street, between Park and Lexington Avenues in Manhattan.

Dr. Ladd was born in Portland, Oregon, but lived most of his adult life in New York where he became a very distinguished physician. His landmark gift in 1947 of what had been tentatively used as his offices not only brought the Club a permanent home of its own but also into the real estate business. Though the New York City Building Department ordered the brass pole removed before we could occupy it, the basic nature of the ancient private fire station was unchanged and the gift prompted the first major fund raising effort on behalf of the 45-year-old club. The Club's Board determined that owning such premises also required the establishment of an endowment that would fund its upkeep.

Dr. Ladd was more widely honored for his achievements in the

152

field of medicine than for his accomplishments as a mountaineer, serving as dean of the Cornell Medical School. But he was also honored in mountaineering by election to Honorary Membership in the Club Alpin Français

1932-1934

Henry Baldwin deVilliers-Schwab (1887-1935) climbed extensively in the Alps beginning with minor ascents in the Tyrol in 1901. From the age of 14, he spent 10 consecutive seasons in the Oberland, around Zermatt, and making climbs from Chamonix; making 20 ascents in the year 1920, alone.

Born in New York of German ancestry, he attended St. Mark's School and Harvard College ('09) before joining the importing firm of Oelrichs & Company, in which he rose to a partnership by 1917 and headed their wool division. During the course of his career, which was cut short by his untimely death from the nephritis which afflicted him for several years, he visited many parts of the world on business and always took time to visit the local mountains in such places as New Zealand, Chile, Peru, South Africa and Australia.

In addition to several other first ascents in the Canadian Rockies Mr. Schwab was a strong and valued member of the party which made the first ascent of Mount Clemenceau in 1923. After his retirement from business in 1926, he served the Club as secretary until 1929, and as a councillor thereafter until his election to the presidency.

He was a respected member of The Alpine Club and acquired his complicated full name by virtue of his marriage in 1912 to Kathrina H. de Villiers, a native of Cape Town.

At the end of his presidency the Club membership stood at 231 of which 11 were Honorary.

1935-1937

Joel Ellis Fisher (1891-1966), was the first, and unofficial, manager of The American Alpine Club's portfolio. As noted above, back in those less rigid days, while serving as treasurer from 1929 to 1934, he might take an occasional risky flyer on behalf of the Club. If, by year end, the stock had risen as hoped, the Club was the winner. If it had not, he would sell it and then make the organization whole out of his own pocket.

A Phi Beta Kappa graduate of Yale in 1911, Ellis (as he was known to his intimates) started climbing at age 15, in the Alps, and returned to these mountains of his youth every year until 1965, when, at the age of 75, he climbed the Riffelhorn. In all, he made more than 150 major ascents.

As president of the Denver Terminal Railroad and treasurer of Melville Shoe Company, he was a prominent figure of the business world. But he also bankrolled personally a great deal of scientific research, particularly into glaciers and glaciology.

Ellis had the distinction of managing the first and to this date only proxy fight in the Club's history. As the senior advisor to a group of renegades – four of whom (80 percent) later became Honorary Members – he sought to insert a By-law amendment that would mandate that AAC annual meetings be rotated about the entire country, not merely among major cities of the East. The proposal failed at the time, but it's spirit came to dominate the organization.

1938-1940

James Grafton Rogers (1883-1971) was the founder of the Colorado Mountain Club and its first president. His knowledge of Rocky Mountain history, in particular that in the vicinity of his retirement home high in the upper valley of Clear Creek, made him a unique source of data on Colorado place names. With this knowledge it was inevitable that he should also become president of the Geographic Board of Colorado.

A distinguished member of the Colorado bar – as well as dean of the Yale Law School – Mr. Rogers was among the most influential of those whose labors and influence brought into being the 10th Mountain Division. It was his personal relationship with Henry Lewis Stimson, the Secretary of War, and his equally long friendship with Chief of Staff General George Catlett Marshall, that broke the bureaucratic logjam and led to the establishment of the 87th Mountain Infantry Regiment in mid-November of 1941. The location of the Club in the State of Colorado, the selection of Camp Hale in the valley of Pando, and the cordial relationship that the Club now enjoys with the alumni of this distinguished military unit are natural fruits of James Rogers' legacy to American mountaineering.

His greater legacy to the nation came from his service on various reconstruction boards in Europe after World War I and his work on planning for the Office of Strategic Services in the sequel conflict.

1941-1943

James Monroe Thorington (1894-1989) was America's ultimate scholar of alpinism. He also served the Club variously as a councillor, vice-president, secretary, editor of the JOURNAL and finally as its president.

An opthalmologist by profession, as had been his father, Roy (as he was known to his friends) came to be THE authority on the "Canadian Alps," succeeding to the mantle of Professor Fay. In 1921, with the cooperation of Howard Palmer, he brought out the first of the long series of guidebooks that The American Alpine Club undertook as "the publisher of last resort" for mountaineers. Among the photographs herein Roy is pictured on one of his many guide-accompanied trips to the less visited mountains of the Alps.

A distinguished and honorary member of numerous alpine societies, Roy produced an enormous list of valued historical publications on alpinists and alpinism. His contributions have served as references for many of the displays at this centennial gathering of the Club and cause he served so long and loyally.

Roy was crusty, a condition which one of his successors as president blamed on a shy streak in his character, but he was thorough in his research and infinitely knowledgeable on the history of alpinism, both in the Alps and in America. That he was asked to write the lead article for the centennial issue of the ALPINE JOURNAL was an international tribute to Dr. Thorington's scholarship.

1944-1946

John Crowther Case (1892-1983) lived the typically long life of the vigorous alpinist. A native of Rochester, New York, he was educated largely in Europe and lived much of his life abroad.

After service as a machine gunnery officer in World War I, he worked for the Socony Vacuum Oil Company in various capacities, culminating as vice-president of production. In this capacity he was responsible for the formation of ARAMCO, the Arabian American

155

Oil consortium.

John's service to American alpinism was very much connected with the establishment of the 10th Mountain Division, in which he played a leading part. But, of all mountain areas, he was most concerned with his native Adirondacks, where he maintained a summer home in Keene Valley and where he died.

His other service to the Club came because of his gentle and perpetually youthful outlook, which enabled him to serve as a trusted and welcome counselor to an amazingly large number of his successors as President of The American Alpine Club.

At the conclusion of his presidency, Club membership stood at 318 and the evening dinner guest of honor at the annual meeting was William Williams, who had attempted the ascent of Mount Saint Elias in 1888 and now heard about the second ascent (and first American ascent) of that striking American mountain.

1947-1949

Walter Abbot Wood, Jr. (1907-1993), like so many of his predecessors, was largely educated in Europe, mostly Switzerland, where he became qualified as a mountain guide. His major impact on alpinism, however, was certainly in North America where he was among the founders of the Arctic Institute of North America.

His interest in high-altitude research led him to assist with establishing the station on Mount Logan, which he visited with great regularity, even to his 81st year. Walter climbed, and practiced his skills as a surveyor, in mountain ranges all over the world, from Greenland to Colombia to Kashmir and finally to the Yukon, where he made first ascents of Mounts Steele, Wood, Walsh, Hubbard and Alverstone.

With the equally distinguished Kenneth Atwood Henderson, Walter was instrumental in the process of testing and certifying mountain guides in the United States in the late 1930s. A number of the Club's later noteworthy members held cards testifying to their competence and signed by this Club committee.

A man of great talent, Walter also served as president of the American Geographical Society and the Explorer's Club. At the final dinner at which he presided, he described his ascent of Mount Vancouver.

1950-1952

Henry Snow Hall, Jr (1895-1987) became the world's most ubiquitous patron of alpinism. During the course of his lengthy association with The American Alpine Club, the living room of his Cambridge home served as a planning office for countless expeditions, major and minor, for many of which he also provided a silent but critical subsidy.

Henry's many years of service to the AAC began with his election to the Council in 1923, extended into his 15-year tenure as secretary, from 1932 to 1946, and culminated in his election as president. However, retirement from the Club's highest office did not diminish his support, financial and spiritual, which continued until his death and even thereafter.

In recognition of his unmatched contributions to this organization, he was elected to Honorary Membership in 1946, and as the Club's first Honorary President in 1974, and shortly before his death he received our Angelo Heilprin Citation.

Henry's actual alpinism was not as wide-spread as that of some others, nor marked with as many notable ascents, but he saw to it that The American Alpine Club stayed afloat during a number of dark periods and was a friend indeed to needy alpinists from all over the world. Subsequent AAC presidents became accustomed to receiving their valued and almost weekly hand-written letter of advice from "our father" in Cambridge.

1953-1955

Bradley Baldwin Gilman (1904-1987) was a descendant of numerous distinguished Americans, including a signer of the Declaration of Independence. Though a graduate of Yale College, he attended Harvard Law School and practiced for many years in his native Worcester, Massachusetts.

Brad was the only functionary of The American Alpine Club to hold every one of its varied offices, concluding with a six-year stint as treasurer after 1961. During his years as secretary in the 1950s, however, he uncovered (and ended) the "plot" to elect a four-footed canine to membership, which had passed the Club's councillors.

Though he climbed extensively elsewhere, Attorney Gilman's name remains known to subsequent generations of New England rock

157

climbers for his pioneering ascent of a route toward the westerly edge of the great cliff of New Hampshire's Cannon Mountain – an ascent which he made in 1928 in company with his cousin, Princeton's topologist/mathematician Hassler Whitney. To this day, though it has undergone several gravity-related modifications, and is off-limits during the eagle-nesting season, the Whitney-Gilman route is a North American classic.

1956 - 1958

John Cameron Oberlin (b. 1914) made his first climb (and first self-arrest) at age 16, on Ben Nevis. In later years he made numerous ascents in the Tetons, often with Fred Ayres. In 1942 he served briefly as a ice climbing instructor with the 87th Mountain Infantry, before being sent to Officer Candidate School and thence to other duties.

After World War II, he made numerous ascents over several seasons in the Canadian Rockies, the Alps and the Andes. During this period he made the second ascent of Mount Alberta, retrieving the "silver" ice axe left there 20 years earlier by the Yuko Maki party. In later years, John turned back to the Wind River Range (where he was struck by lightning) and then ascended Popocatepetl (which was smoking vigorously).

His first duties with the AAC involved helping Helen Buck with the transfer of Club books, etc from its rented offices on 46th Street to the new quarters given us by Dr. Ladd on 90th Street in New York City. Elected secretary in 1953, John assumed the presidency three years later and brought a number of important AAC functions into being. These included the Conservation Committee, under Bill Child; the Expeditions Committee, under George Bell; and convincing H. Adams Carter to take over the editorship of the AMERICAN ALPINE JOURNAL to start his distinguished 39-year reign.

1959-1961

Robert Hicks Bates (b. 1911)became a Club member in 1935 at the instigation of Dr. Thorington. He served on the Club's Council from 1939 to 1943 and was then on the Club's Mountain Warfare Committee. Thereafter he helped edit the AMERICAN ALPINE JOURNAL for many years until his election as vice-president in 1955. Bob served again on the Council from 1963 to 1971 and was elected our second Honorary President in 1988.

After climbs in the Alps and Tetons Bob took part in seven Alaskan expeditions – making first ascents of Mount Crillon and Lucania – on the summit of which his picture was taken with Brad Washburn. His wartime service (rising to the rank of Lt. Colonel) included giving training lectures to troops encountering mountain terrain and winter conditions. He made the first ascents of Mounts Hubbard and Alverstone in 1951 and played a leadership role in two expeditions to K2, those in 1938 and 1953.

A teacher of English at Phillips Exeter Academy by calling, Bob also gave considerably of his time to the Peace Corps and Outward Bound. In 1985 he was still at it and was co-leader of the party that made the first ascent of Ulugh Muztagh

Bob has written five books about mountains – two about K2, one about Belmore Browne, another on the English language literature of mountaineering and one semi-autobiographical THE LOVE OF MOUNTAINS IS BEST.

1962-1964

Carlton Perry Fuller (1898-1984) is remembered in financial circles as the man who made Polaroid. He is remembered in the annals of The American Alpine Club as the man whose wise counsel and persuasive diligence brought the Club from an Eastern and somewhat Europe-oriented organization into the mainstream of American mountaineering.

As a successful investment banker in New York in 1941, he saw the future in Dr. Edwin Land's use of polarized light and "bet the farm" on its success. For the next quarter-century he guided the Polaroid Corporation to its position of world prominence.

Never a spectacular alpinist, he was persistent and partook of several interesting ventures, such as the Carter-Washburn trip in 1957 to retrace and document the route of Dr. Cook's famous first ascent hoax on Mount McKinley.

Carl encouraged the 1963 Expedition to Mount Everest which resulted in great prestige to American mountaineers; but his major legacy to American alpinism consisted in great measure of his recognition and encouragement of a many young "whippersnappers," several of whom came in time to succeed him to the Club's presidency.

By the end of his presidency Club membership stood at 628 and the organization was ready to seriously span the nation.

1965-1967

Lawrence George Coveney (1889-1981) was once asked by one of his successors if he could be counted on to attend the Club's Diamond Jubilee dinner in Philadelphia in 1976. *"Well, I'd like to, [name], but at my age you can't count on anything!"* In the event, he did attend and regaled many of those present with his delightful summary of having finally led The American Alpine Club to hold an annual meeting in the City of Seattle, heretofore believed by Easterners to be uncivilized, distant, rural and almost inaccessible. It turned out to be the first of many.

As an alpinist, Lawrence was deeply involved, along with our Honorary Member, Fritz H. E. Wiessner, in the "opening" of the Shawangunk cliffs during the late 1930s and participated with him in the first free ascent of Wyoming's Devils Tower.

As a Club functionary, Lawrence and his wife, Marion, served as a gracious hosts for several meetings of the Club's board at his home in South Royalton, Vermont, in the years that followed his presidency. His most enduring service to the Club came from serving as a bridge between a number of young "troublemakers" moving into positions of leadership and the Club's financial "establishment."

A graduate of Pennsylvania State College, his business career was largely in the field of foreign trade, from an office headquarters in New York City.

1968 - 1970

Nicholas Bayard Clinch (b. 1930) was the second major expedition leader to be elected as president. Being transplanted from Texas to California he knew a great number of members, both from the East and the West.

During his presidency the public service activities of the Club expanded greatly with the establishment of the Grand Teton Climbers' Ranch. After his term as president he was "forced" to serve one term (1971-1973) as treasurer, *"to atone for my mismanagement"* during the previous three years. Nick also introduced the ice screw into North American climbing usage.

For almost 40 years, starting with a trip into the Coast Range of British Columbia in 1954, he organized and led a variety of major expeditions, including those resulting in the first ascents of: Hidden Peak (26,470 feet) in 1958, and Masherbrum (25,660 feet) in the Karakorum in 1960; Vinson Massif (16,200 feet) in the Sentinel Range of Antarctica in 1966, and Ulugh Muztagh (22,800 feet) in the Kun Lun range between Tibet and Xinjiang in 1985. For his extraordinary services to mountaineering he was later elected to Honourary Membership in The Alpine Club [London].

Between expeditions and playing a strong and ongoing leadership role in support of The American Alpine Club, he has practiced law, run the Sierra Club Foundation and paid close attention to a family business.

1971-1973

John Lathrop Jerome Hart (1904-1986) served as president of The American Alpine Club during the troubled years when students were occupying college presidents' offices and many icons of American society were under question, if not major attack. As President Clinch noted of his successor: *"He did a remarkable job... ...while constantly being criticized by those who did not understand what he was doing, as well as by those who did understand."* Nevertheless, following his turbulent years as president, Jerry became a much admired counselor to his successors.

Jerry brought his calm, legal mind to bear on the anti-establishment trends of that period and undertook the first major revision of the Club's By-laws since its establishment. Under his leadership, The American Alpine Club rejoined the International Association of Alpine Societies (UIAA), of which we had been a founding member and in which we have since played an increasingly prominent role. He was also in the forefront of arranging for climbing exchanges with alpinists from the Soviet Union – a process that came to fruition in 1975.

Jerry was a Colorado Mountain enthusiast and student of the area's climbing history, with some of his earlier literary efforts still being regarded as authoritative. Ill health forced Jerry to relinquish the last few months of his presidency, which were filled out by Charles Hollister.

1974-1976

William Lowell Putnam (b. 1924), a television broadcaster during most of his years as a Club functionary, began his service to the Club as editor of our Canadian guidebooks in 1957. Elected to the Board in 1969, he served on it – in one capacity or another – for 30 years. Previously, he had been an officer and servant of the Appalachian Mountain Club and president of the Harvard Mountaineering Club.

Because of injuries suffered during combat as a member of the 10th Mountain Division in Italy, he was unable to ascend to high altitude, but made scores of first ascents in Western Canada and succeeded Dr. Thorington as THE authority on the mountains of that region. In such capacity he produced several historical reference works on mountaineering in the "Canadian Alps."

During his presidency, the Club adopted a number of major policy statements that remain guidelines for Club policy with respect to the public perceptions and obligations of alpinists. He also organized the first complete membership survey to consider a relocation of the Club offices and headquarters. In the 15 years following his presidency, Putnam served as treasurer and was the Club's principal representative to the UIAA, where he also served as vice-president. His later insistence on the adoption of a special By-Law removed the pressure of short-range interests from the Board of Directors and placed the Club's endowment within the custody of a committee controlled by the past presidents.

1977-1979

James Francis Henriot (b. 1928) was the first Club president elected from the Pacific Northwest, where he has resided all his life. He previously served three years as president of The Mountaineers and as chairman of the AAC's Expeditions Committee. Having climbed actively in his native Cascades since 1955, in 1960 he branched out to other parts of the world and has been atop the highest summits in five continents.

During his presidency, the Club fought off an attempt by the

City of New York to place our premises on the tax rolls, and since leaving that office he has maintained an active interest in Club affairs. He organized and chaired the Club's efforts to arrange international climbing exchanges and has attended many UIAA General Assemblies [including the first held in the United States – at Pinkham Notch, NH, in 1979] to assist with Club representation in that body.

Since his formal retirement from the active practice of the law, specializing in labor and employment issues, Jim has continued a vigorous life as a mediator and arbitrator but has not neglected his ongoing duties as an alpinist and to the Club. He has visited Outward Bound Schools throughout the world as well as CARE projects in Central America.

1980 -1982

Thomas Callender Price Zimmermann (b. 1934), an historian of the Italian Renaissance, was dean of the faculty at Davidson College during his term as president. During his earlier years as a professor at Reed College he climbed widely in the Pacific Northwest and elsewhere.

While serving as chairman of the Club's Conservation Committee and later, during his term as president, he stimulated the drafting and adoption of a number of major and long-lived policy statements on matters such as *Mountaineering Ethics (1972), Mountaineering Access and Use of Public Lands (1974), Alpine Environmental Practices (1974), Management of the National Parks (1975),* and *Mining in National Parks and Wilderness Areas (1975).*

Professor Zimmermann saw the deleterious effect of a trend towards deficit financing of the Club's operations and initiated a fund drive to relieve pressure on the endowment. In this he laid the groundwork for the Club's later (and present) policy of having access to the capital of our endowment restricted by requiring the consent of representatives of the Club's past presidents to any withdrawals other than an annual return based on current yield.

In 1981, much to the joy of several other members as well. Price became joined in matrimony with Margaret, daughter of the Club's distinguished servant, Dr. Benjamin Greeley Ferris, Jr.

163

1983-1985

Robert Wallace Craig (b. 1925) a native of Seattle, began a career of serious climbing and expert skiing in the Cascades at age 11. Returning home after naval service in World War II he picked up where he had left off and made a number of impressive climbs in Alaska and on Mount Rainier.

After the war he served as a park ranger and then acquired the guiding concession on Mount Rainier. Following post-graduate work in philosophy, Bob then served as a civilian instructor for the Mountain & Cold Weather Command in Colorado and made several new routes on Long's Peak before joining the 1953 American expedition to K2. On this venture, he and Pete Schoening established the team's high point. Later that year he undertook the management of the Aspen Institute, where he stayed for 10 years.

In 1974, Bob served as co-leader of the first climbing exchange with alpinists from the Soviet Union, which resulted in his book, STORM AND SORROW IN THE HIGH PAMIRS. In 1975 he founded the Keystone Center, which became a nationally recognized resource in science and behavioral education.

After his election as president of the Club, Bob set another first, by not presiding at the very next Board meeting (he was off on Mount Everest).

1986-1988

James Peter McCarthy (b. 1933) began climbing in 1951 in the Shawangunks with the Princeton Mountaineering Club. The following year he began a decades-long association with Dr, Hans Kraus, a team that made numerous and increasingly difficult ascents, there and elsewhere, pushing the level of free climbing difficulty to over 5.10.

A highly regarded New York City trial attorney by profession, Jim served as a Club councillor from 1962 to 1967, then as secretary until 1972. Back on the Board again in 1984, he also served on the Board after his term as president and until 1994. In addition he has also served as a member – generally chairman – of numerous Club committees.

With Layton Kor, Royal Robbins and Dick McCracken, he made the first of big wall climbs in remote areas with that of Proboscis in the Logan Mountains in 1963 and followed it up three years later with a similar ascent of Lotus Flower Tower.

Jim participated in the ice-climbing renaissance in the East during the 1960s – with Yvon Chouinard, that culminated in his leading the first step-less ascent of Mount Washington's notorious Pinnacle Gully in 1970.

In recognition of his notable place in world mountaineering, he was elected vice-president of the UIAA in 2000.

1989 - 1991

Glenn Edward Porzak (b. 1948) is a past president of the Colorado Mountain Club and served 15 years as chairman of the AAC's Expeditions Committee. When not working for the Club, he is a practicing attorney specializing in western water law.

During his term as president, he concluded the long-simmering question of the Club's headquarters location and spearheaded the relocation to Golden and the very substantial fund-raising effort that went into the move from New York City. His leadership and stimulus were the principal factors in bringing the present American Mountaineering Center into existence and led to the proper housing of the Club's library and museum – after 80 years.

As an alpinist Glenn is the only president of a major alpine society to have attained the summit of Mount Everest during his term of office. In addition, he has played leadership roles in the American ascents of Lhotse, Makalu, and Shisha Pangma, as well as being among the first persons to ascend the highest points of the seven continents. When nearer home he has climbed – often by new routes – all of the 100 highest peaks in Colorado.

1992-1994

John Edward (Jed) Williamson (b. 1939) was raised in New York State but received his higher education at the Universities of New Hampshire and Alaska. Already a skier, while at UNH he fell in with climbers, becoming a member of The American Alpine Club in 1963. His subsequent mountaineering ventures have taken him twice to the top of America, to Canada, Mexico, Bhutan, Tibet, China and Russia.

Jed has been a consultant and practitioner in education and

outdoor pursuits. A member of the United States Biathlon team in the 1960s, he became executive director of the U. S. Biathlon Association in 1987. As a faculty member of the University of New Hampshire from 1873 to 1982 he designed the experiential educational program, "Live, Learn and Teach." He has served on the Boards of the Association for Experiential Education and the National Outdoor Leadership Schools, and in 1996 became president of Sterling College (Vermont).

Since 1974 he has been editor of the Club's notable public service publication ACCIDENTS IN NORTH AMERICAN MOUNTAINEERING. He served on the Club's board from 1974 to 1998 and during his presidency was saddled with the wrenching dislocations that accompanied completion of the move of our headquarters from New York to Golden. His vigor initiated the large increase in membership, staff and services that began in those years.

1995-1997

Louis French Reichardt (b. 1943) was born and raised in Pasadena, the son of a prize winning architect and a mother who became a peace and civil rights activist.

Lou's parents were avid pack backers and began taking him into the Sierra at age ten. He started rock climbing at Tahquitz Rock when he was attending Midland High School. A graduate of Harvard ('64), where he was a member of the Mountaineering Club, he went on to Cambridge as a Fulbright scholar and thence to Stanford, University, where he became a well-known medical researcher and also evolved a reputation as a prominent climber from his ascents in Yosemite and Alaska.

In 1969, he was a member of the ill-fated Dhaulagiri Expedition on which seven of America's best climbers perished in an avalanche. He returned in 1973 for a successful ascent, just months after solving the long-standing mystery of how a cell differentiates itself. His research into neural plasticity preceded his 1976 ascent of Nanda Devi by a new and technically difficult route.

By 1983, Lou was among America's foremost Himalayan mountaineers. He had climbed three 8,000 meter peaks and was the only American to have summited both Everest and K2, the former by the East Face and the latter without supplemental oxygen.

166

Alison Keith Osius (b. 1958) became the Club's first woman president. She began high-angle technical climbing while attending Middlebury College in Vermont and honed her skills at the British Mountaineering Council's Centre at Plas y Brenin in Wales. After obtaining her Master's degree in journalism from Columbia University, she wrote articles for numerous magazines and one biography – that of Hugh Herr.

Since 1988 she has resided in or near Carbondale, Colorado, as an editor of CLIMBING magazine. Married to Mike Benge in 1991, she is the mother of two boys, but has continued her career in rock climbing – up to 5.13a – on short and long routes in North America, Australia and Europe. She has also competed successfully in climbing competitions and World Cups and was a three-time national champion.

During her term as president, the Club undertook its first extended public outreach campaign and followed this up by joining a lawsuit initiated by Tom Frost to stop encroachment on Yosemite's Camp 4. This action was successful in bringing on a more enlightened attitude by National Park managers toward the legitimate needs of climbers in areas such as this park. In a further such effort, she led the Club into rule-making with a reluctant U. S. Forest Service regarding the use of fixed anchors in Wilderness areas.

2000-2002

C. James Frush (b. 1950) began climbing near his birthplace of Trinidad, CO. From the nearby sandstone cliffs and 14,000 footers, he graduated, with time, to all the major peaks of the Pacific Northwest, in both winter and summer, and adjacent areas of British Columbia and Alaska.

After his first venture abroad in 1980, he established residency in Kathmandu and participated in numerous expeditions, making the first American ascent of Cho Oyu and leading the 1988 Everest expedition that placed the first American woman on that summit. He has returned to the Himalaya regularly – even while serving as the AAC's president – and has made several first ascents of 6,000 meter peaks

A club member after 1983, he was elected to the Board in

1995, after service as Chairman of the Cascade Section. On the Board he has been chairman of the Expeditions Committee and in 1997 became Secretary.

During Jim's presidency, the Club undertook the first professional demographic survey of its membership and continued the growth of membership that has also seen the Club's budget reach the $1,000,000 mark and the staff reach a total of ten. Numerous other expansions and innovations have: (1) brought our library to the highest state of accessibility of any comparable facility in the world; (2) resulted in a major expansion of the American Mountaineering Center; (3) enhanced the dialog between climbers and federal land managers; (4) worked toward establishment of an AAC Hut and Campground system, based on the Grand Teton model; (5) made the American Alpine Journal, and other Club services, available electronically: and (6) encouraged the publication of this centennial volume.

Appendix A
HONORARY MEMBERS OF
THE AMERICAN ALPINE CLUB

hose honored by The American Alpine Club reflect the strongly
Anglophilic nature (or biases) of the Club's first two
generations of leadership. The list includes 50 Americans; 21
British, seven French, three Canadians, three Italians, two Belgians,
two New Zealanders, two Russians, two Swiss, one Austrian, one
Australian, one Chinese, one Japanese, and one South African, but no
Germans. The table below gives the year of election to Honorary
Membership, the nationality and a biographical reference.
AAJ = AMERICAN ALPINE JOURNAL   AJ = ALPINE JOURNAL
App = Appalachia   Who = Specified volume of WHO'S WHO
Brit = ENCYC. BRITANNICA   Web = WEBSTER'S BIOG. DICT.

Abalakov, Vitale Mikhailovich (1906–1986)		1976
AAJ XXIX- 348	Russia	
Abruzzi, Luigi Amadeo (1873–1933)		1902
AJ XLV-201	Italy	
Albert, I - King of the Belgians (1875–1934)		1934
App XX-112	Belgium	
Bates, Robert Hicks (b. 1911)		1967
Who Am Tchrs	U S A	
Beckey, Frederick William (b. 1923)		1971
Who Am West	U S A	
Bonington, Sir Christian J. S. (b. 1934)		1986
Who 1990	Britain	
Borisienok, Oleg (b. 1938)		1992
AANews 92-2	Russia	
Brower, David Ross (1912–2000)		1990
AAJ XLIII-453	U S A	
Browne, Belmore (1880–1954)		1948
AAJ IX-216	U S A	
Bruce, Charles Granville (1866–1939)		1923
App XXII-525	Britain	
Bryce, James, Viscount (1838–1922)		1907
AJ XXX-303	Britain	

Buchan, John (Lord Tweedsmuir) (1875–1940)   1938
    AJ LII-122   Britain
Carter, Hubert Adams (1914–1995)   1971
    AAJ XXXVII-1   U S A
Cassin, Riccardo (b. 1909)   1962
    Italy
Chouinard, Yvon (b. 1938)   1979
    U S A
Clinch, Nicholas Bayard (b. 1930)   1979
    U S A
Clyde, Norman Asa (1885–1972)   1969
    AAJ XVIII-540   U S A
Coleman, Arthur Philemon (1852–1939)   1920
    App XXII-395   Canada
Collie, John Norman (1859–1942)   1904
    AAJ V-136   Britain
Conway, William Martin (1856–1937)   1902
    App XXI-420   Britain
Coolidge, William A. B. (1850–1926)   1911
    AJ XXXVIII-278   USA/Britain
Daiber, George Craig `Ome' (1907–1989)   1976
    AAJ XXXII-339   U S A
Diemberger, Kurt (b. 1935)   1989
    Austria
Dyhrenfurth, Norman Günther (b. 1918)   1963
    Cur Bio   Austria/U S A
Escarra, Jean (1885–1956)   1932
    AAJ X-143   France
Evans, Robert Charles (b. 1918)   1956
    Britain
Exum, Glenn (1913–2000)   1985
    AAJ XLIII-450   U S A
Farquhar, Francis Peloubert (1887–1974)   1967
    AAJ XX-247   U S A
Farrar, John Percy (1857–1929)   1928
    App XVII-278   Britain
Ferris, Benjamin Greeley, Jr. (1919–1996)   1974
    AAJ XXXIX-389   U S A

Feuz, Edward, Jr. (1884–1981)   1973
    AAJ XXIV-332   Canada
Field, William Osgood (1904–1995)   1976
    AAJ XXXVII-363   U S A
Freshfield, Douglas William (1845–1934)   1902
    App XX-110   Britain
Fryxell, Fritiof Melvin (1900–1986)   1981
    AAJ XXIX-344   U S A
Gabet, Francisque (1846–1930)   1919
    AJ XLII-337   France
Greely, Adolphus Washington (1844–1935)   1902
    Britannica   U S A
Hall, Henry Snow, Jr. (1895–1987)   1946
    AAJ XXIX-341   U S A
Harper, Arthur Paul (1865–1955)   1937
    AAJ X-190   New Zealand
Henderson, Kenneth Atwood (1904–2001)   1994
    Who World   U S A
Herzog, Maurice (b. 1919)   1953
    Who 1990   France
Hill, Lynn (b. 1961)   1997

                                     U S A
Hillary, Sir Edmund (b. 1919)   1996
    Britannica   New Zealand
House, William Pendleton (1914–1997)   1985
    AAJ XL-408   U S A
Houston, Charles Snead (b. 1911)   1967
    Britannica   U S A
Hunt, Sir Henry John Cecil (1910–1998)   1956
    Britannica   Britain
Jackson, William Henry (1843–1942)   1939
    AAJ V-135   U S A
Jacot-Guillarmod, Jules Charles (1868–1925)   1921
    AJ XXXVII-348   France
Kauffman, Andrew John, II (b. 1920)   1992

                                     U S A
Ladd, William Sargent (1887–1949)   1949
    AAJ VII-476   U S A

Leopold III, of Belgium (1901–1983)   1938
    Britannica   Belgium
Lowe, George H. (b. 1944)   2000
    Who Am Sci   U S A
MacCarthy, Albert Henry (1876–1956)   1948
    AAJ X-137   U S A
Maki, Aritsone `Yuko' (1894–1989)   1959
    AJ VC-302   Japan
Mallory, George Herbert Leigh (1886–1924)   1923
    AJ XXXVI-381   Britain
McAllister, Otis (1889–1980)   1977
    AAJ XXIII-353   U S A
McCarthy, James Peter (b. 1933)   1998
                              U S A
Melville, George Wallace (1841–1912)   1902
    Britannica   U S A
Molenaar, Dee (b. 1918)   1994
                              U S A
Moore, Terris (1908–1993)   1976
    AAJ XXXVI-317   U S A
Mumm, Arnold Louis (1859–1927)   1925
    AJ XL-154   Britain
Munday, Phyllis Beatrice (1894–1990)   1967
    AAJ XXXIII-341   Canada
Odell, Noel Ewart (1890–1987)   1936
    AAJ XXX-320   Britain
Peary, Robert Edwin (1856–1920)   1904
    Britannica   U S A
Petzoldt, Paul (1908–1999)   1999
    AAJ XLII-431   U S A
Pierre, Bernard (b. 1920)   1990
    Qui 1990   France
Putnam, William Lowell (b. 1924)   1991
    Who Am 2000   U S A
Rebuffat, Gaston (1921–1985)   1971
    AAJ XXVIII-327   France
Riggs, Thomas (1873–1945)   1941
    AAJ VI-156   U S A

Robbins, Royal Shannon (b. 1928)		1979
	U S A	
Roch, André (b. 1906)		1959
	Switzerland	
Roosevelt, Theodore (1858–1919)		1906
Britannica	U S A	
Rowell, Galen (b. 1940)		1998
	U S A	
Salathé, John (1900–1993)		1976
AAJ XXXVI-321	U S A	
Schoening, Peter Kittlesby (b. 1922)		1992
	U S A	
Scott, Douglas Keith (b. 1941)		1994
AAN- 204	Britain	
Sella, Vittorio (1859–1943)		1938
AAJ V-414	Italy	
Shackleton, Ernest Henry (1874–1922)		1910
Britannica	Britain	
Shi, Zhan-Chun (b. 1929)		1981
	China	
Shipton, Eric Earle (1907–1977)		1956
AAJ XXI-667	Britain	
Smith, Oliver Perry (1884–1969)		1964
AAJ XVII-218	USA/Britain	
Smuts, Jan Christiaan (1870–1950)		1943
Britannica	South Africa	
Spencer, Sydney (1862–1950)		1936
AJ LVII-410	Britain	
Stimson, Henry Lewis (1867–1950)		1942
Britannica	U S A	
Strutt, Edward Lisle (1874–1948)		1932
AJ LVI-396	Britain	
Terray, Lionel (1921–1965)		1962
AJ LXXI-145	France	
Thorington, James Monroe (1894–1989)		1946
AJ XCVI-193	U S A	
Tilman, Harold William (1898–1978)		1956
AAJ XXII-683	Britain	

Underhill, Miriam Elliott O'Brien (1899–1976)		1961
AAJ XX-576	U S A	
Underhill, Robert Lindley Murray (1889–1983)		1961
AAJ XXVI-344	U S A	
Walcott, Charles Doolittle (1850–1927)		1920
Britannica	U S A	
Washburn, Henry Bradford, Jr. (b. 1910)		1956
Who 2000	U S A	
Whymper, Edward (1840–1911)		1909
Britannica	Britain	
Wiessner, Fritz Herman Ernst (1900–1988)		1966
AAJ XXXI-321	U S A	
Wilkins, George Hubert (1888–1958)		1948
AAJ IX-146	Australia	
Wood, Walter Abbot, Jr. (1907–1993)		1966
AAJ XXXVI-319	U S A	
Workman, Fanny Bullock (1859–1925)		1914
App XVI-186	U S A	
Workman, William Hunter (1847–1937)		1914
App XXI-524	U S A	
Young, Geoffrey Winthrop (1876–1958)		1929
AJ LXIV-107	Britain	

****

In addition to the persons thus elected by The American Alpine Club after its founding in 1902, here follows a smaller (and considerably more catholic) list of persons so honored by the Appalachian Mountain Club in the years when it acted on behalf of American mountaineering interests in international affairs. Only four (*) of the AMC honorees were carried forward independently to The American Alpine Club's roster.

*Abruzzi, Luigi Amadeo (1873–1933)		1898
AJ XLV 201	Italy	
*Conway, William Martin (1856–1937)		1896
App XXI-420	Britain	
Daly, Charles Patrick (1816–1899)		1877
Who Was Who-I	U S A	

Dana, James Dwight (1813–1895)		1877
Who Was Who-H	U S A	
Davidson, George (1825–1911)		1886
Who Was Who-I	U S A	
Dawson, George Mercer (1849–1901		1893
Dict Nat Biog	Canada	
Geikie, Archibald (1835–1924)		1886
Britannica	Britain	
Guyot, Arnold Henry (1807–1884)		1887
Britannica	U S A	
Harrison, Jonathan Baxter (1835–1907)		1891
Who Was Who-I	U S A	
Hayden, Ferdinand Vandeveer (1829–1887)		1886
Britannica	U S A	
Heim, Albert (1849–1937)		1886
Britannica	Switzerland	
Henry, Joseph (1797–1878)		1877
Britannica	U S A	
Hooker, Joseph Dalton (1817–1911)		1893
Britannica	Britain	
Hubbard, Gardiner Greene (1822–1897)		1896
Dict Amer Biog.	U S A	
Keltie, John Scott (1830–1918)		1896
Dict Natl Biog	Britain	
Langley, Samuel Pierpont (1834–1906)		1886
Who Was Who-I	U S A	
LeConte, Joseph (1823–1901)		1895
Who Was Who-I	U S A	
Malte-Brun, Victor Adolphe (1816–1889)		1877
Britannica	France	
Muir, John (1838–1914)		1898
Britannica	U S A	
Nordenskjöld, Nils Adolf Eric (1832–1901)		1886
Britannica	Sweden	
Petermann, August (1822–1878)		1877
Webster	Germany	
Powell, John Wesley (1834–1902)		1886
Britannica	U S A	

Rawlinson, Henry Creswicke (1810–1895)   1877
    Dict Natl Biog   Britain
von Richtofen, Ferdinand Paul (1833–1905)   1893
    Britannica   Germany
Russell, Israel Cook (1852–1906)   1893
    Dict Amer Biog   U S A
*Sella, Vittorio (1859–1943)   1895
    AAJ V-414   Italy
Tuckerman, Edward (1817–1886)   1877
    Dict Amer Biog   U S A
Tyndall, John (1820–1893)   1877
    Dict Natl Biog   Britain
Vallot, Joseph (1854–1925)   1898
    AJ XXXVII-190   France
Whittier, John Greenleaf (1807–1892)   1883
    Britannica   U S A
*Whymper, Edward (1840–1911)   1895
    Britannica   Britaain

APPENDIX B
A Centennial Recitation
of
ANNUAL MEETINGS & MEMBERSHIP STATISTICS
1901 -- 2002

Date	Place	Present	Main Program	Total	Hon	MEMBERSHIP Obit
09/05/01	Philadelphia	12	Plans for Organization	12	-	-
15/03/02	Philadelphia	3	Formal Organization, only			
02/01/03	Washington	18+	State of the Club	57	5	0

Designated in the records as the 1st formal meeting.

Date	Place	Present	Main Program	Total	Hon	Obit
31/12/03	New York City	28	Mt. McKinley	59	6	0
30/12/04	Philadelphia	15+	No formal program	57	7	0
28/12/05	Boston	13+	Mt. Rainier	69	9	0
07/01/07	New York City	8+	The High Sierra	72	9	1
30/12/07	Philadelphia	--	Himalaya	78	9	1
02/01/09	Baltimore	11+	Attributes of Alpinists	82	10	1
30/12/09	Boston	45	Mt. Robson	87	10	1
31/12/10	New York City	29	Mt. McKinley	80	12	1
30/12/11	Philadelphia	23	Mt Blackburn	--	12	1
27/12/12	New York City	46	Arctic Travel	–	12	2
27/12/13	Boston	40	Alaskan Climbing	86	12	0
02/01/15	Philadelphia	30	Alaska Boundary	--	12	2
08/01/16	New York City	30	Peruvian Andes	95	12	2
30/12/16	New York City	41	Purcell Range	93	12	1
29/12/17	Boston	32	Crocker Land	99	11	1

[Due to wartime no 1918 membership meeting was held]				–	10	2
03/01/20	New York City	49+	Wind River Range	110	13	3

Designated in the records as the 17th Annual Meeting.

08/01/21	New York City	39+	Canadian Rockies	110	14	4
07/01/22	Boston	40+	Climbing Movies	117	13	2
29/12/22	Philadelphia	35	Canadian Rockies	121	13	2
05/01/24	New York City	96	Mt. Clemenceau	129	16	2
10/01/25	Boston	87	North Greenland	137	14	2
09/01/26	New York City	108	Mount Logan	152	12	3
29/12/26	Philadelphia	--	Mount Everest	159	12	3
14/01/28	New York City	--	Mexican Mtns.	170	10	4
19/01/29	New York City	94	Alps in 1928	192	11	1
11/01/30	Boston	93	Mt. Sir Alexander	198	11	4
24/01/31	New York City	50	Dolomites	201	10	2
23/01/32	Philadelphia	50+	Mount Fairweather	223	12	1
21/01/33	New York City	106	Nanga Parbat	223	11	3
13/01/34	Boston	76	Mount Crillon	231	11	3
19/01/35	New York City	100	Mont Blanc	221	9	7
18/01/36	New York City	106	Yukon NGS Exped.	229	8	4
23/01/37	Boston	104	Mount Waddington	228	10	4
15/01/38	New York City	126	Mount Hayes	234	9	5
14/01/39	Boston	110	C. Houston -- K2	245	12	1
13/01/40	New York City	175	O. E. Cromwell -- K2	253	11	5
18/01/41	Boston	97+	Mount McKinley	264	10	7
13/12/41	Philadelphia	91	W. A. Wood -- Yukon	265	11	5
14/11/42	New York City	126	Wind River Range	274	11	1

27/11/43   New York City 125   Mountain Training   279 11   4
    Though women had been among the Founders, this year the Club itemized that 47 women represented 17% of the membership.
25/11/44   New York City 127   Canadian Rockies   298 10   8

1/12/45   New York City 150   Riva Ridge (Italy)   302 9   7
    From this meeting for the next 58 years, annual meetings were set for the first Saturday of December.
7/12/46   New York City 185   Mt. Saint Elias   318 9   5

6/12/47   Boston   93   Lloyd George Mtns.   326 9   1

4/12/48   New York City 53+   Palmerland   340 12   7

3/12/49   Philadelphia 100+   Mount Vancouver   356 13   3

2/12/50   New York City 50+   Yerupaja   392 10   5

1/12/51   Boston   186   Mount Hubbard   413 10   6

6/12/52   New York City 256   Mount Augusta   436 10   4
    This was designated as the 50th Annual Meeting, presided over by Henry Snow Hall, Jr.
5/12/53   New York City 227   C. Houston -- K2   445 11   7

4/12/54   Philadelphia 159   W. Siri – Makalu   454 10   5

3/12/55   New York City 120+   Axel Heiberg Island   474 8   3

1/12/56   Boston   183   Lhotse & Everest   488 12   7

7/12/57   New York City 117   Mount Logan   495 12   6

6/12/58   Philadelphia 153   Hidden Peak   496 10   8

5/12/59   New York City 154   Mount McKinley   518 12   4

3/12/60   Boston   180   Masherbrum   530 12   8

2/12/61   Washington   182   Ama Dablam   558 14   4

1/12/62   New York City 180   Walker Spur   569 14   7

7/12/63   Philadelphia 396   Americans on Everest   594 17   5

5/12/64   Boston   220   Eiger Nordwand   628 17   6

4/12/65   Seattle   343   Mount Logan   672 17   6
    From this date forward Annual meeting were rotated across the entire United States.

3/12/66	New York City	232	D. Whillans – Patagonia	707	19	9
2/12/67	Berkeley	304	R. Robbins -- Yosemite	759	23	8
7/12/68	Philadelphia	---	J. Amatt – Alpamayo	811	23	3
6/12/69	Boulder	256	Y. Chouinard – Fitzroy	850	22	9
5/12/70	New York City	68+	Annapurna South Face	880	23	9
4/12/71	Portland	318	C. Bonington – Alps	922	25	8
2/12/72	Boston	229	E. Fukushima – Greenland	940	26	11
1/12/73	Santa Monica	400	J. Morrissey – Dhaulagiri I	992	26	12
7/12/74	Lake Mohonk	300	P. Schoening – Pamirs	1119	26	10
6/12/75	Issaquah	425	G. Rowell -- Gasherbrum I	1171	26	4
5/12/76	Berkeley	85+	W. Unsoeld -- Nanda Devi	1181	30	8
3/12/77	Lake Mohonk	200+	Trango Tower -- Patagonia	1300	29	15
2/12/78	Estes Park	150+	Women on Annpurna	1293	30	13
1/12/79	Timberline Lodge		Gauri Shankar	1368	30	15
6/12/80	Washington	200	Muztagh Ata	1428	31	9
5/12/81	Los Angeles	340	Minya Konka	1424	32	11
4/12/82	Boston	223	Circling Everest			12
3/12/83	Seattle	500+	Kangshung Face			10
1/12/84	Oakland	580	W. Bonati	1584	21	13
7/12/85	New York	600+	Seven Summits			7
6/12/86	Denver	700+	L.Kor – climbs	1613		15
5/12/87	Las Vegas	450	Makalu			11
4/12/88	Atlanta	250+	High Angle Climbs		29	13
3/12/89	Boulder		K. Diemberger			18

Date	Location	Attendance	Speaker/Topic			
1/12/90	San Diego		C. Houston			13
7/12/91	Seattle	500+	Mountain Troops			11
6/12/92	Framingham	325	C. Bonington		28	10
4/12/93	Denver	350	Americans on K2	2187	27	13
3/12/94	Snowbird, UT	510	Big Walls	2323	27	
2/12/95	Oakland, CA	601	K. Diemberger	2787	27	
7/12/96	New York	519	S. Venables	3457		
6/12/97	Bellevue, WA	683	8000m peaks	4340	28	11
5/12/98	Denver, CO	579	Steve Haston	5059	28	6
3/12/99	Washington	481	The Totem Pole	5828	27	19
2/12/00	Denver	341	Donini – Patagonia	6115	26	
02/02/02	Snowbird	368	Dhaulagiri – Humar			
28/09/02	Golden		Centennial Celebration			

The three last columns contain net numbers and take into account those members dropped for non-payment of dues or who resigned. The final column indicates the number of members whose death was officially noted by the Secretary or in other club notices (the number of obituaries in the <u>American Alpine Journal</u> are not necessarily conclusive, as some members escaped the process and some non-members have been included).

Where no number is indicated in the club's records, rather than guess at the facts, we have left any speculation to our successors and offer only the indication -- .

Two special dinners deserve mention in this recitation:

On the evening of 28 May, 1907, 30 members and several guests met Luigi Amadeo di Savoia-Aosta, Duke of the Abruzzi, at the Hotel Astor in New York City to present a testimonial honoring him and his achievements;

On 8 May, 1976, 65 specially invited members met in Philadelphia at the Bellevue-Stratford Hotel (where the earliest AAC dinners had been held) to hear the Club's living past presidents reminisce about the organization -- 75 years after its founding.

Sources of the above data are:

AAC Membership Handbooks of 1902, 1905, 1908, 1911, 1914, 1919, 1923 and 1926.

Annual Reports of AAC activities published in <u>Appalachia</u> from 1910 to 1926;

Secretary's annual reports published in <u>American Alpine Journal</u>, from 1929 forward.

Diamond Jubilee booklet #1, prepared for the meeting of 8 May, 1976.

Miscellaneous statistics derived from <u>American Alpine News</u>.

Appendix C
A Sketch of the Early History of The American Alpine Club
by Henry Grier Bryant
1919

The inception of The American Alpine Club was due to the initiative of Prof. Angelo Heilprin.

An earlier effort to organize the more expert members of the Appalachian Mountain Club of Boston into an Alpine Section, had not met with the success which the project deserved. Professor Heilprin, recognizing the inherent desire of lovers of the mountains to fraternize and group themselves in an orderly association, in the spring of 1902 discussed with a group of friends the project of organizing a club somewhat on the lines of The Alpine Club of London. After corresponding with a number of men in Boston, New York and Baltimore on the subject of the proposed club, he felt encouraged to call a meeting for tentative organization.

This gathering was held at the room of the Geographical Society of Philadelphia on Thursday afternoon, May 9, 1901. At this meeting a statement of the objectives of the organization was formulated, questions of eligibility were discussed, and, among others, the following names were enrolled for membership in the Club: Edwin Swift Balch, Capt. Amos Bonsall, Herbert L. Bridgeman, Henry G. Bryant, Prof. Charles E. Fay, Prof Angelo Heilprin, Prof. Harry Fielding Reid, Prof Israel C. Russell and George Vaux, Jr. Thus another highly specialized organization, whose appeal was necessarily to a small group of nature-loving enthusiasts, was successfully inaugurated.

Following this initial gathering in Philadelphia, a brief circular (the first official publication) was prepared for the information of prospective members. This two-paged prospectus, which was signed by Mr. Balch, Professor Reid and Professor Heilprin as a "Committee on Organization," referred to the preliminary meeting in Philadelphia, gave the names of 11 persons enrolled at that time, announced the objects and named the conditions of membership. It is worth noting that the purposes of the organization and the requirements for membership, as outlined in this circular, are substantially the same as those embodied in the By-Laws today. A striking feature among the announced objects of the Club was the prominence given to "The Scientific Exploration and Study of . . . the regions lying within and about the Arctic and Antarctic Circles" and the making of polar explorers and glaciologists eligible for membership, aside from any qualifications they might possess as mountaineers. This formal recognition of polar exploration and of the importance of the study of glacial phenomena were tenets which differentiated the organization from other Alpine Clubs, whose fields of operation are usually more circumscribed.

This apparently divided allegiance among the founders of the Club – an allegiance which placed Arctic exploration on a parity with Alpinism proper – is explained by the renewed interest in polar exploration which at that time prevailed in Philadelphia, as a result of Peary's various expeditions to the far North. Professor Heilprin took a deep interest in those undertakings and doubtless this interest was reflected in a desire to honor Arctic heroes in the manner indicated. It is conceivable that devotees of mountaineering, *per se*, might resent this inclusion of extraneous activities in such a brotherhood of mountaineers; but experience has shown that this wider field of effort has added a richness and vigor to the Club's life which many of the members would not willingly have missed. In recent years the By-Laws have been amended to widen the class of "eligibles" to include not only those who, excelling in mountain craft, may be regarded as the working members of the Club, but also those who have earned for themselves a recognized place in Alpine literature or art.

This response to the initial circular – which had been sent to a selected list of possible adherents – was so encouraging that on March 15, 1902, a second brief notice was mailed to those who had manifested an interest in the proposed organization. This communication, signed by Professor Heilprin as Chairman of the Committee on Organization, announced that:

"In view of the general endorsement which the prepared draft of laws, etc., has received, the Committee finds in unnecessary to make in it other that verbal alterations, except to establish the two paragraphs: (1) The present seat or home of the Club shall be Philadelphia. (2) There shall be a life membership fee of $50." The

notice goes on to say: *"To facilitate the official organization of the Club . . . the Committee on Organization has taken it upon itself the consideration of the election of officers for the first year, leaving for the first general meeting the official acceptance of the By-Laws as proposed."* A ballot containing a list of officers *"for the term of office extending to December, 1903,"* was enclosed, together with a general membership list. The recipients of the circular were requested to send their ballots, with the names voted for checked thereon, to Professor Heilprin. The officers and councillors nominated in this way – the first governing body of the Club – were duly elected as a result of the mail ballot and included the following: President, Charles E, Fay; Vice-Presidents, Angelo Heilprin and George Davidson; Secretary, Henry G. Bryant; Treasurer, Wm. S. Vaux, Jr.; Councillors, Harry Fielding Reid, John Muir, Israel C. Russell and Harry P. Nichols.

The first booklet of the Club, issued in December, 1902, contained, in addition to the Constitution and By-Laws, a list of 45 active members, and this list appears to be identical with the general membership list issued earlier in the same year.

After all these preliminaries the first business meeting, followed by a dinner, took place at the Colonial Hotel, in Washington, on the afternoon and evening of January 2, 1903. At this gathering the following officials of the Club were present: Messrs Fay, Heilprin, Russell, Reid and Bryant, and among the members participating were: Rear Admiral Geo. W. Melville, U. S. N., General A. W. Greely, U. S. A., Prof. H. C. Parker, Commander and Mrs. R. E. Peary, Mr. A. Lawrence Rotch and Mr. H. L. Bridgman. Our guests at this first dinner were Prof. Wm. M. Davis, General Lawrason Riggs, Prof. Wm. H. Niles, Mr. Emil Deibitsch and Miss Deibitsch.

The Brooklyn STANDARD-UNION of January 3rd, in its account of the dinner, remarked: *"Professor Fay gave a brief resumé of the evolution of the Club from a former unsuccessful effort in the Appalachian Mountain Club, of which he is a past president; Professor Davis spoke upon fields for effective work of the Club, particularly in diffusing a strictly scientific form of description of mountains, so that the same expressions would convey the same ideas the world over; while General Greely described at some length his experiences last summer among the mountains of the Philippines.*

Admiral Melville and Professor Reid also spoke, the evening being one of exceptional interest and evidencing an earnest purpose on the part of those present to develop an organization of serious aim and high standard of achievement."

So was initiated this fellowship, which, born of a common love of the mountains, has survived a score of years amid the distractions of our eager American life. Fortunate in the personnel of its founders, the Club drew to itself a following representative of the finest elements among our alpinists and explorers of the untrodden wilds.

Not to speak of our honored first president, whose attributes of leadership are admitted by all, what names to conjure with among mountaineers are those of Muir, Heilprin and Russell – to speak only of those who have now gone over the Great Divide.

With the gathering years our organization has had a slow but wholesome growth, despite conditions which may be regarded as adverse to the success of such an enterprise in this country. Among such deterrent conditions may be mentioned: the wide geographical distribution of our membership, the distance of truly alpine peaks from the centers of population, and the highly specialized character of the appeal of Alpinism among a people destitute of the mountaineering traditions and opportunities of European countries. That we have nourished this wholesome growth in a soil largely given to the cultivation of more material products must be set down to our credit.

It remains for us, on whom rest the continued success of The American Alpine Club, to continue to answer the call of the mountains, to gather betimes around the festive board to exchange experiences afield, and to take to ourselves the lessons of the eternal hills.

Appendix D
Editing the American Alpine Journal
by H. Adams Carter [1]

The AMERICAN ALPINE JOURNAL was born 27 years after the founding of The American Alpine Club in 1902. The Club had published three monographs called ALPINA AMERICANA: THE HIGH SIERRA OF CALIFORNIA, 1907; THE CANADIAN ROCKY MOUNTAINS, 1911; AND MOUNTAIN EXPLORATION IN ALASKA, 1915. From 1905 until 1925, the Appalachian Mountain Club published for the Club, mountaineering notes and records of Club meetings in APPALACHIA under the heading of "Alpina." The HARVARD MOUNTAINEERING CLUB JOURNAL carried this on from 1926 to 1928.

In 1929, the first issue of the AMERICAN ALPINE JOURNAL appeared. The emphasis was heavily weighted towards the Canadian mountains, although there was one article on the Fairweather range in Alaska and a philosophical article on mountaineering. Number 2 showed an enormous increase in the number of regions covered: Ecuador, Wyoming, Colorado, Montana, California, Mexico, the Caucasus, the Alps, as well as Canada. In this issue, VARIOUS NOTES began; this is the section which is now entitled CLIMBS AND EXPEDITIONS and takes up at least half of the present volumes. The editors were Allen Carpe, 1929; Howard Palmer, 1930-1933; J. Monroe Thorington, 1934-1946; Robert H. Bates and David A. Robertson, 1947-1953; William S. Child, 1952-1955; Richard C. Houston, 1956; Francis P. Farquhar, 1956-1958; and H. Adams Carter, 1959 to the present.

It is interesting to note that the first *AAJ* cost $1.50. The price varied from $1.00 to $2.00 until 1946, when the price began to rise meteorically.

My own involvement began as an Assistant Editor in 1954. I agreed to do the CLIMBS AND EXPEDITIONS. At that time, there were possibly each year, a half dozen expeditions to the great ranges. I could fit my work into one long weekend, which did not disturb my teaching schedule. I agreed to take on the editorship in 1959 until my

---

The Original of this Appendix appeared in the Himalayan Journal, Volume 50.

children were old enough to accompany my wife and me on expeditions. Somehow, teaching, editing and expeditions all managed to get sandwiched in and I continued on as editor.

In my first years (and, of course, later on, too), I was ably helped by those who were older and wiser than I. I got excellent advice from the preceding editor, Francis Farquhar, and from such notables as Marcel Kurz and G. O. Dyhrenfurth. Today I lean heavily on such authorities as Evelio Echevarria, Elizabeth Hawley and Josef Nyka, to mention only three. And I must not omit mentioning the help of my editorial staff and my wife, Ann. Without other mountain chroniclers and expedition leaders, we could not hope to try to publish most of what has gone on in the mountaineering world each year. I do have to prod, and often write several letters to those who hesitate to send me their reports. It is exasperating when letters go unanswered.

Francis Farquhar handed me over the reins with one important bit of advice: "Don't ever forget that you are the editor." I may have infuriated some authors when the editorial blue pencil struck hard. Previous editor Thorington would become irate if I changed a comma of his work, even when he was clearly wrong. Not a few authors, after seeing their writing in print, have written to tell me how well thgeir efforts read in the *AAJ,* not suspecting that what they had written was changed and edited. When I make significant changes, I do send a typescript to the author for his approval. I shall never forget one case when an author submitted a hideously badly written article. A visiting mountaineering friend and I spent every evening for a week, working it over. Hardly an original sentence remained. I thought I would incur the never-ending wrath of the author when I sent him the new version. His reply turned out to be far from sarcastic. It was; "How did you manage to say just what I wanted to but could not?" Strangely enough, he was grateful to me until his death a few years afterward in a tragic climbing accident.

Over the years, I have managed to acquire knowledge of what has gone on in the mountains, having gradually picked up information as it was becoming part of climbing history. I have sometimes been able to note when a "first" ascent was being done for the second time. My climbing in most of the great ranges of the world, with the exception of New Zealand, the Caucasus, the Antarctic and

Greenland, has been an enormous help. I have had the privilege of getting to know a large number of prominent climbers from all over the world. My Facility with foreign languages helps. Writing to climbers in English, German, French and Spanish assists in getting replies. I even write letters in Italian, which I have never studied, and get replies to the questions I have asked. I have translated articles from Catalan into English. Friends who send me letters to translate in such languages as Slovene, believe I can handle all languages. In fact, I never got beyond the fifth lesson in the Slovene grammar book. Knowledge of languages does help in combing through foreign periodicals, something I do with care to see who has done what and where. Knowing that, I can go after specific climbers to get a report.

I have been asked what the future of the AMERICAN ALPINE JOURNAL will be. I cannot answer that. The future is always cloudy. All I know is that all things come to an end. It has taken me a long time to become familiar with the whole subject of mountaineering history. I have been lucky to have had some of the qualities needed for the job. Whom have I been training to carry on? Nobody. All I know is that when I can no longer do the editing, the AMERICAN ALPINE JOURNAL will be different. Not worse; just different.

$$- 30 -$$

Final Note by W. L. P.

I first met the late Hubert Adams Carter in early February of 1943, when he was working for the U S Army Quartermaster in developing and testing equipment and rations for the incipient 10th Mountain Division (very few of which we ultimately came to use when in action in the Aleutians or Italy). He and Ann (who was pregnant with their first child) were slogging up the John Sherburne Trail on Mount Washington dragging a sled loaded with mountaineering impedimenta of various sorts that he wished to test for his then employer.

Andy Kauffman and I had just finished the fall semester of college before going off to war and were in residence for a few days at the old Harvard Mountaineering Club cabin on Boott Spur – the place that Brad Washburn had been instrumental in building. Having just completed the first ascent of Huntington Ravine's lengthy Damnation Gully, we were returning home when the Carters struggled into view at Windy Corner. We two young bucks promptly hitched ourselves into the traces in place of the tiring couple and dragged the sled the rest of the way into the floor of Tuckerman Ravine. There we established Ad's "Tent, Mountain, M-1942" and the four of us crowded inside to escape the 70 MPH winds that gusted through the cirque. With Andy stretched full length along one side to help hold the tent down, and my then much slimmer self on the other side, Ad and Ann were able to move more freely and cooked up a dinner of "Mountain Rations, M-1942," feeding us alternately from two common spoons.

Perhaps we two were young, perhaps we were just starved after two strenuous days on the "Old Rockpile" and our own cooking, perhaps a lot of other things – for at this writing one of us four has crossed the Great Divide and another is tottering on the crest – but in my mind that was the best meal I have ever enjoyed in the mountains, and at this writing – 59 years later – remains one of my fondest mountaineering memories.

INDEX

193